Archives and Library Administration: Divergent Traditions and Common Concerns

Archives and Library Administration: Divergent Traditions and Common Concerns

Lawrence J. McCrank
Editor

The Haworth Press
New York • London

1743

Archives and Library Administration: Divergent Traditions and Common Concerns has also been published as *Journal of Library Administration*, Volume 7, Numbers 2/3, Summer/Fall 1986.

The Haworth Press, Inc., 12 West 32 Street, New York, NY 10001
EUROSPAN/Haworth, 3 Henrietta Street, London WC2E 8LU England

Library of Congress Cataloging-in-Publication Data

Archives and library administration.

   "Has also been published as Journal of library administration, volume 7, numbers 2/3, Summer/Fall 1986"—Verso t.p.
   Bibliography: p.
   1. Library administration.   2. Archives—Management.   I. McCrank, Lawrence J.
Z678.A78   1986   025.1   86-19405
ISBN 0-86656-590-6

Dedication

to
Ann Morgan Campbell

Executive Director of the Society of American Archivists, 1974–1986; in appreciation for professional service to archivists in particular, and to the information community in general.

Archives and Library Administration: Divergent Traditions and Common Concerns

Journal of Library Administration
Volume 7, Numbers 2/3

CONTENTS

Contributors   1

Preface   7
  Lawrence J. McCrank

FROM THE EDITOR   15
  John R. Rizzo

ARCHIVIST PERSPECTIVES ON LIBRARY ADMINISTRATION
  OF ARCHIVES

Archives Under Library Administration: Points of Convergence
  and Conflict   17
  Paul H. McCarthy

*Archives and library administrators perceive each other's operations and adminis-
tration differently, which leads to conflicts and misunderstandings. Librarians often
do not recognize basic distinctions in broad mission and more specific objectives,
operations and procedures, and personnel differences, separating archives from
libraries as types of information organizations. Professional alliance and mutual
interests should not overshadow these divergent traditions and approaches to
information systems. Better understanding of the distinctiveness of an archives from
a library might improve relations and help avoid internal managerial conflicts.*

The Provenance of Archives Under Library Administration:
  Organizational Structures and Organic Relationships   35
  David J. Klaassen

*Archives are frequently located administratively and physically in libraries. Based on
the assumption that environment influences development, the symbiotic relationship
between libraries and archives is explored. Realities observed include: (1) the relationship is unequal, with the library normally as parent, having greater resources, a
larger constituency, and more public visibility; and (2) administrative linkage is
justifiable, but differences are substantial enough to produce numerous tensions.
Placement of an archives in a library affects both. The necessity of organizational
cohabitation does not obliterate the distinctiveness of each from the other.*

RESOURCE SHARING: ARCHIVAL AND BIBLIOGRAPHIC CONTROL

Information Systems for Libraries and Archives: Opportunity
or Incompatibility?   49
Richard V. Szary

*Many factors have delayed the development of archival information systems parallel
to library systems and networks. The requirements of the two may be similar, but they
are not the same. Major differences exist in approaches to collection development,
description and retrieval, and reference, but modern information technology can be
used for all three areas in archives as well as libraries, and in museums as well. There
is potential for cooperation in these functional areas and between these types of
organizations because of a commonality of interests and services, if enhancements
include accommodation for real differences.*

The Impact of Automation: Integrating Archival
and Bibliographic Systems   61
Lawrence J. McCrank

*Automation is a process of dynamic change whereby organizations adopting comput-
erized information technology are systematically and thoroughly changed. Modification in processes produces inextricable change in personnel, procedure, organizational structure, services, and the public perception. Automated networking and the
transfer of archives documentation through the nationwide bibliographic networks
will have profound influence on archives, more than on libraries. Computer
technology is forcing archivists to rethink old theoretical assumptions, professional
values, and organizational strategies, including their traditional relationship with
librarians and the prevalent administrative nexus between libraries and archives.
Several options remain open to archival development in automated information
systems, some of which are alternatives to library-dominated networks and approaches to bibliographic control, while others call for closer archives-library
cooperation and an integration of methodology to produce a new hybrid information
milieu.*

Archival and Bibliographic Information Networks   99
David Bearman

*Library networking was predicated on the achievement of unifying standards for
description and a common basis for communication, MARC formats. The inadvertent
lack of early inter-computer protocols also fostered decentralized organizational
development and the commercial exchange of data. Pre-1976 visions of a national
library system have been modified to the realities of interactive networks. Archives
were largely uninvolved in such developments in the 1970s, until 1977 when the
Society of American Archivist's National Information Systems Task Force was
formed. NISTF prepared the way for archives and library interaction and the
development of the MARC Archives and Manuscript Control format which preserves
archival control distinctions from bibliographic conventions but uses authority
records effectively. Further cooperation is now possible.*

COOPERATIVE PROGRAM DEVELOPMENT AT INSTITUTIONAL AND NATIONAL LEVEL

Government Publications as Archives: A Case for Cooperation
Between Archivists and Librarians   111
Richard J. Cox

Government publication is a method of disseminating the archival record of government action and reporting, and government documents in published form are an extension of government archives. While the federal system of repositories is functional, most of these are in libraries where archival management is compromised by library practices. The condition of state publications, their retention and condition, and dissemination, are inferior to the federal system. Archival appraisal criteria provide an intellectual guide to accessioning and acquiring government documents. Access to government documents is confused by odd mixtures of archival arrangements and descriptive techniques and library cataloging. Archival rather than bibliographic control provides solutions to many library-housed repositories confronting the problem of mass in government materials. Recommendations for cooperation between archives and repositories are provided, with observations on the fusion of archival and library roles into a common professional information endeavor.

Conservation and Collection Management   129
John F. Dean

Library and archives conservation and collection management concerns are similar. Both need to be addressed in institutional policies and well defined objectives for procedures and priorities in selecting materials for long-range preservation. Collection weeding, withdrawal from primary use to low-use retention facilities, and decisions about treatment, are key ingredients in a conservation program which is well integrated into collection management. Successful programs in either archives and libraries must be embedded into the policies and activities of the organization, rather than being ancillary and remedial. The administrative emphasis must be on sustained, systematic, and programmatic approaches to the conservation problems facing both archives and libraries.

Funding Resources and Priorities for Cooperation:
Toward a National Records Program   143
George L. Vogt

Archives and libraries have emphasized their differences rather than commonalities, and have so specialized within their own developmental traditions that cooperation has been an illusive ideal. Archivists are now moving toward a national or more accurately nationwide system of information exchange, after a decade of false starts and consensus building. The National Historical Publications and Records Commission has been a major stimulus for cooperative development. By 1985 the key elements for a national system were identified, and now questions of actual development and leadership are being discussed. Funding is always critical for such developments, but planning must face continued austerity and yet proceed.

EDUCATION AND PROFESSIONAL DEVELOPMENT

The Relevance of Archival Theory and Practice for Library
Education: An Argument for a Broader Vision   155
Francis X. Blouin, Jr.

*Archivists during the past decade have been greatly concerned with archival
education and professional development, and the proper context of archives training
programs: History, Library Science, or independent Archival Science degree programs. Library schools offer the most reasonable possibilities because of their move
toward new information technology and management strategies, and a broadening of
the older library-centered core. If their curricula can accommodate the differences
between libraries and archives, and alter their dominant focus on the book and
traditional library procedures such as cataloging, then archival concerns can be
included. Such inclusion would enhance library science curricula by providing
divergent professional vantage points, alternative strategies, and multi-disciplinary
discussion about common issues such as the organization of information, shared
problems, and policy implementation. Archivists are at a crossroads, with choices to
remain separate and exclusive, or to work for alliances and cooperation. Technological developments make the latter choice imperative.*

Librarians and Archivists: Organizational Agenda for the Future   167
Robert M. Warner

*The historical development of archivists and librarians, although related, has always
been substantially different. Past experiences, reactions to different needs and
problems, separate professional development, and divergent philosophies work to
keep them apart today. Modern problems of professional identity, massive collections
and limited financial resources, and adjustments to new technology, force archivists
and librarians to re-examine old habits, values, and bias. Commonality in the kinds
of technology being used for information services, types of materials kept by both
archives and libraries, and education trends, further such reconsideration. The
education issue looms large at present. Speculation about future development includes
predictions that separate fields like archival and library science will blend into a
larger, holistic information profession. Education programs will do the same, if not
to promote such convergence, then as a consequence of it.*

Abbreviations and Acronyms   177

Index   179

Archives and Library Administration: Divergent Traditions and Common Concerns

Contributors

David Bearman is the deputy director of the Office of Information Resource Management at the Smithsonian Institution in Washington, D.C., where he was also in charge specifically of Policy and Planning. Previously, he directed the Society of American Archivist's National Information Systems Task Force, and he has served as an automation consultant for the Institute of Education at the University of London. He was educated at Brown University in Intellectual History, and thereafter worked toward the Ph.D. in the History of Science at the University of Pennsylvania. He has enjoyed various honors, such as being elected in 1985 as a SAA Fellow in recognition of his contributions to NISTF.

In 1986 he will be a Mellon Fellow at the Bentley Historical Library, University of Michigan, to complete a book on archival automation based on the NISTF experience. This interest is reflected in articles for *The Conference on Archives, Automation, and Access* (1986), *Archivaria*, *The American Archivist*, and the NISTF working papers. His other publications reflect his interest in the history of biological science and the history of ideas.

Francis X. Blouin, Jr. is director of the Bentley Historical Library at the University of Michigan where he holds concurrent positions in History and Library Science. He was educated at the University of Notre Dame and received his M.A. and Ph.D. in History from the University of Minnesota. He teaches in urban history in the Department of History and archives and manuscripts administration at the University of Michigan library school and was instrumental in creating the three-year Carnegie-Mellon fellowship program on Modern Historical Documentation at the Bentley Library. He is active in several professional organizations, most notably the Society of American Archivists as a member of council and in particular the SAA Education Committee.

His research interests pertain to social and labor history in the upper midwest, urban history, and to professionalization and training of American archivists. In addition to several guides to manuscript collections, he has written about sampling methods in archival appraisal, case methodology in teaching archival science, business records appraisal, and he was co-editor of the well-known SAA publication, *Archivists and Machine Readable Records*.

Richard J. Cox is one of America's most published archivists. He was educated at Towson State University in Baltimore and completed his M.A. in History from the University of Maryland, in addition to several seminars and institutes in archives administration and records management. He began his practical career in historical St. Mary's archeological site, and then edited the Calvert Family papers for the Maryland Historical Society where he became the curator of manuscripts. In 1978 he became the city archivist and records management officer for the city of Baltimore, and subsequently in 1983 became the head of the Archives and Records Division of the Alabama Department of Archives and History. In 1986 he joined the staff of the New York State Archives in Albany as Associate Archivist for External Programs.

His publications have appeared in diverse journals, from Marylandia to genealogical periodicals, local history sources, and most notably in *The American Archivist*, *Manuscripts*, *The Public Historian*, and the *Midwestern Archivist*. His focii have been the condition of state and local government records, the history of archives, and the relationship between archivists and historians. Professionally active, he has served as the book review editor for *Manuscripts*, the new notes reporter for *The American Archivist*, and editor of the Society of Alabama Archivists newsletter. He is an instrumental member of the American Association for State and Local History's Advisory Committee on Local Government Records, and participates on several Society of American Archivists committees.

John F. Dean was born in Yorkshire, England, and was educated initially at Oldham's Municipal School of Arts and Crafts. While completing a six-year bookbinding apprenticeship with Lee Whitehead Ltd., he specialized in the same field at the Manchester College of Art and thereafter returned to Oldham to study art history and heraldry in connection with his interest in the book arts. While serving as the bindery foreman for the Manchester Public Library, he turned his academic attention to management at Victoria University in the same city. In 1969 he came to the United States to head the binding operations of the Newberry Library, and while there he completed his M.A. in Library Science at the University of Chicago with a thesis on "English Language Bookbinding Manuals . . ." In 1975 he moved to Baltimore to establish the preservation and conservation programs, including a five-year bookbinding apprenticeship program, at the Johns Hopkins University libraries. He also completed a Master of Liberal Arts from Johns Hopkins, with a focus on the history of science to support his interest in conservation. He became in 1985 the chief conservation officer for the Cornell University libraries.

John Dean is known nationally for his role in conservation education, consulting, and provision of numerous workshops. He taught as an adjunct lecturer of library science at the University of Maryland's College of Library and Information Services, and in collection management at Georgetown University; in summer 1986 he will be a visiting lecturer at the library school of the University of Alabama and teach bookbinding in its M.F.A. program in the book arts. He has published extensively on the role of bookbinders in preservation programs, about collection management techniques, and binding standards.

David J. Klaassen is a curator and assistant professor at the University of Minnesota's Social Welfare History Archives. He received his undergraduate education at Tabor College in Kansas and his M.A. in History from the University of Minnesota where he has continued his graduate studies in social history. He has also served as archivist for the University of Minnesota and as a visiting instructor in history at Bethel College in the Twin Cities. He has worked on various archival guides and has published articles in American social history. He has been active in the Midwest Archives Conference and the Society of American Archivists, most recently as chairman of the 1985 conference program. His past SAA activities are noteworthy in the areas of archival reporting standards, confidentiality issues in archives, education and professional development, and institutional evaluation.

Paul H. McCarthy is the archivist of the University of Alaska and curator of manuscripts in the Rasmuson Library, with particular administrative responsibility for the university's Alaska and Polar Regions Department. His administrative experience includes work with library building projects and university-wide committees. He is well-known as the treasurer of the Society of American Archivists, work on Council, and on various committees; as well as parallel professional activity with the Alaska Library Association, of which he has been vice-president and on the board of directors; and the Alaska Historical Society, which he served as both secretary and president. He continues to function in a variety of advisory capacities, in Alaska and elsewhere.

He was educated at St. John Fisher College and received his M.L.S. from Syracuse University, and his education has been continued in several institutes and workshops as well as by further graduate studies at the University of Alaska. His publications include several registers and guides to collections with which he has worked, as well as bibliographies, oral histories, and studies of archival and manuscript programs. He has also appeared in several state and federal public hearings, testifying about the importance of records and documents programs.

Lawrence J. McCrank is the dean of the AUM Library and Resource Center at Auburn University at Montgomery. Previously he was head of the Department of Rare Books and Special Collections at Indiana State

University's Cunningham Memorial Library where with an NHPRC grant he founded the university archives, and he served as the consultant for the Mt. Angel Abbey Library rare book and manuscript project. As an assistant professor at the University of Maryland College of Library and Information Services, he worked with the late Walter Rundell in the pioneering Advanced Studies Program which combined the M.A. in History and the professional M.L.S. for specialization in the fields of archives administration, manuscripts, and rare books, historical editing, related work in cultural resource management. He has taught History at Whitman College and the universities of Kansas, Virginia, Oregon, and California (Berkeley), and has been a visiting professor in library and archival science at the universities of Western Ontario and Alabama. He was educated as an historian in Minnesota, received his M.A. from the University of Kansas and an M.L.S. from the University of Oregon, and he earned his doctorate in Medieval and Iberian History from the University of Virginia.

This edition of essays complements an earlier compilation and pro-ceedings of note, *Automating the Archives . . .* , which sought to crystallize then-current fragmented developments in archival automation so that more directed progress could be made in cooperation with bibliographic information systems. These works number among seven monographic publications, over forty articles, and a dozen reviews, split between the fields of medieval Iberian history, history of the American West, and studies in library and archival science focusing on educational issues, conservation, rare book and manuscript cataloging and descrip-tion, indexing strategies, and networking. He just completed a book for 1986 release: *From Totems to Books and Libraries: Instructional Media in the Catholic Mission to the Oregon Frontier, 1835–55.*

Richard V. Szary is the Associate Archivist for Information Systems in the Smithsonian Institution archives, Washington, D.C. Since 1985 he has served as the deputy project director in the Smithsonian's Office of Information Resource Management for the Smithsonian Bibliographic Information System with specific responsibilities for the archival com-ponents of SIBIS. As an archivist at the Smithsonian he was previously in charge of nontraditional media, and earlier he worked with the records of the National Museum of History and Technology. He was educated first at Georgetown University and De Paul University, before complet-ing an M.A. in Asian Studies at the University of Illinois where he first worked in archives as a graduate assistant. More recently his academic interests have turned to programming and information systems. He compiled the guide to the National Museum of History and Technology manuscript collections, and has presented several papers during the 1980s on archival automation and archives/library information systems.

George L. Vogt is the director of the Historical Records Program at the National Historical Publications and Records Commission in Washington, D.C. He earned his B.A. in History from Yale and his graduate degrees, the M.A. and Ph.D. in American History from the University of Virginia. While at Mr. Jefferson's university, he worked in the Manuscripts Department of the Alderman Library, before going to the capital as the assistant to the executive director of the NHPRC. After 1982 he supervised the second edition of the *Directory of Archives and Manuscripts Repositories* while serving also as the assistant director of the NHPRC Publications Grant Program. He moved into his present position in 1984, and now supervises a two million dollar program.

He is active in several professional organizations in archives, editing, state and local history, and served as president of the Manuscripts Society (1984–86). His writings and editorial work reflect these same interests, with the additional excursion into humor with Roger Bruns as co-author of *Your Government Inaction* (1981).

Robert M. Warner is the dean of the School of Library Science at the University of Michigan, where previously he directed the Bentley Historical Library before serving as Archivist of the United States (1980–85). At the University, where his experience began as an assistant curator in 1957 and where he completed his M.A. and Ph.D. in History, he holds the rank of professor in both History and Library Science. He has served in various capacities on the board of visitors to the Case Western Reserve University library school and the Syracuse University Maxwell School of Citizenship and Public Affairs, as well as a member of council of the American Historical Association. He has been director, vice-president, and president of the Society of American Archivists, and served the Historical Society of Michigan in the same capacities.

His publications include ten books authored, co-authored, and edited on various topics related to Michigan history, the collections of the Bentley Historical Library, migration studies, and archives and historical manuscripts collections. His work with Ruth Bordin, *The Modern Manuscript Library*, is especially well known. His thirty-two articles cover a similar breadth of learning and administrative concerns, and he continues to be an active reviewer of Michigan-related works. Life-long contributions to historical studies, archives and libraries, are reflected by his numerous professional positions, awards and honors, including honorary doctoral degrees.

Preface

The genesis for this book goes back several years when I was an assistant professor at the University of Maryland's College of Library and Information Services. There I became acquainted with Professor John Rizzo, editor of *Journal of Library Administration*, in his capacity as director with Professor Paul Wasserman of the well-known UMCP-sponsored annual two-week institute for library administrators at Port Deposit, Maryland. I had always thought that archivists should avail themselves of this institute or something similar, and that archival literature should pay more attention to administration and management as a focus of their scholarly efforts. I went so far as to encourage the Society of American Archivists' central administration and its education committee to explore the possibility of repeating the institute specifically for archivists, records managers, and those in public records administration. The overture was never explored by SAA, even though John Rizzo was receptive to the idea. I was convinced that archivists had lost a real opportunity, especially when Rizzo published his book, *Management for Librarians: Fundamentals and Issues* (Westport, CT: Greenwood, 1980), which seemed so appropriate for archives administration as well.

Undaunted, I approached John Rizzo with a second overture, this time unhampered by SAA's inaction. We discussed the possibility of devoting a special issue in the *Journal of Library Administration* to current issues in archives administration and to relate these to a readership primarily of library administrators. This would be in line with the topical focii of *Library Trends*, which had devoted one very useful issue to archives (Richard Lytle, ed.), and other dedicated issues of the *JLA*. The opportunity came in the hiatus between the editorship of John Rizzo, who resigned in 1986, and the transfer of editorial responsibility for the journal to Dr. Sul Lee, director of libraries at the University of Oklahoma. A special, sizeable double-issue turned over to a guest editor at this juncture was a benefit to all three parties.

In its original conception, this volume of essays was to update and revise, and hopefully pull into more coherent form, myriad issues in archives administration as they related particularly to library administration, as attempted earlier in Robert L. Clark's edited collection, *Archives-Library Relations* (NY: Bowker, 1976). I approached respected colleagues who were in administrative positions, whose vantage points would provide a variety of professional and technical perspectives on the issues separating and simultaneously joining librarians and archivists. Ten topics were outlined, and each contributor was asked to address these from an administrator's perspective with attention to: (1) resource allocation, (2) personnel management, (3) adoption of new technology, (4) defining clienteles and services, and (5) cooperation and networking. Our readers will have to judge whether we were successful in producing a coherent set of essays which brings into focus key issues confronting archives and library administrators today.

I wish to thank those who contributed to this effort, for the timeliness of their contributions and tolerance of my prodding, heavy-handed reading and editing, as well as their willingness to do so with enhancement of our professional literature as their only reward. As administrators all, everyone was pressed for time to make this effort with relatively short notice and to comply with very short turn-around time for reviewing, proofing, and editing work. I must thank John Rizzo for making this production possible as a dedicated issue of *Journal of Library Administration* and a spin-off hardbound monograph as well, and to the publisher, Bill Cohen, for his support of a substantial volume despite the constraints of today's publishing costs.

Let me finally call your attention to the dedication of this edition of essays fittingly devoted to issues of archival administration and librarianship, to Ann Morgan Campbell, executive director of the Society of American Archivists from 1974 to 1986, upon her leaving an office well-served and with the gratitude of professional archivists everywhere.

INTRODUCTION

In the original outline of topics to be discussed in this forum, the idea was to create a much needed dialogue across professional lines about the commonalities and differences of archives and libraries, and how these points of splintering and convergence affect managerial and administrative decision making. At first the introduction was going to consist of a brief historical background of the divergent traditions and common concerns demarcating libraries and archives, but this retrospective glance at how the two came to share the same environments and yet remain different, even distant in attitudes, seems to be covered well enough in the following essays. Consequently, freed from obligations of historian, this editor has elected to provide an editorial introduction.

Students of administrative history, as much as anthropologists, have noted that entities which co-exist in proximity with each other often develop symbiotic relationships; or else one moves into dominance over the other and ultimately destroys it consciously, or simply dominates it so completely that the smaller of the two ceases as an independent unit. It is absorbed, or so transmuted by the overpowering influence of the dominant party, that it can no longer be recognized for what it once was. This theme of inferior vs. superior, and the resulting inferiority complex of archives within library organizational structures, pervades these essays. Although the original conspectus sought to balance two polarized vantage points, one of libraries under archives administrations, and the other of archives under library administrations, the latter situation prevails to such an extent that the former perspective seems to represent only the views of historical societies and a few select institutions. Consequently, this editor sought to get two complementary viewpoints of archivists who by the nature of their placement in libraries and by virtue of their functions and activities, could share with library administrators their professional viewpoints from "down under" in typical library administration hierarchical structures.

Paul McCarthy and David Klaassen do this nicely, first by contrasting metaphorically perspectives attributed to library and institutional administrators against the practical realities of archival administration; and then by using the archival concept of provenance as an analog to suggest how the context of a library environment influences the development of an archives. Both authors, and others in this collection, indicate the continuum of archives, archives *qua* library or manuscript library, and library, is uneven and imbalanced, with a preponderant power, prestige, administrative bias, resource allocation, and size, at the library end of the spectrum. Can one read into these essays a sense of envy? frustration? Or filial devotion? admiration and respect? The overriding sense is that archivists view libraries as parent organizations very much cast in the role of proverbial stepmothers, if not actually wicked, at least uncaring. In many instances what is left unsaid is as important as what is articulated, since the major tone of the arguments herein is one of distrust, misunderstanding, and lack of communication.

This attitudinal problem may be as important as any specific managerial problem identified in these essays. Whereas it might have been interesting to present the viewpoint of the library administrator (somewhat reflected in my own essay which might put archivists on the defensive), that perspective seems to have been amply documented and represented in this essay by impressions from the so-called Levy Report presented to the 1985 conference of the Society of American Archivists. This albeit sketchy survey indicates how archivists are perceived by resource allocators, library administrators included; in turn, these current essays reflect how archivists see themselves as being perceived. Neither is really complimentary. Self-image is part of the problem, a defensiveness, in creating a genuine dialogue between librarian and archivist administrators. This may strike librarians as ironic, since library literature itself abounds with documentation of a widespread inferiority complex among librarians as information professionals, with low self-images, and a problematic public image. What an ego-booster for librarians, to understand the depths from which archivists perceive library administrations as powerful, large, and technically adroit organizations!

This theme of defensive posture, distrust, and misunderstanding is most important in assessing the failure, past and present, of a constructive dialogue and partnership between libraries and archives. Library administrators may not realize the undercurrents in their organizations which force archivists, perhaps allied with manuscripts curators, rare book librarians, and conservators, to react defensively to their administrations. Both are inherently interested in information services, but the latter natural coalition is more interested in cultural resource management than merely information management which is seen to dominate the modern library perspective. Of course, in accusing library administrators of misunderstanding the nature and role of archives, archivists leave themselves vulnerable to the countercharge of misunderstanding the nature of library administration and its perspective from on-high, according to archival perspectives, when library administrators often perceive of themselves as middle-management.

Like all forms of cohabitation, no matter how domestic, friction is commonplace in problem solving and problems abound in the modern information service professions and organizations. Cooperation is essential for the common good, but cooperation itself is labor intensive, time consuming, and dependent on common shared goals and educational backgrounds. In the same vein that archivists complain about how misunderstood they are by their library counterparts, librarians could turn the argument by suggesting that modern library trends and technology, both influenced by an increasingly sophisticated and holistic information science, are perhaps not well understood by archivists, especially those whose backgrounds are rooted in traditional historical studies. These essays hint at, if they do not always attack them directly, many problems in professional and continuing education related to these frictions from personnel management *per se* to more general group dynamics of archivists within libraries.

The second cluster of essays concentrate on technical services, primarily on information exchange about information resources. They all go beyond merely discussing holdings information, however, to more complex questions of compatibility in description, standards, and data formats, and to factors of human engineering which include user and staff education. Everyone agrees that technology is pushing both archives and libraries into accelerated change, and that the rapidity of technical adaption is putting strains of archives and library personnel and organization as a whole. Most see such technology as propelling archives and libraries toward closer ties, out of necessity and instinctive survival as much as for more altruistic motives. Whereas libraries are proceeding without much regard for archives, the latter are playing a game of catch up to the pace set by libraries and bibliographic networks. Both, however, feel awkwardly behind the changes prompted by technology in areas of government, business, and industry outside traditional information services as encompassed by archives and libraries. Indeed, archivists are just now thinking about themselves as part of the information field, with natural reservations since so little in information science and management relates well to the ideology of cultural resource management and to documentation in its European sense. American archivists understandably lack trust in the theoretical library and information science world to care for archival interests because of their experience at home, so they are cautiously considering a *rapprochement*. On the other hand, they seem also to lack a firm grounding in the larger, historical antecedents of their values, methods, and assumptions, so that they harken back to a very few principles which are projected as immutable virtues of archivy against what they see as an equally intransigent standard in libraries for information sharing. Those polarized attitudes appear to be rooted emotionally as much, if not more so, than in reason, and may appear to someone outside of archives as being too introspective and self-limiting.

The three essays on information systems, automation, and networks by Szary, McCrank, and Bearman respectively, all challenge archivists to think differently about information resource sharing and about modern technology will undoubtedly change the very nature of archives. Those challenges lay in abstract notions and ideology, and on the other hand, in basic, pragmatic concerns of daily processes and services. They also beckon library administrators to think, perhaps for the first time, about the special circumstances of archives and their requirements of information systems. Equally important, although perhaps assumed as too self-evident on the part of all three authors, is the fundamental assumption that of course archival resources are rich in information, potential use, and inherent or "intrinsic value." The critical reader of these essays may not always agree with such underlying assumptions, and will therefore find the arguments therein to be lacking a certain convincing *tour de force*. This is because at times the authors assume that their readers already are familiar with archival concerns, processes, and principles; and at other times, they address a supposed neophyte audience. Although this inconsistency in address may reflect the editor's lack of proper advising, it may also reflect a much larger problem of the actual uneasiness characterizing the dialogue this volume seeks to stimulate.

The third set of essays, especially the duo by Richard Cox and John Dean, speaks to many of the same issues but in terms of collection management. In one case, government documents are characterized as published archives which are controllable by archival strategies especially suited for the growing bulk and endless geometric expansion of governmental series. This problem of mass is equally important for general book collection management and conservation, where administrative options allow libraries to treat their collections archivally. Little in library literature reveals that government documents in libraries are commonly treated archivally rather than bibliographically; even the basic textbooks by government document "librarians" fail to understand or articulate why the inferential process of retrieval, based on provenance, in government information is so different from general monographic collections and cataloging. Nor do advocates of remote storage realize that their positions are fundamentally archival, in advocating a second appraisal for a retention decision, a withdrawal and revised description and perhaps re-arrangement, before being deposited into a low-use, high-preservation stack area. These essays serve to remind librarians and archivists alike that the supposed difference of methods between libraries and archives is not as well marked as some suggest.

Vogt's third essay in this cluster brings such issues from inside an institution to the national arena, and simultaneously to the all-pervasive issue of funding. It is in considering a nationwide records program that one confronts the problematic fusion of issues pertaining to archival and bibliographic control to the concrete realities of collection management and preservation. The key elements of an overall policy are outlined, and they look not altogether dissimilar from goals and objectives discussed in the library world for coordinated collection development and management.

The final essays address education and professional concerns. So often education is seen as the single cure for problems of poor communication, non-cooperation, misunderstanding, and dissension within the ranks. The foregoing essays, however, indicate that the differences in archival and library approaches to similar problems are real, as are differences in the mission of the two types of information agencies and in the kinds of materials they accession and acquire. Education may serve to make people more acutely aware of these differences and in other instances commonalities, but such awareness does not guarantee resolution of those attitudes, principles, and methodologies which keep archives and libraries apart. Indeed, as Francis Blouin notes, a segment in the archival profession very much wants educational programs which are separate from either foster curricula, History or Library Science, and might emphasize the divergence rather than integration.

The idea of convergence, however, does not entail the absorption of one into the other, but cognates a working together, a partnership, and acknowledgment of overriding common goals as information providers. Blouin suggests as well that such cooperation in educational program development is necessary, arguing the observation that the united have a better chance of success and survival than the divided. He notes that new forms of information management coming from business, government, and engineering sectors of education and organizational development outside higher education, are possible threats to archives and libraries as they have been defined traditionally. The non-archives, non-library oriented information people are oriented to new technology and management schools, and hence do challenge the professions of archival administration and librarianship unless these non-allied fields are co-opted.

Robert Warner sees such technology as forcing on splinter groups within the still ethereal information profession a greater convergence which will affect professional identities. As this identification undergoes revision and technology outside libraries and archives continues to evolve faster than these institutions can keep pace, a common defensiveness may indeed draw archivists and librarians closer. It would be nice if both groups could see in their disciplines and heritages more positive motivation to inspire cooperation. The future course of both archivists and librarians is still very open, with the exception that everyone sees automation, the largest sense of computer technology applications in information settings, as the current wave and dominant force in behavioral change and professional development.

Such an observation admits that external developments are exerting more pressure on archivists and librarians to change than is being generated from within these fields to control their own destiny. Both are largely reactive. These essays make it clear how archivists are reacting to changes in libraries which affect them, some good and others less so; but archivists perceive libraries as being largely uninfluenced by archives. Interaction is wanting, seemingly on a daily unilateral basis as well as at the national and professional organizational levels. This volume hardly outlines ready solutions, but these essays do point to current intersections of activity, recognition of a universal common cause, and some recent progress in using modern information technology and networking to mutual advantage. If these essays serve as a point of departure for further discussion and exploration of new ways for collaboration, then the purpose of this project is accomplished.

Perhaps in another decade, a third attempt should be made to bring into focus the relationship between archives and libraries, to continue the reflection begun in Clark's *Archives-Library Relations* and carried forward in this volume, *Archives and Library Administration: Divergent Traditions and Common Concerns*. At present archives and libraries are developing along parallel lines, as indicated by the essays' reminders of past divergence and possible future convergence. It would be interesting to know in ten years if this parallel course holds steady, or if, as many of the current contributors suggest, past divergence may be altered into convergence and the evolution of an all-embracing information profession. If such predictions come true, it will be interesting as well to assess the relative position of archives and libraries to each other and how much professional identification still coalesces around these two divisions, or if current questions about their relationship are muted by the onslaught of new technology, multi-media, and information managers who lack sufficient regard for cultural preservation or the transfer of information through time in addition to the dominant concern of information crossing space at one time for particular, immediate needs.

Lawrence J. McCrank
Guest Editor

FROM THE EDITOR

A huge gap in my own education and experience precludes me from making substantive comments on the articles of this special issue of *JLA*. Much of what I know about archives and about relationships between archivists and librarians comes from reading the papers that lie ahead. For this and other reasons, I will attempt to neither summarize nor criticize the contents of this important work.

From my own managerial perspective, however, I am struck by several themes which appear like a drumbeat across the papers. These themes are reflected in terms such as "differences," "similarities," and "cooperation." Permit me to briefly reflect on them.

A number of authors in this issue openly acknowledge differences between archivists and librarians, or between archives and libraries. These differences are particularly interesting to note given the frequent occasions in which the two are located in the same organization. There are numerous sources of differences, including those that bear on values, education, priorities, materials, descriptive language, classification schemes, client characteristics, to name a few. It is not for me to judge whether these differences are real or imagined; in either case they operate at a sufficient level to warrant attention. The salient issue is whether the differences will ultimately spell dysfunctional separation, or whether they can be used to benefit the archivist, the librarian, and most important, the users they serve. As a consummate idealist, I prefer to foresee the latter. As a student of management and organization, I know that for conflict to be dealt with effectively, differences must be openly acknowledged, respected, and processed if constructive resolutions are to emerge.

The acknowledgement of differences, combined with some added reflection, inevitably generates a number of similarities. Librarians and archivists appear to recognize similar needs surrounding issues such as preservation, types of materials, classification schemes, access to materials and information, technological advancements, among others. Sometimes these similarities draw librarians and archivists together in a natural fashion. But this is not always the case. If the papers in this issue are an accurate barometer, similarities have not guaranteed interaction nor have they been exploited in regularized, widespread ways. The existence of similarities is an insufficient condition for interaction; it takes additional ingredients to prompt productive relationships.

Perhaps this explains why the third theme, cooperation, stands as a separate issue. Cooperation appears to have at least two general sources of impetus. One is reactive. Such is the case where technology is forcing and fostering interdependencies. The other is proactive, and takes many forms. Among these are committees of professional associations, programs and projects, conferences, and a variety of other exploratory discussions and experiments. Both reactive and proactive conditions call for dialogue, and both call for leadership. This special issue is a good example of proaction. From a managerial point of view, cooperative efforts in charting new and untested paths are among the most demanding. The problems and opportunities faced by librarians and archivists are complex and varied. It will take sustained, reasoned, and intelligent efforts to increase cooperative efforts and to utilize every mechanism to learn and to disseminate this learning to others. It is hoped that this journal issue takes one additional step in the right direction.

There is much more to the papers in this issue than the foregoing commentary acknowledges. They cover a wide variety of topics beyond those I chose to discuss above. The authors, to whom I would like to express my sincere appreciation, worked diligently to bring attention to many important issues worthy of attention and action. They offer many solid possibilities for future exploration. The major credit for this issue belongs to Larry McCrank. It began as his idea, and it came to fruition because he took all the necessary initiatives. He put in many hours of his own writing, and coordinated the work of other authors. He framed the idea, put structure on the work, identified his contributors, and got the task done. I might add that he did so with a plan that met deadlines that almost no one meets these days. I therefore extend deep appreciation to Larry for this undertaking, and predict that he will be sought after and remembered for his contribution.

John R. Rizzo

Archives Under Library Administration: Points of Convergence and Conflict

Paul H. McCarthy

CONFLICTING PERSPECTIVES

Archives and their role within the library have been perceived quite differently by administrators, other librarians, and archivists. Archives and other "special collections" have been cast by some as the jewel in the rich information crown of the sophisticated research library. This "jewel" was thought to bring sometimes a sense of completion and maturity to the library program. During the affluent days of the late sixties and early seventies, administrators seeking prestige and stature in the scholarly community, recognized the genuine contributions to research that an archives could make. Rich in unique and rare primary source information, the archives were seen as adding the final lustre to the "compleat" research library and announcing its scholarly maturity.

The more skeptical have seen the development of archives and other special collections programs as the Biblical "pearl of great price" while others, especially some archivists, disappointed by a perceived lack of understanding or support, take an even more cynical view. To these more skeptical observers, some administrators have engaged the pursuit of this prize without heed to its total cost and the relatively limited number of

Paul McCarthy is the Archivist of the University of Alaska and curator of manuscripts, directing the Alaska and Polar Regions Department, Fairbanks, AK.

students it would affect. While not quite capable of fulfilling the Biblical charge to "sell all you own" in pursuit of this "pearl," many were seen as mortgaging the future financial health of the library by expansion into a specialized program of limited impact and appeal. The jewel was as expensive in upkeep as it was in pursuit. Its richness proved useful only on limited occasions.

The most cynical archivists may sense that archives are more appropriately viewed, to change the metaphor, as an unsuccessful and disillusioned Cinderella. Brought into a family already living in desperate circumstances, her unique gifts and talents went unappreciated. Typically she is assigned less desirable quarters and expected to accomplish her work without reasonable assistance. She comes to the attention of those in power who apparently appreciate her virtues, however momentarily, only through the good offices of her fairy godmother, Celebration. While she is particularly valued for her stunning features which enhance the kingdom's great social occasions, this Cinderella is forced by time and circumstance back to her impoverished setting. Because of the Prince's attention and patronage, the archival Cinderella may be eyed suspiciously by less secure and occasionally jealous family members; yet, unlike the fairytale, this Cinderella finds herself pursued only on significant occasions by an opportunistic and inconstant Prince. Chastened by the inconstancy of the regal administration and unsure of the support and understanding of her step family, the archival Cinderella searches for a suitor who will appreciate her real virtues and assist her with her efforts to escape from what seems an untenable situation.

Whether the archives is seen as the "crowning jewel," the "pearl of great price," or the "unsuccessful Cinderella," each of these metaphors may well reflect only the bias or perspective of a particular viewer. A closer examination of the library environment in which so many archives operate suggests a more realistic experience in a number of areas where there is a real convergence of values and ideas, and other areas where differences continue and require not agreement, but a realistic appreciation of and respect for the differences.

During the past one and a half decades, we have seen trends in resource and personnel allocation within libraries which have exacerbated traditional conflicts between libraries and archives under library administration. These years also have seen the development in areas such as networking and access to collections, a concurrence of values and a convergence of interest. In some way the re-definition of clienteles and services have brought these institutions to new understandings and an appreciation of their complementary value.

A large plurality, if not majority, of archives exist within the library corporate culture. To the degree that the environment, values, and interests are shared, we can expect to find convergence of understanding;

to the degree that these factors differ, there may be significant sources of conflict.[1] While sharing the same facilities, administration, budget apparatus, and personnel policies, the overall environment in a cultural sense, in which archives and libraries operate, the values which each esteem, the heroes which each holds dear, and methods of communication to which they are accustomed, may at times be different enough to promote distinct subcultures, significant conflicts, and misunderstandings. On the other side an appreciation of the positive effects of a nurturing environment, such as developments in technology, similarities in communication, and an understanding of each profession's role in the emerging information sciences and fields, should promote shared interests and collegial understanding. The large number of archival programs established since 1970 within library settings, especially within this country's institutions of higher learning, have had a significant impact on both the development of the archival profession and the preservation of the American cultural record.[2] The drive toward professionalism in archival administration has often seen the use of the library science model for comparative and contrasting purposes.[3]

PROGRAMMATIC DIFFERENCES

Archival operations compared or contrasted to typical library counterparts, indicate areas where the library and archival environments as well as values differ or complement one another. The developing sense of archival professionalism and the need to define differences as well as similiarities with allied fields, has provided vexing personnel management problems to library administrators and frustrations to individual archivists. Archivists engaged during the 1970s in three significant initiatives to define more precisely and develop the profession: (1) the certification of individual archivists: (2) recommendations for basic elements in archival education programs: and, (3) the development of standards for the operation of archival institutions.[4] These are all significant steps in modern professionalization. Although three initiatives have had strong support within the Society of American Archivists, they have faltered or floundered until recently. The situation of most archivists within their parent institutions has provided neither the incentive nor administrative muscle necessary to attain the goals initially envisioned.

Individual archival programs developed within a library setting usually have been modest in scope and staff size. Cumulatively, however, the growth in the number of programs initiated has had a tremendous impact on the profession. The major developments through the mid-1960s in theory, practice, education, and experience came from the National Archives and from strong State archival or Historical Society programs.

Theory and practices adopted by these units to meet the demands of increasingly voluminous public records, anticipated by a generation the problems that would be encountered during the 1970s in developing archival and manuscript programs within libraries. New archivists of the 1960–1970s received their training at such institutes as those sponsored by the National Archives and Records Service, and initial experience at the hands of practicing archivists steeped in archival theory and a practice developed to handle public records. Traditional manuscript programs already housed in libraries gradually adopted archival practices which focused on the respect for the order, integrity, and arrangement of records. They abandoned efforts to treat these records as items or to approach them on a subject basis, both of which may be seen more traditionally as library practices. Archives and manuscript repositories might be seen in retrospect as differentiating themselves for the past generation from the practices of their parent library institutions. This was caused both by practical need and theoretical concerns. This shift in primary focus from the user to the material as the determinate of how service would be provided, posed a serious conflict and challenge to traditional library values. It still increases the likelihood of misunderstanding.

Libraries and archives approach collection development in fundamentally different ways. The chief "limiting step"[5] or restricting factor in archival or manuscript collection development is the limited availability of sources to build a research collection. The solicitation of manuscripts occurs in a highly competitive market. Good research materials are always difficult to locate; one or two geographic areas and several states, such as New York,[6] have done a needs assessment but nothing which might even begin to approximate a market analysis. Knowledge of this highly individualized and ever changing market is gained by good research, connections, sensitivity to the people and institutions likely to be good prospects, as well as happenstance, luck, and tremendous patience and determination.[7] Once identified, some donors need to be made aware of the historical and intellectual value of the materials they possess, be convinced that the materials should be made available for public research use, and be assured of the integrity and capability of the institution represented. The process takes weeks, months, and even years. Personal and legal hurdles must be overcome; the process, however hopeful, can be discontinued at any time through a change of heart or will. It can be complicated by competing family members or competing institutions. There is no assurance of success until the collection is received and legal title is gained. The environment is competitive, the market unknown or at best known vaguely, and the success rate low. Probably less than ten percent of all solicitations by a modestly aggressive manuscript program prove successful. Competitiveness, diligence, ability to relate well to a variety of people, the ability to appraise unique materials, and confidentiality are the prized values. The same pertains to the development of archival collections. The competitiveness is mitigated, but the same persuasive talents are needed. The records to be transferred to an archives are usually seen as so important to at least one person in the originating office to make him or her resist the transfer.

In contrast, the limiting step (particularly in times of declining revenues and budgets) in book collection development is availability of funds for acquisitions. The market for libraries is definitive and largely non-competitive, except for rare books. There is an incentive for the seller and a pre-established rationale for the acquisition of library materials, a method to develop a sustained flow of books from producers to repositories, and an ability to plan which may be lacking in archival operations. Finally, there are incentives for the development of cooperative arrangements with the thought of sharing materials, in original or facsimile.

Bibliographic knowledge, careful market appraisal, and the ability to understand the needs of students and faculty, allows library collection-development personnel to design more carefully their acquisition program to meet immediate and future demands. They are therefore more likely to engage other libraries in cooperative strategies for collection development and resource sharing. Current trends in collection appraisal and conspectus development hold promise for more intelligent and deliberate development of collections both by individual libraries and cooperative groups.[8] The existence of an external, knowable universe against which collections can be measured, and extrinsic subject oriented schema against which progress can be measured, is critical to the effort. Cooperative ventures have evolved more slowly in the manuscript arena. The universe of available materials is largely unknown, collection development much more opportunistic, and as yet, there are no external subject schema by which to measure progress or coverage. Manuscript collection development policies have thus tended to be necessarily imprecise. Incentives for cooperative ventures have focused the obligation to preserve as much of the critical historical record as possible, while recognizing the limitations of the participating institutions. The transfer of archival collection data in any sophisticated form has been a relatively recent development; the transfer of original materials is extremely rare. The transfer of content for any but the smallest collections, while technically feasible, is far from being cost effective.

Incentives for cooperative projects among libraries include cost effectiveness, and because of current protocols and technologies, enrichment of the information base for their users. In contrast, cooperative projects among archives have been motivated by cost avoidance while insuring at the same time that a larger portion of the historical record will be preserved as a result of the effort of the cooperating institutions. Few libraries see themselves as responsible primarily for the preservation of the record of the American publishing industry, or for even one publisher; they focus primarily on fulfilling the perceived needs of their clientele. The *raison d'être* of all archives and manuscript repositories is the assumption of responsibility for the preservation of the record of an individual, family, or corporate entity. The primary library emphasis on fulfilling user needs and the archive's maintenance of the record is a division that constantly differentiates between their divergent approaches to collection development, access, personnel management, resource allocation, and cooperative ventures.

Consequently, one of the most vexing problems for archivists is the apparent lack of the different environmental situation of an archival operation and the values involved. The identification of unique collections and the development and maintainence of a strong ongoing relationship with prospective donors are key elements in any aggressive manuscript program. While library acquisitions might be compared with a purchasing office, archival development would be more closely compared to directing a sales program and a service operation. Indeed, an archives is selling a service: preservation of a particular historical record in exchange for a donation. Travel is an important component in the development of this type of program. The general reduction of travel in the last several years within libraries is seen as an annoying problem for most librarians; archivist and most manuscript curators would see it as a blow to their ability to maintain even a basic acquisition or solicitation program.

PERSONNEL DIFFERENCES

The recruitment, development, and mobility of archival professionals offers several areas of comparison and contrast between library and archival environments and values. At this time perhaps one insight into areas where the respective professions converge and where they still differ is gained by looking at pre- and post-employment educational patterns.

Regardless of degrees and previous library employment experiences, professional work commences once the standard professional degree, the M.L.S., has been achieved. The focus of education concentrates on understanding basic library operations and responsibilities, the nature and organization of information, and the utilization of standardized processes to provide bibliographic access to library holdings. The application of increasingly sophisticated strategies to obtain information from holdings as well as those retrievable from elsewhere through other databases, and studies of the information seeking behavior of their users, are also increasingly important. The emphases would seem to be on organization, facilitation, and service.

The tempo of efforts by archivists to differentiate themselves as a profession has increased in the last generation. Traditionally the archivist would likely arrive at his or her first work assignment with a much greater subject discipline orientation and much less specifically professional background. For many years the preparation for archivists was aligned closely to the specialized interests served, in history which has dominated the enterprise, or specialty subjects such as physics or sociology for more subject focused archives and special collections. The development of organizational and information skills of a technical nature were, for many, post-employment expectations. Thus, annual conferences, workshops, seminars, and other courses have always been a more critical factor in the development of archival expertise than in librarianship, partially because of the widespread lack and availability of graduate archival education. The value of these continuing educational offerings is likely to persist because of the normal appointment process in many smaller archival and historical institutions and some libraries as well. In-house candidates familiar with the organizational history, and with years of experience in the organization, are likely to be appointed to archival responsibilities. Their archival training often comes after their subject specialization. Regular offerings in basic archival professional education will continue to demand the time and attention of the Society of American Archivists as the field matures because of this appointment process, which, unlike general library science, is based rather heavily on a subject field.

Recently, with the growth and development of graduate programs which include archival concentrations, all libraries and academic ones in particular, can demand for beginning positions adequate academic preparation from competitive candidates. The consolidation and articulation of archival theory and practice during the last decade have helped to identify the key elements that need to be included in a graduate school archival curriculum.[9] Several graduate library and history programs have integrated archival administration into their course offerings either as an area of emphasis or as a major concentration. SAA's Committee on Education and Professional Development has been actively working with archival educators to develop evaluation and accreditation procedures for graduate archival education, although so far without success. The political constraints, expense, lack of incentive, and liability that are involved in accreditation, particularly when this education occurs within schools whose dominant focus on professional education is elsewhere, may doom any external review process. Recent renewed enthusiasm by archival educators may presage wider agreement and further progress in this area.

Many archivists, lacking standardized measure for archivist qualifications, recently have renewed interest in instituting a certification process. The current proposal before SAA would involve the post-employment certification of archivists using a combination of criteria: experience, education, and a comprehensive examination.[10] SAA seeks to preserve the valued freedom of access to the field by professionals from widely varying backgrounds, along with equally prized value of basic professional competence. Many younger professionals see certification as the recognition of competence already gained, which can provide a competitive edge in an increasingly crowded job market. Many also see the institution of certification as a profession-wide responsibility that allows employers to use appropriate credential in the recruitment process. Those opposed to the certification process see it as a laudable and well-intended effort, but less than effective in the effort to establish a position of power and prominence for the archival profession. Sensitive to the currents of de-regulation, some see it as a restrictive process countervailing current social and economic tides. Others see a significant lessening of the distinctions between the several professions engaged in a more loosely defined and integrated information industry. They see a blurring of the distinctions which have existed between traditional library and archival formats and more recently, computer-based data. With the advent of the electronic office and electronic publishing, the deluge of machine-readable data that is appearing, some archivists foresee a future that will require a re-thinking of basic approaches, techniques, and values in both archives and libraries. This re-thinking will require all of the information-based professions to develop understandings and interests which more closely coincide. For them, the move toward certification seems counterproductive when technical evolution seems to be moving us toward information-based rather than format-based professions. Regardless of point of view, the certification thrust does indicate the basic urge of many archivists to articulate more clearly the need for specific professional recognition and the definition for a profession that has been, at times, over-shadowed or influenced by its two allied professions, history and library science.

Because of early cooperative collection building and development of networks to facilitate resource sharing, librarians have anticipated archivists perhaps by several years in seeing themselves as information providers and brokers. Refocusing from format toward service requires a paradigm shift by both professions. F. Gerald Ham in his 1981 challenge to archivists, emphasized changes which could occur in the "post-custodial era."[11]

Regardless of the move toward viewing archivists and librarians alike as allied information professionals, the two are likely to retain significantly different approaches toward this information. The culturally "sacred" character of the book and intrinsic importance of records are likely to remain. The demise of books and records have, like marriage, long been predicted, yet are not likely to occur. Books are more widely available than ever before; the paperless office is not. However, fundamental changes can be expected in the storage and delivery of some kinds of books and most forms of records as we proceed into an age of more intense communication and data sharing. These latter trends will have profound effects on archivists and the archival record.

The situation of archivists in whatever parent agency has long been a source of concern and frustration among archivists.[12] Archives within agencies well-positioned to exert power e.g., executive agencies in government and administrative offices in universities seem often to be cultural wastelands to most archivists. The emphasis on economy, housekeeping and current information often conflicts with the cultural values that attracted most archivists into the profession. Libraries, while proving to be more culturally conducive to archival values, seem to deprive archivists of power and position. Usually relegated to the administrative and geographic outposts of the library, the archival staff, particularly if their training and education differ markedly from that of their colleagues, feel isolated in the cultural framework of the library.

Some archivists may find themselves in matters of academic promotion marching to the beat of two different drummers, neither playing a tune that echoes fondly in the archivist's ear. A heritage of discipline-based education may prompt the archivist to a markedly different approach to promotion than expected of many librarians, but heavy work loads and position requirements may prevent the archivist from matching the pace established by academically based departments. Promotion may be seen as easier or more difficult than that of their colleagues, depending on how and where criteria are established. A prime consideration for an archivist recruiting professional staff into a library based archival program must be to measure carefully the applicant's ability to survive special interests within and without the library. The M.L.S. has become *de rigeur* for the academic archivist, a criterion not shared by the rest of the profession.

The upward mobility of archivists within library systems is quite limited. Even the most expansive archival or manuscript programs within libraries have a small number of professional staff, so opportunities for promotion must be sought elsewhere unless the archivist is willing and prepared through education or experience to undertake some administrative metamorphosis. Promotion for many means a journey from one institution to a more prestigious one, or from a less to a more sophisticated one, or occasionally from a university to a public corporate archives. Too frequently career advancement means leaving the field entirely. Even with relocation, rarely do archivists penetrate the higher echelons of library administration. Whether by temperament, professional dedication, lack of opportunity, or lack of degree, few archivists have assumed positions of significant administrative responsibility in major libraries at any policy-making level above department head. Only within the last few years have any well-known archivists made this change; but even now the number can be counted on one hand.[13] This lack of upward mobility is perhaps one reason many archivists perceive their needs and their perspective as seldom represented in a library's administrative consciousness, or at the state and national levels, even though libraries so heavily influence the welfare of archival programs.

This devalued position of archivists within organizational structures has been described most sharply by Sidney Levy in a report to the Society of American Archivists.[14] In a survey concentrating on resource allocators' perceptions of archivists, Levy characterizes resource allocator's view of archivists as having "the impotence of virtue, which is supposed to be its own reward, leaving allocators to address themselves to more pressing concerns."[15] Archivists have maintained a position of virtue, not one of power. Archivists have assumed for too long that the unique character of the records and the importance of their work would make resource allocators sensitive and responsive to their needs. Whether it be Rodney Dangerfield's "I get no respect," or the scenario of the disenchanted Cinderella previously described, archivists are now becoming keenly aware of their need to compete for resources, even or especially within a library context given the strained resources of most libraries. None of the positions suggested by the metaphors at the beginning of this article are workable! Through professional initiatives and studies that focus on the archives and the society served, or on goals and planning for the profession, archivists more than ever before are involved in developing demand, support, and use of archival services.[16]

COLLECTION ACCESSIBILITY

The arrangement, description, and access to collections are areas where traditional approaches have differed substantially, but where modern technologies make similar approaches more feasible. This is one area where the library environment has been increasingly supportive of archival aspirations and values. Incentives for cooperation such as economic savings occurred historically earlier for libraries than for archives. Printing and the wider distribution of identical copies of the same works made the development of great library collections possible. While the growth of libraries with many duplicated materials thus accelerated, archives continued to accumulate the original historical record, the only document of the past for an individual family, organization, or government. The book provided an ideal vehicle for transmitting ideas: it conveys the prefocused, distilled, concentrated perspective of a writer in a manner that facilitates distribution and communication, and thus demand. The growth of collections, the similarity of materials, a commonality of approach, limited funds and staff, and the possible replacement of materials, naturally provides incentives to establish standard bibliographic elements, for shared processing and data exchange. The evolution of modern communications networks from mail to phone, and then electronic data transmission, have all facilitated the efforts of libraries to share resource data and the actual materials. The incentives have been economic, the focus service, and the results fruitful.

Few of these same incentives until recently inspired archives to cooperate. Knowledge about the material within a particular collection was limited to those privy to their contents through personal examination or through the word of other scholars. Organization was idiosyncratic, content was dissimilar, approach was individualized to function, communication limited, and the uniqueness of the material prevented any widespread sharing except through massive duplication and publication programs. Only with the modern volume has form been forced onto format, less by the archivist than by the records creator. Modern records generators are being forced to structure and organize their records in a more uniform fashion during their creation to cope with volume, in a struggle printers and publishers underwent years ago. The volume of material has likewise forced corporations and organizations to think more clearly about the organization. Improved communications have helped archivists realize the universality of problems dealing with organization, arrangement, and descriptive practices.

The move toward standardization of practice and data elements in description has few of the economic incentives for archives so apparent to the libraries. No central agency has had the power and influence in the archival field that the Library of Congress has had within the library community. The sharing of data generated by others does not effect cost savings within any other archives; the adoption of uniform practices must be seen more as a professional responsibility and eventually as a user service for others than members of the parent organization rather than of any primary benefit to the institution itself. The focus on user service becomes viable and professionally rewarding only as communication among archivists increases, and as archivists see themselves as professionals in an emerging information field with particular responsibility to assist scholars seeking primary source material, regardless of location.

This broadly perceived reference function is a relatively new element in archival thinking.

Because of the increased communication and the emergence of a more cohesive archival community, significant accomplishments have marked the past decade. Sharing finding aids plus discussion and debate over appropriate elements has led to the adoption of more uniform approaches. A growing archival literature available through the Society of American Archivists and the various regional archival groups has produced a body of common knowledge about arrangement, description, acquisition, appraisal, security, and other subjects that has produced more unified consensus about archival practices.[17] The SAA basic manual series has had an enormous impact on the large number of new professionals who have entered the field in the last decade and a half.[18]

Within the last five years archivists have devised an acceptable MARC format for Archives and Manuscript Control (AMC) to share collection data through bibliographic utilities.[19] While late by library standards, the standard was forged because archivists perceived previous library solutions to manuscript descriptions as unacceptable approaches. This effort by SAA's National Information Systems Task Force of archivists associated with many of the larger research libraries, will significantly change the role and self-perception of many archivists. Previously archivists were seen primarily as custodians and interpreters of the collections at hand; any assistance to researchers about collections in other repositories was limited to the valued but dated *National Union Catalog of Manuscript Collections* or through their personal knowledge. With network capabilities and access to shared collection data, archivists will have more incentive to become active partners in their clients' search for primary sources. Their approach to preliminary arrangement and description of collections may be re-focused to take advantage of new computer capabilities and to gather data suitable for AMC as the collection enters the archives. In this way information on incoming collections will be available regionally or nationally almost immediately, rather than delayed until the information is compiled as an end product after processing is complete. Computerized network technology increases the effectiveness and speed of communication. This sharing of a common information environment and values among archivists should provide a tremendous catalyst to archival development, and may stimulate greater rapport with librarians who assume such exchange is commonplace. It is a new one for most archivists.

While librarians long ago agreed on creating subject access to materials, archivists and manuscript creators are still in the process of determining an acceptable approach to subject access. The use of traditional Library of Congress subject headings is perceived by many archivists, somewhat reluctantly, as a tolerable and useful approach. The development of a more particularized or geographic oriented subject approach still maintains a high importance for most archivists. Traditional LCSH headings provide valuable but general access points, not the very specialized approach important to most archivists to exploit fully regional collections. If much of the data gathered during arrangement is going to be useful for additional access, the use of appropriate MARC tags in AMC that are suitable for local adaptation will be necessary. Provision of such particular descriptors will continue to be much more important for archives than for libraries. This will involve all archives to some degree in establishing their own descriptors, and perhaps thesaurus also. Recent efforts have been made to develop a standardized list or vocabulary of functional activities that generate records within bureaucratic organizations.[20] A method for sharing these additional access points by network technology will be an important next phase.

MANAGEMENT CONCERNS

Efforts to deal with modern records more theoretically has also had its benefits for management practices. Libraries have long been subject to external reviews by both funding agencies and accrediting organizations. Review has become systematic; operations have been analyzed to a point where appropriate data is produced so that both the library and agencies can measure the effectiveness and costs of various operations. Unlike libraries, no accrediting agencies have taken note of archives, except as an adjunct to resources available in the book and periodical collection. However, the data requested has been so generalized so as not to give much of a picture of the capabilities and strengths of the archives. Funding agencies, while interested and concerned about archival operations, have been largely unable to provide incentives for archives to undergo an accreditation process. Within the last few years there has been a move to provide an effective and comprehensive evaluation of archives. A systematic approach has been developed by SAA's Task Force on Institutional Evaluation.[21] Although its use has been limited, the formal evaluation process has been utilized by archivists seeking to improve their own programs and by some administrators concerned about the operation and direction of archival programs under their control. The evaluation process also gives funding agencies a measure against which to compare archives submitting grant requests. On an informal level the evaluation outline has allowed some archivists, such as at the author's institution, to review their operations in terms of staffing, processing costs, layout of facilities, and user services, without going through the extensive formal review process.

Librarians have also taken the collection of institutional data for granted. Access to such statistical and comparative data is unknown in the archival field. The presence of a large influential national library and a long established and substantially funded professional organization has facilitated the development of standardized library terminology and appropriate measurements for institutional resources and processes. Federally funded grant programs have provided additional incentives. As the technology presented the opportunity and the need became more apparent archivists began formalizing elements, definitions, and reporting practices.[22] These efforts were especially influenced by library models, as might be expected. Efforts by SAA's Committee on Standard Reporting Practice, and then a sub-committee of its Task Force on Institutional Evaluation, sought to develop standard terms and measurements for operations. As a result SAA was able to conduct the first national census of archival repositories.[23] It will establish a number of archivial benchmarks. These data, when available and presented by the institution, will have an enormous impact on individual archivists and their ability to compare and contrast their operations with other institutions. For the first time archivists will have management information long available to their colleagues in the library field.

Planning, whether institutional, statewide, or national, is another area of convergence between librarians and archivists. Because of the complimentary mission of their institutions and cooperative values, librarians have long engaged in a dialogue at the local, state, and national level in an effort to improve the future of libraries and librarianship. More recently, archivists, faced with massive record selection and preservation challenges, a "scarce resource" outlook, and the need to develop more tangible public use and support, have embraced planning as a way to effect the archival future as well. State planning efforts and record surveys funded by the National Historic Publications and Records Commission of the National Archives and Records Service (now the National Archives and Records Administration) were the first publicly funded planning grants in the archival field. The archival profession more recently, undertook the initial analysis of planning needs on a comprehensive basis through SAA's Task Force on Goals and Planning.[24] This seminal work has brought to the attention of the individual archivist the need for broadbased planning in a way no other document or effort has been able to effect.

CONCLUSION

There are common interests and a convergence in values within libraries and archives that will bring these two professions closer together. Librarians recently have become particularly aware of their need to address the physical safety and preservation of materials in order to serve user interest on a long term basis. Archives, with the expanding horizon that technology offers, are beginning to realize an opportunity to focus much more closely on users' needs and desires. There are at least two challenges in the near future to the archivist in the library setting. First, we will need to adopt and adapt the library approaches and technologies and those of other information systems to ones appropriate for the unique nature of archival materials, and seek original solutions to problems posed by that format. While electronic publishing will have a significant impact on libraries, particularly those focused on research use rather than the more popular materials, the effect of the electronic office will have a profound impact on archives of the future. The progressive archivist will be called upon not only to insure the preservation of the record but also to take a role to insure that the records created are complete, available and are integrated with the myriad of other records created by an organization. As we move into an information future, record creators will need effective and perceptive guides for the creation and maintenance of their documents in order to maintain accurate records of their work. With a "half life" of computer technology which now seems to be between six months and one year, this entails no mean challenge. The constant push toward centralized systems, and the equally powerful pull toward more decentralized systems with the evolution of microcomputers, pose significant challenges to preserve the archival record.

In the last fifteen years archivists within library settings have gone a long way in defining their mission and capabilities and how these are distinct from as well as related to librarianship. The profession itself has made significant progress in the last five years in its ability to be of greater assistance to users by providing better access to diverse collections. The profession-wide management data soon to be available should provide archivists with the ability to analyze, compare, and then seek changes in their environment; a higher level of service should evolve. An appreciation of the need to balance the role of the preserver or custodian of the record with that of information server or broker has been recognized. In a promising note: new archivists coming into the field are better trained than ever.

The information arena will continue to evolve rapidly. The second and perhaps greatest challenge is to be open and grasp the opportunities of the future in archival information management. As radical changes occur in both institutional and commercial marketplace, both formal and informal education and an openness to change will allow archivists as well as librarians to play a dynamic and significant role in the information field. While libraries and their constituent archives have functioned well in a number of areas the assumption that librarians and archivists shared the same environment and values has led to a number of frustrations and misunderstandings. A fuller appreciation of the differences and recognition that we must negotiate an allied future in terms of our "interests"[25] will allow both professions to play significant, distinct, yet complementary roles in our information future.

REFERENCES

1. The specific criteria for defining a corporate culture by environment, values, heroes, and communication, are taken from Terrence E. Deal and Allen A. Kennedy, *Corporate Cultures: The Rites and Rituals of Corporate Life* (Reading, Massachusetts: Addison-Wesley Publishing Company, 1982), cf., for library corporate environs: Howard E. Aldrich and Jeffry Pfeffer, "Environments and Organizations," and Beverly P. Lynch, "The Academic Library and Its Environment," in *Management Strategies for Libraries*, ed. Beverly P. Lynch (New York: Neal-Schuman Publishers, Inc., 1985).

2. Membership data from the Society of American Archivists were not collected in the early seventies to permit easy documentation of the increased number of university archivists in the Society over the 15-year period. Since SAA's re-organization in the seventies when university archivists could be more easily identified, the group has grown into one of the largest and most active groups in the Society.

3. A number of studies discuss archival education in the context of library education; the literature is also resplendent with opposition to that model. Frank G. Burke, "Similarities and Differences: Education," in *Archives-Library Relations*, ed. Robert L. Clark, Jr. (New York: R.R. Bowker, 1976; J. Goggin, "That we shall truly deserve the title of profession: the training and education of archivists, 1930–1960," *American Archivist* 47 (1984): 243–54; Nancy E. Peace and Nancy Fisher Chudacoff, "Archivist and Librarians: A Common Mission, A Common Education," *American Archivist* 42 (1979): 456–462; and Lawrence J. McCrank, "Prospects of Integrating Historical and Information Studies in Archival Education," *American Archivist* 42, no. 4 (1979): 443–455, provide several different points of view.

4. A very good recap on SAA's activities on the accreditation of educational programs and the certification of individual archivists is: "Education Committee Submits its Summary Report," *SAA Newsletter*, March 1982. pp. 10–12. Efforts of SAA's Task Force on Institutional Evaluation to develop an effective self-evaluation mechanism and instrument are described in *Evaluation of Archival Institutions: Services, Principles, and Guide to Self Study* (Chicago: SAA, n.d.), p. 10. This extremely useful process has not been more widely utilized because of the lack of incentives.

5. The concept of the "limiting step" to identify the factor or condition that will determine the shape of an intellectual process or production, is from Andrew P. Grove, *High Output Management* (New York: Vintage Books, 1985), p. 4.

6. New York State Archives, *Toward a Useable Past: Historical Records in the Empire State*. A report to the governor and the citizens of New York by the State Historical Records Advisory Board (Albany, New York: State Education Department, 1984).

7. An excellent work describing the intricacies of a manuscript acquisition program is Edward C. Kemp, *Manuscript Solicitation for Libraries, Special Collections, Museums, and Archives* (Littleton, Colorado: Libraries Unlimited, Inc, 1978).

8. The major conspectus is Nancy E. Gwinn and Paul H. Mosher, "Coordinating Collection Development: The RLG Conspectus," *College and Research Libraries* 44 (1983): 128–140. Alaska has been quite active in adopting this approach to the evaluation of individual library collections and for resource sharing environments. This regional use is described in Dennis Stephens and Daniel J. LaRoe, "Enlightened Self-interest: Planning for Cooperative Collection Development in Alaska and the Pacific Northwest," paper presented at the ALA Resources and Technical Services Division, Resources Section's program on Coordinated Collection Development, July 7, 1985, Chicago. Use of the RLG schema to assess manuscript collections and how they contribute to a number of subject areas within the RLG Conspectus might offer an attractive subject-appraisal study.

9. Cf., "Proposed Program Standard for Archival Education: The Practicum," *SAA News-*

letter, July 1979, pp. 19–21; Guidelines for Graduate Archival Education Programs in "Education Directory," *SAA Newsletter*, March 1983, p. 2, a report prepared by the Committee on Education and Professional Development.

10. For the current proposal on individual certification, see "Certification," *SAA Newsletter*, July 1985, pp. 7–10.

11. F. Gerald Ham, "Archival Strategies for the post-custodial era," *American Archivist* 44 (1981): 207–16.

12. The administration of archives within the framework of the library during the mid-seventies is discussed in Clark, *Archives-Library Relations*, pp. 155–165, where the placement of archives within state, university, and public libraries is analyzed.

13. An attempt to explain the lack of movement of archivists into major library administration is difficult indeed. Ann Morgan Campbell, SAA Executive Director, and other archivists were able to identify only a small number of well-known archivists who have made that transition, most within the last two to three years.

14. Sidney J. Levy and Albert G. Robles, *The Image of Archivists: Resource Allocators' Perceptions*, A report prepared for the Society of American Archivists Task Force on Archives and Society by Social Research, Inc., December 1984. This study was requested by the Society's Task Force because of its concern about the image resource allocators had of archivists and archives. The study was based on interviews with forty-four individuals in five major urban areas. While administrative responsibility was not absolutely clear in the sample description, at least 40%, +/− 4% appeared to have administrative responsibilities in or for library services.

15. Levy, "Report," p. iii.

16. SAA's Task Force on Archives and Society was formed during David P. Gracy's tenure as President in response to the real concern over the image of archivists and archives held by their various constituencies. These concerns and some solutions were well articulated in David Gracy, "Archives and Society: An Address by the President of the Society of American Archivists at the annual meeting of the Society of Mississippi Archivists, May 1, 1984," *The Primary Source* 2, no. 2, (May 1984): 1–2, 12–18. The task force saw as important development of a statement explaining the importance of archives: see the draft in "Archives: What They Are, Why They Matter," *American Archivist* 46 (May 1984): 6–7.

17. Frank B. Evans, comp., *Modern Archives and Manuscripts: A select bibliography* (Washington: SAA, 1975), still quite valuable, is updated by Richard B. Kesner, *Information Management: Machine-Readable Records, and Administration: An Annotated Bibliography* (Chicago: SAA, 1983). Covers office automation, videodisc technology, and networking in addition to information management with a bibliography of over 900 citations.

18. SAA's Basic Manual Series has consistently sold well since its introduction in 1977; copies sold represent several times the individual membership of the Society.

19. The work of the National Information Systems Task Force is brought to the attention of the greater archival public by Nancy Sahli, *MARC for Archives and Manuscripts: The AMC Format* (Chicago: SAA, 1985; and Max J. Evans and Lisa B. Weber, *MARC For Archives and Manuscripts: A Compendium of Practice* (Madison: State Historical Society of Wisconsin, 1985).

20. In February 22–23, 1986 eleven participants from major archives and representatives from RLG and SAA met at the call of David Bearman, Smithsonian Institution, to develop a list of functional activities that generate records within bureaucratic organizations.

21. Cf., SAA, *Evaluation of Archival Institutions: Services, Principles and Guide to the Self Study* (Chicago: SAA, n.d.), presents an outline for a comprehensive self-study of an archival program.

22. The consensus reached by SAA's NISTF Working Group on Data Elements is David Bearman, comp., *Data Elements Used in Archives and Records Repository Information Systems: A Dictionary of Standard Terminology*, rev. ed. Nancy Sahli, (Chicago: SAA, 1985).

23. In the summer of 1985 SAA's Task Force on Institutional Evaluation conducted a census of archival institutions to profile and document major administrative functions. The 549 responses to the fifteen-page census are now being analyzed by Paul Conway of the Gerald Ford Library, a member of the Task Force. Studies reflecting the information gained in this major effort should become available in summer 1986.

24. The first efforts of the Task Force were published as "A Statement of the Mission and Goals for the Archival Profession," *SAA Newsletter*, March 1983, 6–7; the major work was published as

an "Initial Discussion Draft," *Planning for the Archival Profession: A Report of the SAA Task Force on Goals and Priorities,* (Chicago: SAA, 1984), 63 p.

25. An extremely interesting strategy for resolving differences by focusing on "interests" has been developed by Roger Fisher of Harvard University, who directs the Harvard Negotiation Project. A brief description of his approach is "Our Group Finds that Negotiating Means Agreeing Not to Disagree," *Wall Street Journal,* 24 December 1985, p. 11; a fuller treatment is Roger Fisher and William Ury, *Getting to Yes: Negotiating Agreement Without Giving In* (New York: Penguin Books, 1983).

The Provenance of Archives Under Library Administration: Organizational Structures and Organic Relationships

David J. Klaassen

Archivists, more than most people, should appreciate that no administrative unit is an island. Unsuccessful efforts to impose external, preconceived classification schemes on the inactive files of institutions, organizations, and individuals led archivists to realize that the key to effective management of records lay in understanding and presenting groups of records as the product of a particular administrative entity or activity. This principle of provenance—arguably the most basic, enduring, and unique archives concept to emerge from archival experience—was developed to guide decisions about the selection of records for archival custody and their subsequent management, but it can be applied equally well to an analysis of the circumstances in which an archives itself operates.

Consider provenance as a useful way of thinking about archives under library administration. Simply stated: where you are affects what you are and do. Any complex modern institution assumes the existence of a hierarchical structure with interdependent specialized divisions, all of them controlled to a degree by the institution's standard operating procedures. The administrative setting in which an archives is placed will affect its operation. Conversely, the presence of an archival unit should, to some degree, shape the nature of the parent institution as well. There should be a symbiotic relationship between libraries and archives when they are administratively linked.

Archives and archivists almost by definition report to someone else. They are not ends in themselves, nor do they normally deliver goods or services that might be considered end products. They exist instead to provide access to information needed by someone else to shape a product or inform a decision. These observations apply equally to libraries; they constitute a succinct summary of the affinity between libraries and

David Klaassen is a curator of manuscripts and an assistant professor at the Social Welfare History Archives, University of Minnesota, Minneapolis, MN.

archives. The responsibility of archives for the inactive records of their parent institution may define their mission primarily as serving administrative informational needs, or the charge to acquire and preserve historical records that are in no way associated with activities of the parent institution may reflect a commitment to support scholarly, genealogical, or general research interests. In either case, archivists are normally subordinate to someone with a nonarchival background and with primarily nonarchival responsibilities.

The Society of American Archivists acknowledged this subordinate condition recently when it commissioned a study to determine how persons who allocate institutional resources perceive and characterize the archivists who report to them. The findings were concise and painful: archivists are perceived as virtuous but impotent. In the view of their administrative superiors, archivists are good at what they do but tend to be "out of sight, out of mind," and they lack clout in comparison with other departments—a perception that both confirms and reinforces their subordinate status.[1]

Thus an analysis of archives under library administration should be undertaken with the understanding that administrative self-determination is seldom an option for archives. Although a few archivists report directly to high-level administrative officers, archives are typically subsumed in a division having general purposes believed to coincide with archival purposes. The reporting line often runs through an administrative operations, public relations, or legal office, reflecting an expectation that the archives exists primarily to serve administrative information needs. Occasionally an archives unit reports through academic teaching-and-research channels, such as a history department or an academic affairs office. The most common circumstance finds archives units placed in libraries, both physically and administratively.

This situation predominates in academic institutions. Nicholas Burckel and J. Frank Cook's profile of college and university archives in the United States demonstrates the pervasiveness of the archives-within-a-library model. They found that the overwhelming majority are located physically (89%) and administratively (82%) within college and university libraries and that a similarly high percentage (82%) of archivists surveyed believed that libraries were the appropriate location for archives.[2] It would be misleading to imply that archives and libraries are administratively linked only in academic institutions. Similar connections exist within state government, businesses, religious bodies, and public libraries as well.[3]

For the most part, the nature of the relationship of libraries and archives can be captured in two general statements:

1. The relationship is fundamentally unequal, in that the library is

normally the parent unit, has greater resources, serves a broader constituency, and is more sharply etched in the public consciousness;

2. Libraries and archives have enough in common to account for their frequent administrative linkage, but the distinctions are substantial enough to produce certain tensions, which can be creative or destructive.

The first proposition is not without exception. There are cases where libraries and archives operate essentially in tandem; this happens most notably in state historical societies or state historical departments where library and archives-and-manuscripts divisions may operate on a separate-but-equal basis or as closely linked units reporting to a common division head.[4] These arrangements reflect a situation where the scale of library and archives operations are relatively balanced, in contrast to the typical archives-and-manuscripts unit in a large research library. The cases of library units contained within an archives are so rare and operate within such narrow limits as to warrant no more than passing mention. The effect of archives normally being subordinated to libraries is profound but often subtle.[5]

THE NATURE OF LIBRARIES AND ARCHIVES

Libraries and archives do have much in common. Both deal with information primarily as recorded in written form; both are concerned with orderly arrangement of their holdings so as to facilitate retrieval; and both ultimately exist to serve as a collective memory, preserving accumulated knowledge for the benefit of present and future generations. The basic functions of both—acquisitions, technical services, preservation, and reference—are roughly analogous. Even in regard to the materials contained in libraries and archives, the distinctions are not as sharp as is sometimes assumed. Archival holdings often include printed matter, and both libraries and archives can contain maps, audiovisual materials, and machine-readable data.[6] Admittedly the commonalities identified here exist mostly at the broad conceptual level and begin to display significant distinctions when examined more closely. Even so, the general purpose shared by libraries and archives provides an adequate base from which to make a credible case for joining them administratively.

Operating on a corollary to the time-honored principle that things not broken should not be fixed, there is more value in analyzing the areas in which archives and libraries differ, in substantial degree if not in kind. These differences fall in three categories:

1. the nature of the materials;
2. the method of selecting and controlling materials;
3. the mission or purpose of the library or archives, as embodied in its perception of its users' needs and how it relates to them.[7]

Frank Burke correctly suggested that the distinction between materials contained in libraries and archives has to do not so much with their form as with the purposes for which they were created.[8] The printed matter contained in libraries is normally created to inform, entertain, or otherwise enrich a diverse, external audience. Individual items can be assumed to be self-contained and self-explanatory, leaving the librarian free to arrange them in accordance with the desired classification scheme, with little concern for their relation to other items. Archival materials, on the other hand, are created for a more limited audience and purpose. In most cases they are a part of the activities that they record, intended to communicate to a specific recipient for an immediate purpose. Creators (the term is used purposefully; "authors" implies a literary intent that is inappropriate here) of individual documents "say what needs to be said," seldom giving thought to the needs and interests of a broader readership. The resulting documents are frequently not self-contained or self-explanatory, and can be understood only if the context of surrounding, related documents is preserved. The limited purpose and audience of documents gives rise to another important archival characteristic. Each grouping of archival records is unique, as are many of the individual items contained in it.

These characteristics have been the basis for much of the distinctiveness in how archivists evaluate and administer the records in their custody. That distinctiveness is most apparent in three areas:

1. The rejection of the concept of a universal classification scheme into which individual items can be assigned;
2. the necessity of shifting from an item orientation to a respect for the integrity of related groupings of items that are bonded by a common origin;
3. a related shift in focus from analysis of the intellectual content of materials to analysis of the process by which materials were created.

All three of these points are embraced in the principle of provenance which is so central to the archival endeavor. In its narrowest definition, provenance prohibits the intermingling of the archives of a given records creator with those of another. In its broader application, it acknowledges the interrelatedness of documents and the necessity of preserving as much contextual information as possible.

Archivists arrived at this point by trial and error. Richard Berner has effectively exposed the duality of past approaches to archives and manuscript materials by identifying two main strands in the development of archival theory and practice in the United States.[9] One, the "historical manuscripts tradition," evolved from librarianship and library responsibility for historical manuscripts, with an emphasis on item-level control, subject classification, and a card catalog as the primary finding aid. The other, the "public archives tradition," adapted European archival practices to the administration of state and federal government records. It emphasized a hierarchical, collective approach to massive quantities of records and utilized the inventory as the primary finding aid.[10]

In the years since World War II there has been substantial intertwining of the two traditions in an effort to develop a generic approach—"the one world of archives" was the phrase applied by a president of the Society of American Archivists—that is equally applicable to everything from massive institutional archives to small collections of personal papers. This attempted unification has exposed some important professional crosscurrents. It would be futile to ignore the important differences between archives and manuscripts. One maintains the archives of the parent institution, primarily for their administrative usefulness, while the other acquires manuscripts primarily for cultural and educational purposes. These differences should not obscure the common conceptual base that informs the work of professionals working in either setting.[11]

It should be clear that the archival profession and its constituents have been better served by the attempted integration than if the two traditions had ignored each other and continued their separate development. As Berner demonstrates, exposure to the public archives tradition sensitized manuscripts curators, from the Manuscripts Division of the Library of Congress on down, to the necessity of shifting away from item-level analysis, while public archivists have come to appreciate the need to supplement their inventories with integrative finding aids modeled on the card catalog. If the results have fallen far short of perfection at either the theoretical or applied level, at least they represent progress. The productiveness of this interaction suggests the potential for similar benefits resulting from continued interaction between archivists and librarians.

Another means of understanding the powerful implications of applying the principal of provenance is afforded by the work of Richard Lytle, who identified two basic methods of intellectual control employed by archivists.[12] The "content indexing method," which derives from Berner's historical manuscripts tradition, attempts to anticipate users' demands by focusing on analysis of file contents and by recording, in index entries, the precise location of materials identified with a given subject. Clearly it relies heavily on an intellectual control system imposed on the records after they have been acquired by the archives. The "provenance method," which is linked with Berner's public archives tradition, depends primarily on exploiting existing characteristics of the records to provide the basis of intellectual control. By recreating and describing the structure and origins of records, emphasizing context over content, it establishes an inferential system that allows the user to anticipate where desired information might be located.

The mass and complexity of archival materials preclude the possibility of comprehensive indexing. The cost of such an undertaking would be wildly prohibitive, but even if the resources were available, the user would have extreme difficulty selecting among the myriad of entries offered. The retrieval capability of the content indexing method is always limited to the entries provided by the indexer. In the provenance method, however, the whole is greater than the sum of its parts. The clues that the provenance method provides to the existence and location of desired information are less precise and certain, but it transcends the subjectivity of content indexing and supports an open-ended variety of retrieval possibilities. It also enhances a researcher's ability to engage in external criticism of documents. The two methods are not mutually exclusive; a provenance-based control system can be enhanced by an index which cites specific selected documents (collection content) or provides cross-referencing to descriptive elements in the finding aid.

Lytle's analysis of content indexing and provenance concentrates on intellectual control, but his dichotomy also brings into focus the way in which the archivist's approach to collection development differs from the librarian's. The distinction between institutional archivists and manuscript curators is most evident in the area of acquisitions. The former is obligated to accept and preserve the permanently valuable records of the institution, while the latter is free to collect from a wide range of sources. Underlying this difference however, is a shared basic approach. Whereas a librarian approaches collection development by seeking to identify what has been published *about* a particular subject or field and then selects from that universe, the archivist must begin by conceptualizing a universe consisting of the written records generated or accumulated *by* the participants and observers of the defined field. No equivalent of a bibiographic or publisher's information network exists to call attention to what has been produced. Thus the question, "what has been written or recorded?" must be preceded by the question, "who would have had reason to write?" Once again, the archivist attends to the act of creation as much as to the resulting record.

Interwoven with differences between libraries and archives in regard to the nature of their materials and the way those materials are selected and controlled are differences in mission and constituency. As already noted, both exist to provide effective access to recorded information; but archives, with their accumulation of historical raw material, can also appeal to and serve users on another level altogether. In her 1985 presidential address to the Society of American Archivists, Andrea Hinding called for a greater appreciation of the affective, noncognitive power and appeal of documents, observing that for many users of archives the appeal is something more, or other, than information content.[13] The value of establishing a physical link with the past is something that information professionals have generally been content to relegate to their museum counterparts, but the trend toward the interpretation of artifacts for informational purposes should have as its counterpart a reciprocal appreciation for the artifactual value of written and printed items.[14] The potential effect of this is relatively limited for librarians—rare books and special collections materials can evoke a tangible sense of linkage with the past—but it is much more profound for archivists.

Differences between libraries and archives in regard to mission and constituency can emerge on another level. For example, a university archives contained in a university research library can find its operational priorities defined by distinctly different clients and needs than those of the library in general. The archives' administrative, as opposed to research, orientation is particularly strengthened if it administers a records management program for the university.[15] The issue here is not a generic difference between libraries and archives—a special library might serve an administratively oriented function analogous to that of an archives—but the juxtaposition of a unit with a primarily administrative orientation within a research setting.

ORGANIZATIONAL STRUCTURE

The differences between libraries and archives are important to individual practitioners who seek to understand the conceptual base for their own professional activity and to the individual researchers whose effective use of library collections and archives depends on an understanding of their nature and relationships. The differences assume added institutional significance when administrative linkages of libraries and archives effectively require one to play by the other's rules. The relationship and its effects are reciprocal, but given that an archives is almost always the junior partner, the effects are felt more fully there.

In any modern organization, libraries not excepted, there exists a hierarchical structure, functional specialization, and an implicit or explicit set of operating procedures. Given the predominant twentieth-century western world view, these structural elements are necessary to provide stability and efficient operation. Standards and definitions provide a base from which to approach both familiar and new circumstances. Archivists under library administration must accommodate to general library goals, objectives, and policies. The policies or policy-makers are not necessarily hostile or insensitive to specialized needs of archivists, but library values and assumptions naturally predominate.[16]

Job descriptions for library-based archival positions are more likely to require an M.L.S. degree than they would in another administrative setting, sometimes because the position entails substantial responsibility for, or interaction with, other library units and sometimes out of simple adherence to standard policy. The library-based archivist is more likely to define his professional membership and publishing activities at least partially in terms of library organizations than would otherwise be the case. Career development opportunities for archivists include the possibility of advancement to a library administrative position, which may offer more residual involvement with archival activity than would a similar up-and-out advancement in another setting.

The competition for limited institutional resources requires a compelling justification. Such a presentation, to be effective, must demonstrate the present and potential contribution to the library's overall program objectives. Statistical evidence can be critical, and this works to the archives' disadvantage when crucial standard reporting categories to measure size of holdings, workload, productivity, and volume of service fail to provide an accurate reflection of archival activities. The archivist can respond to such a situation by passively accepting the disadvantage to the detriment of his or her program, by modifying the program to achieve a better fit with library measures and expectations, or by suggesting modifications in the measuring instruments. Only recently has the archival profession begun to develop statistical reporting standards that provide a meaningful measure of archival activity.[17]

Automated library bibliographic information systems have become a powerful element in the library infrastructure; they present archivists with an enticing opportunity to improve their ability to share information. Past efforts to develop national standards for cataloging manuscripts, notably the *National Union Catalog of Manuscript Collections* and the first and second editions of *Anglo-American Cataloging Rules*, encountered stiff criticism from the archival community, but there was general recognition that the concept of standardized description, if not its then-current application, was vitally important to archives and their users. The USMARC Archival and Manuscripts Control (AMC) format is being accepted more readily because: (1) the potential contained in national online library information systems far exceeds anything previously available to archivists, and (2) the Society of American Archivists' National Information Systems Task Force helped to define the AMC format with sufficient attention to archival concepts and user needs.

Reliance on library-based national online systems such as the Research Libraries Information Network (RLIN) provides a powerful incentive for strengthened ties between archives and libraries. It will likely motivate archives to accept administrative location within libraries or, at the very least, to make other arrangements permitting their participation in online information networks.[18]

Although the structural effects of archival existence in a library are felt more profoundly by the archival unit, there are implications for the host library as well. Potential benefits include the visibility and prestige associated with unique research resources that can enhance the library's overall reputation and ability to support research, assuming that the nature of the archival unit is consistent with library's mission. On the other hand, the archives will always be something of a square peg in a round hole. Its unique expenditure patterns defy simple application of standard budget categories and practices. Collection development expenses in a manuscript repository, for example, involve travel and shipping expenses rather than purchases and subscriptions; and the necessity of responding quickly to an unanticipated opportunity makes the projection of expenses difficult. Specialized supplies and equipment needs add marginally to administrative headaches and overhead costs. These issues are nuisances rather than insurmountable problems, but they require a certain amount of administrative resolve that must be based on a sense that the archives contributes to the library's mission and thus warrants the added effort.

An archives requires substantial financial support, because of the labor-intensive nature of arranging, describing, and preserving records.[19] The sheer bulk of archival records requires significant investment in supplies and equipment, and for space as well. Acknowledgement of the impossibility of replacing unique materials must lead to the provision of adequate environmental and security controls.

ORGANIC RELATIONSHIPS

Any organization has biological as well as mechanical characteristics. While the structural, hierarchical elements provide necessary stability and operating efficiency, they also shape human interactions, encouraging or impeding creative and innovative effort. Just as the functional specialization of the mechanical model requires that different parts work together in synchronized "clockwork" fashion, so also life and health in the organic model depend on a combination of diversity and compatibility.

There is in this modeling an application for the placement of archives in libraries. It assumes that there is an organic benefit to be realized from internal diversity. Sociologist Charles Perrow identified the potentially stultifying effect of organizational structure and standard operating procedures:

> An organization develops a set of concepts influenced by the technical vocabulary and classification schemes; this permits easy communication. Anything that does not fit into these concepts is not easily communicated. For the organization, ''the particular categories and schemes it employs are reified, and become, for members of the organization, attributes of the world rather than mere conventions.''[20]

The archival profession, let alone any individual archival operation, has not matured to the point where it has had cause for serious worry about this eventuality. To the contrary, Berner's exposition of the interweaving of the historical manuscript and the public archives traditions suggests the stimulative power generated by the interaction of contrasting sets of assumptions. Archival theory and practice have been informed and enriched in the past by the librarian's perspective and they will continue to be, if for no other reason than their inability to resist the preponderant position of academic libraries over so many archives.

There is a largely unrealized potential for reciprocity in this relationship. If archivists can effectively and consistently articulate the implications of their provenance-based thinking, they may stimulate their library colleagues to re-examine their controlling assumptions beneficially. Librarians and their users for the most part have been well served by the efficiency and comprehensiveness of bibliographic control systems. They have been victimized to some extent by their own success. There are signs of such systems collapsing under their own weight, in ways even online systems with sophisticated search capabilities may not be able to support. Too often librarians' capability to identify and retrieve individual items has robbed them of the ability or desire to retrieve the whole; that is, to see the forest as well as the trees. Of necessity archivists have learned to look for related groupings and to focus on the process of creation as well as the content of the resulting documents. Such a perspective is unlikely to become the new library orthodoxy, but it deserves serious consideration. Two examples illustrate possible applications.

A project to microfilm selected nineteenth-century popular novels for preservation purposes would typically proceed by compiling title and author lists and comparing them with citation patterns, sales figures, critical reviews, or some other presumed measure of significance or impact, as the basis for selection. An alternative approach more likely to be suggested by an archivist might begin by recreating the publishing patterns, i.e., identifying major publishers and analyzing the extent to which each specialized in a particular type of novel or appealed to a particular audience, and use that information as the basis for selecting titles. Whether or not the latter approach is superior to the former is debatable, but considering it might lead to yet other possibilities for an improved project.

Much of the library reference service focuses on providing a user with a requested item, presumably one containing desired information. Bibliographic instruction often aspires to prepare users to achieve similar results without staff assistance. Again the emphasis is on the item, primarily because that is what the bibliographic retrieval system is geared to retrieve. Without seeking to dismantle the system, the archivist's natural inclination would be to supplement it by attempting to describe and analyze broader patterns observed in available published sources and to present reference tools collectively as an interrelated resource, hoping to provide the user with a framework in which to evaluate item-specific bibliographic citations as part of developing a research strategy.

There is no need to challenge the rational basis for placement of archives under library administration. The two have enough in common to coexist peacefully, and yet are distinct enough to provoke each other to more considered applications of their respective principles. The challenge is to achieve the mutual sensitivity which might accommodate differences, and to realize the creative potential of substantive interaction in exploring the assumptions and principles that underlie practices in both.

REFERENCES

1. Sidney J. Levy and Albert G. Robles, "The Image of Archivists: Resource Allocators' Perceptions," Report prepared for the Society of American Archivists Task Force on Archives and Society, December 1984, by Social Research, Inc. Copies are available from Society of American Archivists. The findings were based on interviews with forty-four people who control and/or influence the funding of archival operations, of whom fourteen could readily be identified in the report as library administrators.

2. Nicholas C. Burckel and J. Frank Cook, "A Profile of College and University Archives in the United States," *American Archivist* 45 (Fall 1982): 410–428. Their findings were based on a questionnaire survey of a random sample drawn from a 1980 directory of college and university archives in the United States. The directory and the survey both defined college and university archives to include repositories that collect materials not related directly to the parent university.

3. Robert L. Clark's description of the varied institutional settings for library management of archives, in his *Archive-Library Relations* (New York: R. R. Bowker Company, 1976), pp. 155–165, is somewhat dated by now but still instructive. His description was based on a survey for forty-four state, university, and public libraries which reported the presence of archives and manuscripts operations within their jurisdiction. His omission of any reference to business and religious settings is a limitation, but perhaps was more understandable when he undertook his volume.

4. Of twenty state archives covered in an assessment of the conditions of historical records in 1983, only two were under state libraries. Seven were under state historical societies and two were

divisions of state historical commissions. The remainder were in a variety of other administrative settings ranging from the office of the secretary of state to the education department. Edwin C. Bridges, "State Records Programs," in *Documenting America: Assessing the Condition of Historical Records in the States*, ed. Lisa B. Weber (Albany, NY: National Association of State Archives and Records Administrators, 1984), p. 2.

5.   I struggled without success to identify an appropriate metaphor that would capture the effect of this fundamental inequality of archivists and their profession compared with librarians. No analogy to minority group status seemed particularly apt, and I rejected the Biblical injunction to be "in the world but not of the world" because of the unintended implication that librarians were eternally damned. The most enticing is the statement often attributed to Canadian Prime Minister Pierre Trudeau about living next door to the United States, paraphrased as: it is like sleeping with an elephant; even though it is friendly, it tends to roll over.

6.   See Clark, *Archive-Library Relations*, particularly the section by Frank Burke on "materials and methodology," pp. 31–50.

7.   This is hardly a voyage into uncharted waters. My analysis of archival distinctiveness draws in a general way on three other introductions to archival theory and practice, written primarily for librarians: Clark, *Archive-Library Relations*; David B. Gracy II, *An Introduction to Archives and Manuscripts* (New York: Special Libraries Association, 1981); and Richard Lytle, ed., *Management of Archives and Manuscript Collections for Librarians*, a special issue of *Drexel Library Quarterly* 11 (1975), subsequently reprinted by the Society of American Archivists, 1980.

8.   Clark, *Archive-Library Relations*, p. 35.

9.   Richard C. Berner, *Archival Theory and Practice in the United States: A Historical Analysis* (Seattle: University of Washington Press, 1983). More abbreviated versions of the same approach, also by Berner, are "Arrangement and Description: Some Historical Observations," *American Archivist* 41 (1978): 169–181, and "Historical Development of Archival Theory and Practices in the United States," *The Midwestern Archivist* 7 (1982): 103–117.

10.   An archival inventory describes the contents of a record group, i.e., a body of records emanating from a common source. The description normally includes a brief history of the institution or agency and a narrative description of the contents, first viewed in their entirety (scope and content note) and then focusing on each subdivision (series description). The inventory may include a more detailed listing of the contents of selected series if they are judged to be of special significance. Manuscript repositories have adopted a similar format, sometimes calling it a register, for their collections, i.e., the records of an organization or the personal papers of an individual or family. They are more likely to include a container list of folder titles, and they may provide an index, either to the inventory/register itself or to selected items in the collection.

11.   As a reflection of this distinction, the term "archivist" is used to embrace all members of the profession, whether they deal with records of a parent institution or with externally collected materials. In cases where the distinction is vital, I have differentiated between "institutional archivists" and "manuscript curators."

12.   Richard H. Lytle, "Intellectual Access to Archives," *American Archivist* 43 (1980): 64–75, and 43 (1980): 191–207.

13.   Andrea Hinding, "Artifacts or Information? Some Antiquarian Thoughts on the Uses of Historical Records," Presidential Address at the Forty-Ninth Meeting of the Society of American Archivists, Austin, Texas, October 29, 1985.

14.   Cf., Thomas J. Schlereth, *Artifacts and the American Past* (Nashville: American Association for State and Local History, 1981) and Schlereth, ed., *Material Culture Studies in America* (Nashville: AASLH, 1982).

15.   In Burckel and Cook's survey, twenty-three percent of the college and university archives had records management responsibility while another eighteen percent reported the existence of a records management program outside their jurisdiction: "Profile of College and University Archives in the United States," pp. 420–422.

16.   The following discussion of specific effects of a library organizational structure on archivists draws on Nicholas Burckel, "Archivists in a Library Environment," paper presented at the spring meeting of the Midwest Archives Conference, Chicago, May 1985.

17.   The "Recommendations for Reporting on Archives and Manuscripts," *SAA Newsletter*, (November 1983), pp. 13–16, offers a suggested standard that is serving for continued work on the part of the SAA's Task Force on Institutional Evaluation.

18. Nancy Sahli, *MARC For Archives and Manuscripts: The AMC Format* (Chicago: SAA, 1985) unpaginated.

19. William C. Maher, "Measurement and Analysis of Processing Costs in Academic Archives," *College and Research Libraries*, 42 (1982): 59–67, offers the most careful measure of processing costs, based on the experience of the University of Illinois-Urbana Archives.

20. Charles Perrow, *Complex Organizations, A Critical Essay*, 2nd ed. (Glenview, IL: Scott, Foresman & Co., 1979), p. 146, cited by Michael A. Lutzker, "Max Weber and the Analysis of Modern Bureaucratic Organization: Notes Toward a Theory of Appraisal," *American Archivist* 45 (1982): 119–130. Lutzker demonstrates how an understanding of the nature of bureaucracy can be applied to archival theory. In that discussion I first saw the basis for distinguishing between organizational structures and organic relationships.

RESOURCE SHARING: ARCHIVAL AND BIBLIOGRAPHIC CONTROL

Information Systems for Libraries and Archives: Opportunity or Incompatibility?

Richard V. Szary

A noteworthy feature in the current development of the archival profession has been a conscious attempt to emphasize differences distinguishing the role and responsibilities of custodians of original and primary materials from those of persons whose main responsibility is the care of published, secondary resources. The impetus for stressing these distinctions comes not only from the normal course of professionalization which demands the definition of a unique niche for self-identification, but also from an intuitive appreciation for the differences in context and characteristics between historical and published materials.[1] While this distancing exercise has occurred, however, archivists have recognized a commonality of interests between themselves and the library world, rooted in the selection, classification, description, and use of documentation.

The wider knowledge and visibility of the published world and demands for paths to and through it have fostered library practice and standards development, and provided the resources for their implementation. The archival world, on the other hand, is a much more exclusive domain with fewer persons recognizing its existence and demanding

Richard Szary is Associate Archivist for Information Systems, Smithsonian Institution, Washington, D.C.

access to it. Its scope appears to be much narrower than the published world, especially when considering an individual repository or a given set of materials. The benefits of cooperative collection development, shared cataloging and common descriptive standards, or the compatibility of access tools, have never had the driving force that they assumed in the library world. The clientele for an archive's records and services, especially outside the parent institution, has always appeared too small for any serious, sustained demand for resources sharing, the type of demand that would lead to the adoption of standards and networks for information exchange. The development of archival information systems as a result has never had the support that library systems have enjoyed. A similar set of circumstances has dictated the later development of information systems for other forms of material (e.g., visual materials) as well.

The library profession has attempted on occasion to fill this void by assuming no significant differences amongst different forms of documentation that could not be accommodated within the model it had developed for published materials. In the area of information systems to support archival practices the result was either an inappropriate treatment of archival materials and methods as variations on books and library practices, or attempts to develop systems specifically for archival materials. While archivists resisted attempts to fit archives into the library model, they were unable to define the benefits of a shared archival model concretely enough or to gather sufficient resources within one institution to construct an independent archival information system model. Substantial beginnings were made in individual repositories and small groups, but archivists never developed the profession-wide model that has sustained library information systems development.

The success of library standardization for information systems, the promise of better management and intellectual control through automation, and the realities of resource availability for the construction of an independent archival system, have forced archivists to re-examine the feasibility of generalized bibliographic systems able to accommodate both published materials and unpublished, non-print, historical materials. Archivists are bringing to this exercise not only their professional experience and judgement about the nature of historical records and ways of managing them, but also a readiness to re-examine that experience and determine what is essential about it and what accidental. They may find themselves in that process not merely agreeing with librarians on the requirements for effective management and control of documentation, but also contributing unique perspectives that will enhance library practice as well.

In this comparison of library and archival practice and the resulting requirements for information systems, two factors color perspectives and should be noted explicitly. First, even though the term "archives" and its various derivatives have been used throughout this dialogue, many of the same principles apply to the manuscripts world as well. The world of official records is not so regular, nor the world of personal papers so irregular, as much of the literature would have one believe. The characteristics of historical documentation transcend legal and philosophical boundaries between persons and organizations; nothing seems to make the requirements of information systems for the two substantially different.

There is no suitable archival analog for the general public library. The client of an archival repository is invariably a specialist of some type, usually well-versed in his field. Thus, the segment of the library world most concerned with archival development is the academic or research library which serves a knowledgeable and focused clientele. It is only in this context that useful comparisons can be made. Three areas of library and archives practice may be considered: (1) collections development, (2) bibliographic description and retrieval, and (3) reference service, to compare the information system requirements that flow from them. The emphasis in such comparison is on unique or incompatible requirements that archival practices might bring to an information system designed on the standard library model.

COLLECTIONS DEVELOPMENT

In examining the forces that drive collection development activities in libraries and archives and the environments in which those activities take place, similarities are evident, but one must see if they are strong enough to derive benefits from a shared information system. The acquisition of library holdings is a user-oriented process, geared to anticipating and satisfying the needs of the library's clientele which in many cases knows the specific materials that it wants and requests them directly.[2] Once desired materials are identified, the acquisitions process is straightforward, with all of the actors and lines identified. Ordering, receiving, claiming, and paying for published materials, are routine operations subject to well-defined procedures.

The acquisition of archival collections has some similarities to this model, especially in the records management process by which many archives attempt systematically to accumulate their holdings. In many cases, however, the similarities are more apparent than real. For example, the archival "vendors" or the offices creating the records, do not have the same impetus to be as responsive to the "customer" or the archival respository, as library book suppliers. There are no alternative sources to which an archives can turn if the offices in its parent organization are unwilling to cooperate in records scheduling and disposition. In an ideal situation, the records management process would operate with the same regularity and predictability as the book purchasing process is supposed to, but this is the exception rather than the rule.[3]

Archives which collect from sources outside their own organization must also follow the model of manuscript repositories. An information system that can support donor relations may share some of the features of both the library acquisitions and archival records management systems, but neither the actors nor the procedures are as well-defined and regular. A repository may have a standard procedure for dealing with potential donors, but the circumstances surrounding each gift will be so varied that rigorous adherence to the mechanics of that procedure are rare. For example, where a library can send progressively more demanding claims notices when an ordered publication does not arrive, and an archives can with considerably less hope of success send reminders to offices that a particular series of records is due to be transferred, the repository soliciting a gift of personal papers can do little more than gently nudge a donor to make good on a promised gift. Similarly, both the library and records management program can resort to fill-in-the-blanks notices, but donor reminders need to be personalized. While the function of "claiming" may be present in all three situations, its rigor and regularity varies across a wide spectrum.

Library acquisitions also are tied to financial and accounting constraints. In many ways these systems closely resemble standard procurement systems, with the same type of procedural and recording capabilities needed to track the obligation and expenditure of funds and assure that ordered services and items are received. In contrast, the acquisition of archival materials is less directly tied to an expenditure of funds. Funds are necessary to provide the human and physical resources to solicit, ship, store, and manage archival materials, but archives rarely purchase their holdings in the same way that libraries must. Consequently, archival acquisitions systems do not require the same degree of funds control necessary for library-based systems.

Aside from the mechanics of tracking and processing the addition of holdings, there is still a fundamental difference between the collection development approaches in libraries and archival repositories. Because library acquisitions are basically user-oriented, focusing on anticipating and satisfying the needs of their users, a library's collections policy and book selection decisions might be considered failures if the additions to its holdings were not used by the patrons. The library's decisions are made somewhat easier by their reversibility; if the library were to err in anticipating the needs of its clientele for a particular publication and did not acquire it, chances are that it can either still be obtained or is available from another repository.

The archival situation does not present the same type of clearly defined criteria or timely feedback for appraisal decisions. While the fashions of current scholarship and the demands of active users undoubtedly play their part in the selection of materials to be retained, archivists are also constantly aware of the irreversibility of their decisions and must anticipate the judgement of future users. In place of the library profession's emphasis on public service as the touchstone of its acquisitions policy, the archivist appeals to the adequacy and patterns of documentation in determining whether records are worthy of retention and attention. Use patterns may play a primary role in determining processing and conservation priorities, but they are clearly a secondary factor in developing appraisal guidelines. Archivists are more likely to conduct comprehensive records surveys that delineate the records that are available to document a particular activity or organization, and then use their professional judgement and experience to determine which sets of records are most valuable in providing an accurate historical composite record and how to assure their retention.

The selection of manuscript materials is more susceptible to the vagaries of chance and opportunity than archival appraisal and scheduling. The archivist not only has to comprehend and document a limited universe, the world of the parent organization, but also has an organizational mandate for demanding compliance with his decisions. The manuscript curator, even in a restricted subject area, must deal with a more nebulous world of documentation, where responsibilities for the creation and maintenance of records are not fixed, and where persuasiveness must take the place of appeals to legal or organizational policies.[4]

BIBLIOGRAPHIC DESCRIPTION AND RETRIEVAL

It might appear at first glance that the differences in ways that library holdings are classified and cataloged and archival holdings are arranged and described preclude any significant benefit from a cooperative bibliographic description and retrieval system. Criticism of shared systems often focuses on incompatibilities in the sources of information that are used to derive bibliographic descriptions for the two types of materials, the inability to preserve contextual information in traditional library-based systems, and in the types of bibliographic products that are essential to the effective retrieval of archival materials.[5] Recent developments in archival arrangement and description standards and practices, however, are discovering a commonality to form the basis for cooperative efforts. A realization is emerging that while practices, approaches, and products may vary, the type of structure needed to support them can be shared.

While it has been recognized for some time that shared access to information about archival holdings requires a standardized format, it was also believed that such a structure would be unique to archival materials.[6] This belief was reinforced by the inadequacy of attempts by the library world to fit archival materials into its system of standards for published print materials.[7] One result of studies and discussions conducted by the Society of American Archivists' National Information Systems Task Force (NISTF) from 1977 to 1983, focusing on the requirements for archival information exchange, was the replacement of the MARC format for manuscripts with the Archives and Manuscripts Control format.[8] The new format, drawing on NISTF's investigations into archival description practices, attempts to provide data elements and capabilities needed to accommodate the specific characteristics of those practices in a data structure which had been successfully used and was widely implemented in other bibliographic networking applications.[9]

Archivists have also begun the process of codifying their descriptive practices. The definition of common data elements and how they are used is underway; this promises compatibility of archival descriptions within and across repositories.[10] While those standards will vary significantly from those established for published materials, their existence will provide designers of shared bibliographic information systems with documentable differences to be accommodated.

The same effort unfortunately has not been applied to an investigation of the types of bibliographic products needed to support access to and research in archival materials. Current efforts focus on the possibility of generating traditional archival access tools, i.e., guides and inventories, from standardized bibliographic descriptions. While there seems to be no technical or structural impediments to their production, no system yet supports an ongoing mechanism to produce them. Like librarians who first used computers to support production of catalog cards, archivists are reluctant to explore the effectiveness of new methods and products until existing practices and products can be replicated in automation.

Smithsonian Institution drew up the following set of requirements for the enhancement of a standard library catalog system to handle archival materials:[11]

1. Compatibility with national standards (primarily MARC-AMC and MARC for Visual Materials),
2. Ability to record, display, and maintain large records containing long text fields;
3. Ability to link records describing the same materials at different levels of aggregation;
4. Ability to provide appropriate intellectual access to catalog descriptions (flexibility in indexing and display formats);

5. Ability to maintain cataloging consistency and authority control;
6. Ability to maintain security of data;
7. Ease of data entry and proofing;
8. Ability to provide management control over holdings; and
9. Ability to interface with image retrieval systems.

Such features that are required to support archival arrangement and description practices in a bibliographic information system are enhancements rather than incompatible modifications to existing functionality. A few examples will help illustrate the applicability of some of these enhancements to non-archival environments. The functionality needed to support the multi-dimensional arrangement and description of archival materials is also needed by libraries to support series and analytical cataloging at collection levels. Displays and other bibliographic products tailored to the characteristics of the described materials rather than defined solely by the characteristics of published print materials, are as important for music, visual, and other forms of material as for archives. Research and other specialized libraries require the same flexibility in the number, choice, and control of access points that archival repositories need.

By providing these capabilities, bibliographic information systems would not only make it possible to integrate and support the description and retrieval of archival materials, but they would also provide the opportunity for supporting other forms of material and specialized bibliographic projects in ways appropriate to their particular nature and characteristics. Assuming a generalized bibliographic information system of this type, administrative support requirements are considerably less complex and expensive than if individual systems were designed and implemented for each type of material. The cost of operations, equipment, data entry and quality control procedures, and similar technical requirements are such that an institution will not be able to support a separate catalog system for each type of material for which it is responsible. Realistically, a generalized, shared system often will be the only opportunity for the implementation and maintenance of adequate information systems for all materials.[14]

Archivists will continue to insist, justifiably so, on independent bibliographic information retrieval systems until it has been demonstrated that shared systems can not only accept and store descriptions of their holdings, but also manipulate, retrieve, and display them in useful and appropriate ways. It is becoming evident, however, that those capabilities are useful not only in handling archival description, but also in enhancing the flexibility and scope of standard library description and the description of other forms of material as well.

REFERENCE MANAGEMENT

Libraries and archives have different perspectives on the amount and type of reference service that should be provided to their clienteles. The catalog plays a role in the library environment that is not matched by any single tool in an archives. The closest parallel to the library catalog is the archival repository guide which describes and provides access to archival holdings at a collective level; both describe the basic units of holdings in the repository. A fundamental difference between the two, however, is that while the library catalog aims to provide its users with a mechanism that will answer a high percentage of bibliographic reference questions without the intervention of a reference librarian, the archival guide provides only a starting point in identifying holdings relevant to the user's query.[13]

The size and nature of most archival collections require that the repository provide supplementary help to the user once a collection has been identified as a likely source of relevant materials. This help may take the form of more detailed inventories, lists, calendars, or other finding aids, prepared by either the office of origin or the repository, which the user can peruse in attempting to find the specific materials of interest. Often, however, a staff person familiar with the materials themselves and the subject area of interest to the researcher will work with the user to help narrow the focus of the query and translate it into terms in which the finding aids and the materials themselves can be addressed. While the reference librarian performs the same function, especially in specialized, research libraries, or with users unfamiliar with library practices, the percentage of patrons requiring the services of the reference archivist is considerably higher, nearly total, than for the librarian.

Besides the differing roles of the reference staff in the two types of repositories, the types of material they control also affect the reference workflow. Archives are basically closed-stack repositories, providing strictly controlled access and use of their holdings. Materials rarely leave the custody of the archives in the same way that published materials circulate. The recording of information about patrons and their use of materials is, however, essentially the same in both cases.

A number of exceptions to this similarity may be noted. The value, complexity, and confidentiality of many of the materials in their care, require that archives retain information linking patrons to the materials they used much longer than libraries must. Archives are unique and irreplaceable records, and archivists have a greater interest than most librarians in tracking the use of those materials very specifically. The unit of material that circulates—a box, folder, or set of these—generally contains many discrete pieces, and precise information about contents is impossible to maintain. Consequently, damage or theft of archives is often difficult to detect at the time a researcher finishes using them, and may only show up at a later date and in indirect ways. The archives' responsibility to administer restrictions on who and how materials may be used also requires the maintenance of usage records that will document their adherence to such conditions.

The citation of archival materials in historical literature is another rationale for creating and retaining comprehensive use records. Despite the best efforts of a repository to suggest ways to cite records in their custody, so that those records may easily be found again, users of archives are notorious for their inexact and misleading citations. A citation that reads, "Letter from Mr. X to Mrs. Y, January 17, 1905," often provides insufficient information for repository staff to track down the cited item, especially if it is filed by subject in Mr. Z's Papers. Knowing which collections, boxes, or folders that a researcher used, however, will usually narrow the search considerably.

Archivists are also interested in identifying and tracking the queries that their users bring to the archives. The amount of time that reference staff must spend responding to queries and the limited resources archives have for detailed processing and description place a premium on the information that researchers are able to cull from the holdings. It is not unusual for a researcher to know considerably more about a narrow segment of a repository's holdings than the staff itself. One does not have to go so far as to suggest that a patron's research record should be open to other patrons, to recognize that the success or failure of a patron's research may provide reference staff with information which might prove useful in answering other queries.

An analysis of reference management activities of the Smithsonian Institution in seven units responsible for archival-type holdings, revealed the following general requirements for an archival reference management system:[14]

1. Report on number, types, and research projects of patrons to support program planning;
2. Record and retrieve information on which materials have been used by a particular patron to support collections security and verification of research;
3. Report on which patrons have examined a specified set of materials;
4. Classify reference transactions by type to support program planning and monitoring;
5. On-line recording and display of user and transaction information;
6. Link reference transactions to queries to support future reference activities;

7. Support selective dissemination of information about new holdings to patrons;
8. Track research in progress to record where materials have been used or cited;
9. Track loans outside the repository;
10. Track usage of holdings as a guide to future allocation of processing resources; and
11. Report extent of materials consulted in a specified time span.

Many of the capabilities identified in this discussion are very similar to those now present in automated circulation systems for libraries. As with cataloging requirements, most enhancements needed to support archival reference management would allow libraries to do more comprehensive reference and use studies than current systems allow. The major incompatibility introduced by archival requirements is the need to keep historical records linking patrons with the materials they have used. Libraries have a justifiable fear of keeping the types of circulation information that might lead to the invasions of privacy of their users. Many would be reluctant to implement such a capability.

CONCLUSION

An analysis of practices in libraries and archives as presented here, cannot be the only determining factor in deciding whether archives and libraries should undertake shared development and maintenance of information systems. Local variations from practices described here and differing emphases will play as important a role in deciding the worthiness of specific projects. This analysis points out, however, that there are some areas where cooperation will be easier and the chances of success more likely.

The ability to generalize functionality between the two practices at a very high level is an academic exercise. It is only when generalization can be taken to the procedural level that it becomes useful for system development. Keeping this in mind, one can rank the feasibility of shared system development in each of the three areas discussed.

Of the three areas, bibliographic description and retrieval appears to present the most commonality. As noted, the enhancements to standard library systems are features which would also be necessary for the integration of other non-print materials and for the support of desirable features in catalogs of published print materials as well. This is especially true for academic and research libraries where there is likely to be a demand for and more detailed cataloging and specialized access beyond what a standard library catalog system can support. Cooperation in this area is also becoming increasingly possible as archivists begin to recognize the advantages of building on existing standards and structures in the library world rather than designing their own. The realities of resource availability and the promise of visible results in the short-term provide the impetus for archivists to approach cooperative ventures with more open minds than has been the case in the past. The chance of such cooperation succeeding and continuing, however, will disappear unless systems are enhanced to support the capabilities that archivists need to control their holdings effectively.

The next most likely area for cooperation is in reference management and circulation systems. With the exception of the need for archivists to maintain indefinitely links between patrons and used materials, there are few incompatibilities between the requirements for a library circulation system and an archival reference management system. The enhancements that archivists need to current library circulation systems, again, are features that would benefit library operations as well.

There is compatibility between library and archival requirements in collection development at a very high level of generalization, but the procedural details of how the collection development functions work in each case are different enough that individual development may be warranted. The flexibility required for archival and manuscript collections is of secondary interest to library operations except perhaps in gift and exchange systems; and the rigorous financial requirements of the library approach are of little use to archival operations. While there are obviously instances where the capabilities of each would be useful to the other, they appear to be insufficient to offer substantial benefits from shared systems.

The benefits of integrated systems extend beyond the operational and physical resources needed to support multiple systems, and beyond the less concrete benefits of shared access to bibliographic information. This analysis suggests compatibility of certain functions to warrant thinking of sharing professional and technical resources as well. The maintenance of bibliographic formats, the design and implementation of on-line catalogs and other bibliographic products, data entry, authority maintenance, patron registration, and similar functions can also be supported in an integrated environment. The intellectual and resource-saving benefits of such cooperation will only come about, however, as professionals and administrators in both communities are willing to look beyond their traditional and immediate environments, and recognize a commonality of interests and opportunities.

NOTES

1. See Richard C. Berner's *Archival Theory and Practice in the United States: A Historical Analysis* (Seattle: Washington University Press, 1983) for a discussion of the development of archival thought and its relationship to library practices.

2. See for example, the emphasis on determining "wanted" materials in Keyes D. Metcalf, "The Essentials of an Acquisition Program," in Michael M. Reynolds and Evelyn H. Daniel, *Reader in Library and Information Services* (Englewood, Colorado: Microcard Editions Books, 1974), pp. 409–428.

3. While successful records management programs do exist, they are located primarily in business environments or deal with routine types of records such as forms and accounts. In both of these situations the parent organization or creating offices benefit directly from cooperation with the records management program, providing the impetus for good "vendor performance."

4. There is probably more similarity between an archival records management program and a manuscript solicitation program than is generally acknowledged. The importance and influence of the records management program in an organization is often such that the archives program must approach the records-creating offices with the same level of persuasiveness as a manuscript repository must with its donors.

5. Berner summarizes many of these criticisms in his *Archival Theory and Practice*, especially pp. 112–117.

6. The uncertainty about archival descriptive standards and their relationship to those of the library community is clear in the comments of archivists asked to discuss archival automation needs and priorities in Lawrence J. McCrank, ed., *Automating the Archives* (White Plains, New York: Knowledge Industry Publications, Inc., 1981), pp. 225–252.

7. Few archivists used either the MARC format for Manuscripts in its original 1973 version or AACR, Chapter 4; both drew heavily on library practices in defining data elements and rules.

8. Issued as part of Library of Congress, Automated Systems Office, *MARC Formats for Bibliographic Data [1980]*, Update 10 (Washington, D.C.: LC, 1985).

9. Some of those specific features include multi-dimensional relationships between sets of records (whole-part, hierarchical, chronological), attribution and titling standards that rely on the understanding of how materials were created rather than transcription of title page information, and notes specific to the characteristics of unique historical materials.

10. Elaine D. Engst, Standard Elements for the Description of Archives and Manuscript Collections. A Report to the SAA Task Force on National Information Systems, September 1980, Society of American Archivists; Steven L. Hensen, comp., *Archives, Personal Papers, and Manuscripts: A Cataloging Manual for Archival Repositories. Historical Societies, and Manuscript Libraries* (Washington, D.C.: Library of Congress, 1983).

11. Listed in R.V. Szary, "SIBIS-Archives: Description of Current Capabilities," unpublished evaluation report, May 20, 1985, Smithsonian Institution.

12. Within the Smithsonian, for example, the implementation of the Smithsonian Institution Bibliographic Information System, using an enhanced version of a standard library information system, is offering sophisticated bibliographic description and retrieval capabilities to a number of small archival, manuscript, and bibliographic units that would otherwise be unable to develop and maintain them.

13. See Frank G. Burke's contrast between library and archival reference service in Robert L. Clark, Jr., ed., *Archive-Library Relations* (New York: R.R. Bowker Company, 1976), pp. 45–50.

14. Taken from Austin Moller, Report on reference management requirements prepared for the SIBIS-Archives Users' Group, 1984, Smithsonian Institution. The results of Moller's analysis also included a data dictionary, transaction definitions, and record definitions.

The Impact of Automation: Integrating Archival and Bibliographic Systems

Lawrence J. McCrank

INTRODUCTION

Cooperation and Reciprocity

Automation has wrought significant change for all information professions and the institutions they administer. This is already apparent in systems and operations in libraries and it is becoming more evident in archives as well.[2] The recent breakthrough of archivists into the inner sanctum of library networking, i.e., the cataloging operation, through the invention of the U.S. MARC Archives and Manuscripts Control (AMC) format, is more of an intellectual and political than technical achievement.[3] It opens new possibilities for multi-type networks embracing archives and libraries to exchange holdings information via the Research Libraries Group (RLG, a utility supporting its own online network, RLIN), and the Online Computer Library Catalog (OCLC, a vendor offering the same services through a host of regional sub-networks). Both OCLC and RLG are enhancing their services daily. The latter has actively promoted archival interests as part of its research focus, while OCLC through its so-called "Oxford Project" has undertaken a remodeling to introduce an array of new capabilities such as Boolean searching and subject access.[4] Project LINK, representative of the movement toward open systems, suggests new possibilities for participation in multi-type information networking between archives and libraries.[5]

Archives by themselves have been less successful in network development, despite noble efforts in the upper midwestern United States and the encouragement by the National Historical Publications and Records Commission (NHPRC).[6] Unlike libraries, archives have not been able to justify machine-readable cataloging because they cannot use each other's master records for copying. This led to the mistaken notion by archivists that archival data are all unique, when indeed types of data are similar; and by librarians that cooperation with archivists could not include data seen as incompatible with how books were described. Cost saving, rather than added information value, has dominated the thinking of both librarians and archivists in approaching automation and cooperation.[7] Such notions have been outgrown at last, and the stage is now set for some interesting cooperation.

The AMC format offers tremendous potential, although not all possibilities, for greater information sharing between archives and libraries if they start using it regularly and if archives can afford to convert extensive manual inventories and guide entries to the AMC format. This requires a massive retrospective conversion effort more monumental than that undertaken by libraries in turning from AACR1 to AACR2.[8] While archives now have a way to share information about archival holdings as aggregates, at the collection and series levels, there is no counter-move on the part of libraries to begin using an archival approach to description in providing parallel information online about their special collections *qua* collections. This is unfortunate, but not surprising given the current situation and lack of concern in library thought about access to primary documentation.

Libraries have led the way in computer applications and appear to archivists as leaders in automation, but libraries have often approached this new technology in very limited fashion, and have often failed to develop fully integrated systems which support auxilliary enterprises like archives. Consequently, while archives are allying themselves with libraries partially for the benefits of automation and access to large systems development, the alliance may be inherently limiting. There is a lack of reciprocal borrowing of archival tools and strategies by librarianship as possible solutions to collection management in libraries and their consortia, and until recently communication has been very one-sided.[9] Indeed, rather than approach archives in an eager effort to tap their vast information resources and to extend their influence throughout the fabric of an institution through a records management system, libraries have shied away from such involvement. Librarians, following heralds in information science, proclaim their move into the larger world of information management but have problems putting words into action. Few of the limitations are technical, some are fiscal, but most are intellectual and professional.

Automation Concerns

This one-sided rapproachment seems to have a greater impact on archival operations than on libraries, so that four concerns now confronting archivists might be addressed in order to highlight the larger issue of integrating archival and bibliographic information systems. These are:

    1. Archives are being forced by the new information
    technology to reconsider basic archival assumptions

and methods, which may alter the traditional relationship between archives and libraries. This would be especially true if librarianship paid more attention to the intellectual ferment in archival science.

2. A substantial change occurring in archivists' thinking is a move away from warehouse or stock management, toward keener interest in user access. As archival control, like its bibliographic counterpart, becomes more a matter of intellectual access tied to physical control, libraries and archives will continue to focus attention on the language and conceptual issues of document retrieval and the creation of information systems allied to, but not necessarily the same as or dependent upon collection management.

3. Archives and libraries face very similar management problems in the implementation of automated information systems and the formulation of policy controlling those systems. Archivists, more than manuscript curators, should be adroit students of organizational behavior and management systems, capable of dynamic contributions to overall archives and library administration; yet they are often excluded because of the non-integration of archives within library structures.

4. Expectations about automation must be realistic to avoid disillusionment with the rapid change-over of technology and the machine's inability to solve our human, intellectual, and organizational problems. These are matters of education, both preparatory and continuing, which recognize that archivists and librarians must work together, with more ambiguity, perceptual rather than concrete models, and flexibility which is itself habitual.

Archivists and manuscript curators have either recoiled from the onslaught of computer technology or they have argued for its adoption with a sense of urgency that without automation their archives would be hopelessly outdated. Opportunities have been lost in the first case and abused in the latter. In other cases, archives have been forced to use bibliographic systems and cataloging conventions without the proper modification of software or entry formats to accommodate archival description. Instead the library item-approach was used to stuff collection data into formats designed for individual books, as in the production of the *National Union Catalog of Manuscript Collections* with its skewed focii and limited subject access. Such earlier experiences still make archivists wary of library intentions and misconstruction of archival methodology, compounding misconceptions voiced by the once dominant government-archivist position in the archival community which was untrained in library methodology. Consequently, the contemporary rapprochment is not only one-sided, but it is very cautious.

The context is difficult enough, but it is complicated further by the tendency to consider automation and networking foremost in terms of hardware and software rather than organizations and people. Technology itself occupies the spotlight, rather than organizational goals, objectives, and what computer applications can do for an operation. The really difficult problems, often unrecognized and therefore unresolved, are methodological and managerial, intellectual and philosophical, professional and political, and all too human.[10]

Automation is a process, not an act, which embraces more than mechanization of what was done previously.[11] It includes education, standardization, systematization, implementation, testing and modification, before information dissemination.[12] None of these are accomplished automatically, or simply through a computer application; they require detailed forethought, strategic planning, direction, and constant intervention. Work in our electronic age is being transformed radically from manual, physical labor into the intellectual sphere with accompanying mental stress and organizational tension.[13] The transition demands thoughtful management, not just an adequate budget and the ideal machinery.[14]

CHANGING ASSUMPTIONS AND NEW OPERATIONS

Traditional archival functions can be collapsed into documentation, preservation, and information dissemination—not dissimilar from library operations.[15] The dominant focus of past archival concern has been on record storage techniques and preservation rather than retrieval, whereas librarians have worried less about these and concentrated instead on services and information dissemination. Now a reversal can be detected, as librarians adopt preservation and collection management concerns always central to archival thinking, when archivists are turning to issues of subject access, more efficient retrieval, and greater awareness of user needs.[16]

Older accusations by archivists against librarians were that their approach to classification destroyed original order and cataloging disregarded provenance, cardinal propositions in hallowed archival theory. Library cataloging was seen as so removed from narrative description or faithful abstraction, that the surrogate distorted a document's language (e.g., standardized subject headings rather than natural language descriptors or key-word indexing) and could be misleading. Moreover, catalogs seldom produced the associative linkage desired by archivists, and the item-level approach to description did not allow for aggregation except through subject searches. While librarians were trying to condense whole books into one or two headings for subject access, or to rely on direct retrieval through main entries, archivists rebelled from what was regarded as a simplistic approach to mass information. The limitations of library cataloging, of course, are being felt as librarians too confront the problem of massive collections.

Archivists argued also that they should not interpret their sources, mostly to differentiate their roles from historians without recognizing how such a position also segregated them from librarians. Both sets of colleagues, librarians and historians, in reaction thought of archivists as "mere" records managers. Regardless of such misconceptions which have splintered the professions in the past, there is today more regard for commonalities in problems and solutions to information issues confronting both archivists and librarians. It is now more openly recognized that interpretation, value judgements, and other subjective analysis are all part of archival appraisal as much as in library selection and acquisitions, and that these influence access. They come into play no less in term assignment during archival arrangement and indexing than in the assignment of subject headings in cataloging. It is also recognized that automatic indexing and free-text searching are forms of word retrieval, often lacking the sophistication derived from controlled term assignment, preferred vocabularies, translation, and concept formulation characteristic of thesaurus control over an index in a retrieval system. Index languages, like ordering in subject headings, operate with greater precision when syntax is also controlled.[17] Much of what is mistakenly construed as technical problems in automation is really one of language applications, vocabulary and syntax controls, semiotics, and semantics.[18]

Appraisal

The archival counterpart to library selection and collection development, appraisal, has been forced to accommodate the features of machine-readable data. Form as well as content must be evaluated whether for archival accessioning or library acquisitions. Data stored in discrete units enhance the probability of mutliple future uses, often differing from the purpose of original creation, so that in both cases this is a cardinal criterion for retention. In both libraries and archives appraisal criteria have therefore shifted from purely content analysis for evidence, provenance, aesthetics, and traditional historical and legal values, to technical considerations of form, format, compatibility, and flexibility, for maximizing use and linkage to other information resources.[19] This is an example of how automation has accelerated changes in archival thinking, and is now forcing a reconsideration of time-honored notions, including the division between librarians and archivists who both handle machine-readable data bases. There seems to be a lessening difference between libraries and archives today, with the multiplication of media formats, in the kinds of materials each keeps.[20] There is a corresponding coalescence of thought in dealing with new forms, while old divisions about the proper treatment of older forms continue to frustrate archival and library cooperation.

Appraisal of machine-readable data, moreover, has challenged some of the most seminal notions about the archival nature of records. In order to retain the most useable data files, rather than merely to keep the raw data in its original form, often the primary, first-run data set is discarded in preference for a more refined or discretely defined version. Utility may take precedence over chronological primacy in such appraisal decisions. In short, archivists in charge of machine-readable data bases must sometimes substitute one version for another, in choices not intellectually too dissimilar from a bibliographer selecting a revised edition of a text for the authoritative record, rather than the draft or some other intermediary version.[21] Indeed, since so many texts are now being created in machine-readable form, the hypothetical juxtaposition of librarian and archivist in such cases may be no longer valid. Commonplace notions about the archival nature of a document may be put to serious tests, just as we may have to arrive at new definitions for evidence and proof.[22] Certainly old distinctions between primary, secondary, and tertiary documentation are eroding, just a bibliographer's idea of an edition, state, and issue, are becoming obscure whenever modern computer technology is employed.

Because automation includes the conversion of data resources from and to machine-readable form, as well as a process of substitution and surrogation, it must *ipso facto* entail the generation of machine-readable archives for the record of the operation.[23] The very process of automation plunges information managers into the world of machine-readable archives. These may consist of a small desk-top set of a few hard or floppy discs, or a cabinet of tapes, but no one should be fooled that an automated archives M–R file will forever remain inobstrusive just because it is compact in size. The impact of automation on archival thought, objectives, and practice, promises to be pervasive. In addition to challenging basic assumptions underlying current practice, indeed striking at the heart of archival theory as it has evolved thus far, automation threatens the distinctiveness and individuality of the archives and library professionals.[24]

Common Problems and Merging Roles

Since modern technology allows society to produce staggering quantities of records (not necessarily information or knowledge), it has been natural for archivists and librarians alike to turn to technology for the means to save more, and as the bulk grows, to develop ever more efficient ways to search the mass with whatever precision is required. Archivists, less than librarians, have had so little impact on technological development that few production systems have had built-in accommodations for bibliographic much less archival control. Archives have little advance control in records creation and management similar to the advantage of libraries using pre-publication cataloging. Manuscript curators have no hope to achieve the illusive goal of archivists to extend their influence to records creators who might initiate archival control. Moreover, software for specific archival operations has been lamentably limited, and archives components in larger bibliographic packages have been noticeably absent. Librarians in their quest for online catalogs, automated circulation, and support of acquisition and cataloging operations, have had little regard for archives having to use their software and hardware. For that matter, few libraries operate their own *bona fide* records management systems and archives (that is, for themselves, not only for the parent institution). The need for such is not inculcated in their professional library educations, either in administration and management coursework or in systems and operations research. Not only has this lack hindered library historians, but more importantly it explains partially the lack of longitudinal institutional and organizational research in library science. Consequently, archivists have not been able to rely on library administrators to look after the best interests of archives when the library undertakes automation. Small-scale intra-archives computer applications do not guarantee integration of archival systems into the larger world of information systems which would enhance the accessibility and utility of archival resources. More tragic than the happenstance parallel development of archival and library systems, is that librarians still do not recognize commonalities in archival thought and practice with their own; and archivists continue to discuss technological innovation in terms of administrative control more than with high regard for user access.[25]

Being part of a larger information system and profession is both luring and threatening for archivists and librarians alike.[26] Both compete now with data processors, records managers, more powerful information systems officers, and other new breeds and pedigrees, for the management of information resources in computer-based environments. Tensions exist between the two in a competition to control M–R records in an archives, with archival controls, description, and arrangement prevailing; or in libraries as special collections or centers, with cataloging and classification.[27] Other tensions underlie the merging of such job roles, competencies, and reporting lines, as reflected in the designations of archivists as "archival librarians" and the increasingly frequent subordination, in academic environs especially, of archives under libraries.

Archives faced the problem of mass in modern records production before libraries had to consider mass publications or volume problems resulting from aggressive manuscript solicitation. Now that libraries often contain sizeable special collections and are serving as umbrella structures for archives, archival problems are being thrust upon library administrators who often have little acquaintance with the issues or the archival nature of the problems they must confront. Once the magnitude of the problem is in perspective, many library administrators recoil and have second thoughts about their extension of authority over archives. The very largest of American research libraries are considering seemingly unsolvable problems created by massive book collections, to which archives responsibilities add sometimes unwelcome burdens. Neither archives or libraries have been adroit in using automation as an aid to preservation.[28]

It has been estimated that the average office worker in the United States during 1982 produced four file drawers or their equivalence of records in one form or another; that is 72,000,000 files or an estimated 216,000,000 linear feet per year, and the rate of growth is exponential! Based on federal government production, such bulk is increasing at 20% per year. Despite predictions of a paperless office, 90% of all records is still preserved on paper, even when the original state was machine-readable. Libraries have traditionally been on the receiving end of an information-generating spectrum, having to deal only with the distilled aggregration of such voluminous production. However, library involvement in archival enterprises broadens the traditional role into information services based on non-published material. It substantially increases the problem of mass, both for physical collection preservation, technical processing, and information storage and retrieval. When librarians contemplate what is before them, their attitude toward item-level approaches can be persuaded toward alternative choices. Among these are traditional archival approaches using aggregate control.

This most incomprehensible issue of mass is one reason why archivists regard library solutions as unfeasible and the past tendency to force manuscript retrieval into bibliographic rather than archival control mechanisms as unrealistic.[29] If librarians will not be persuaded by archivists' arguments, their mind set will be changed by the cost of mass storage and preservation. Both professionals are looking to technology for answers, ironically when it is automation itself which is contributing to the overwhelming magnitude of the problem. Mass storage with increasing density has evolved at a phenomenal rate, both in miniaturization through reprography and in conversion to machine-readable form. Digitization and optical disk storage media may have transitory relief, but even before their full development, their replacements are in sight: biochips, DNA and plasma structures, etc., perhaps providing, so it is speculated, 800,000 gigabytes (one billion characters each) per cubic foot. Such new storage media are labor intensive and create new problems in the conversion to and from one medium to another, for effective retrieval, and for structuring myriad data into information that humans can comprehend. Moreover, the mechanism to store more has a proportional effect on wanting to save more. The problem seems infinite.

Merging Technology and Approaches

It is also apparent that the current phase of development in automated information systems with its reliance on personal computers will be as fleeting as the previous stage characterized by sole dependence on mainframes, and that the microcomputer revolution is spawning user expectations beyond the capabilities of archives and libraries for immediate response.[30] In this era of converging technologies, the mini-computer will not disappear; it will undergo rapid development as it stays small and convenient, but builds capacities now associated with microcomputers; at the same time, the latter medium-sized machines are taking on the tasks of older mainframes.[31] It would be unfortunate to fall into the trap that small and medium-sized computers are a totally satisfactory solution to current problems just because they can do what previously required mainframes.[32] Our problems are not remaining static any more than is our technology: both are growing in complexity and magnitude.

Very shortly a third phase in automation development will be evident everywhere: the distributed system where intelligent workstations are largely independent and are dedicated to specific functions and tasks, with some sort of networking between stations, and a backup and support from a mainframe computer.[33] By the close of the millenium systems are more likely to be a hybrid combining very sophisticated "smart" workstations with mini- and micro-computers in interactive clusters, with micro-stations that are largely communication intersections routing data to individualized stations and to mainframes which monitor the whole system. Mainframes may be themselves clusters rather than single machines, with unheralded interactive capacity. Storage and rapid retrieval abilities are predicted to develop faster than our ability to use them. One much-quoted prognasticator, John Naisbitt, in commenting on the information age before us warns that our perceptions must change as rapidly as this technology: instead of thinking about physical space crossed by automobiles, we must comprehend conceptual space to be traversed electronically.[34] Some fear that such "megatrends" will be the demise of archives and libraries; others see them as transformed but surviving, as in the case of current libraries becoming tomorrow's archives.[35]

Such technology is challenging. Its particularism threatens the conveyance of holistic information and may spawn a fragmentation and over-specialization which defies the ideal of integration in information systems formation. On the other hand, integration creates such a spectre of mass that the stress on appraisal and retrieval is awesome. The problems now faced by archivists and librarians alike in information storage and retrieval seem perpetual and insolvable in terms of current approaches and thinking, in either archival or bibliographic information systems. Can archival thinking, theory, and invention evolve with production technology? Can portions of our economic wealth be moved from production to preservation technology, since we know that much of what is exploded in the acclaimed "information explosion" of our era comes not from the generaion of genuinely new sources, but from the accumulation and re-use of data in a variety of different ways? How seriously can archivists be taken in their consideration of traditional finding aids, primitive as they are, if they do not develop totally new approaches with the sophistication allowed by state-of-the-art technology? Are libraries and archives to evolve a functional specialization for the dissemination of current and retrospective information respectively? If so, cooperation now seems mandated by the impending changes wrought by automation. These changes might be planned and directed, rather than thrust upon our information organizations and professions.

In such cooperation it seems that the issue should not be which methodology prevails, archival or library/bibliographic, but how to blend the two and create integrated, multi-level and multi-functional systems.[36] The "post-custodial age of archives," to borrow F. Gerald Ham's phrase, should be, but is not yet here in the sense that archivists are still too passive, powerless, or reactive.[37] The problem is to insure the custody of valued information and cultural resources by influencing their very generation. That problem is not solely an archival issue: it is shared by libraries as well. Both must purge the mistaken, prejudicial connotations of caretaker, custodian, or keeper, to rehabilitate its original Latin-based meaning which is active, responsible, and progressive. The latter qualities may be reconstituted in the archival and library professions through effective use of automation to achieve compatible and similar goals of service and information dissemination geographically and chronologically. The negative concept of archival data as unused and perhaps worse, unuseable, can be altered to re-useable, used differently and more intensely, and in other dimensions. The idea of *inactive* records must not apply to archivists themselves or their archives. Nor can they afford to be seen as isolationist and non-interactive.

Flexibility and linkage are therefore seminal ingredients of automation and role transformation for both archivists and librarians. Minimally automation means to use computer-assisted retrieval to link resources and users, but more, to transfer information about information or to create intellectual access to it. As intellectual devices archival and bibliographic systems are ideally compatible and interactive.[38] The end result for archives should be the ability to integrate, or at least relate, one archival information system to another and into a much larger system, and ideally into a multi-type information system transcending the temporary isolationism of different information institutions—archives, libraries, galleries, museums, online services and clearinghouses, and other centers. The evolution of competing bibliographic, museum or artifact, and archival systems should be avoided.[39] The older goal of a national system seems notonly untenable, but undesirable; a nationwide super-system of compatible, cooperating, and interfaced documentary (records), bibliographic, and artifact information systems is, on the other hand, feasible and ideal.

How can archivists and librarians move toward such a goal? First, archivists must continue to rethink their traditional assumptions about archival methods and engage alternative solutions and strategies from allies like librarians, both to influence the latter to improve by adopting the best of archival thought and to borrow the best from both. Librarians, who extoll interdisciplinarity, need to create a more genuine reciprocity with archives and become better acquainted with archival principles and values, approaches, and shared problems. Fundamental assumptions and methodologies in both areas need to undergo continued re-examination.[40] Secondly, and more practically, political and economic coalitions need to be formed and maintained for a common good, especially in making the sizeable financial investments required in automation. Despite lip-service to the latter goal, genuine extensive integration and collaboration between archives and libraries are hard to identify.

A decade ago simple turn-key systems did electronically and more efficiently what mechanical and before that, manual, means could accomplish. Turn-key systems were, and are still designed for a limited number of specific tasks and repeated operations.[41] Now modern DBMS software on micro- and mini-computers do what previously had to be run on mainframes, and the latter do more than what was previously believed possible. The selection seems bewildering especially for archivists to survey office systems rather than limit themselves to ready-made library systems, but the choice today is not mainframe vs. minicomputer, but rather what kinds of combinations serve best the accomplishment of specific goals and objectives.[42] Likewise, software selections no longer mean choosing between an archival or bibliographic solution, since any package handling MARC formats could be used for both. Library system vendors, however, do not seem to be designing components of their systems specifically for archival functions other than user access.

Distributed systems using combinations of hardware and software, MARC and other text-retrieval and indexing strategies, allow for greater options than ever before. Customized workstations with their own memory and processing capacities tied into central facilities allow for the simultaneous running of several kinds of software and the maintenance of dual systems with varying degrees of integration and independence. Some systems, such as SIRSI's UNICORN system based on the UNIX operating system, seem already to accommodate indexing strategies with controlled retrieval mechanisms, free-text searching of narrative documentation such as the more traditional archival finding aids, with or without the use of tags for more direct searches of specified data elements, and can integrate formatted records such as MARC variants in the same files as unformatted text.[43] Such non-menu driven systems operate by commands closer to natural language than ever before, which makes them eminently ''user friendly.'' Old delimitors in software which accentuated differences between archival and library methodologies are fading away. Professional identities, social leavages, work habits, persuasions, and false perceptions may be more persistent.

Consequently, the array of equipment and software provides archivists and librarians alike with such a varied selection that evaluation of them must now include a re-evaluation of the assumptions brought to bear on the choice.[44] Some literature advises that such decisions must be based rationally on very precisely defined goals and objectives, but critics also see this as a sure means of acquiring obsolescence unless overriding goals are flexibility, expandability, linkage, and modular design. Those approaching automation, regardless of library or archives perspective, must envision their undertaking as a process of continuing change and perceive systems evaluation and modification as evolutionary. Phase approaches are not only feasible, they are mandatory. Implementation perceived as one-time, comprehensive solutions will be disappointing. Systems themselves must be regarded as flexible sets of interchangeable subsystems, continually upgradable, and relative to each other. While an archival information system itself may have subsystems (e.g., for records management), the archives system may be a subsystem in a larger superstructure such as a bibliographic or multi-type network.

Monolithic approaches need no longer dominate our mentality, because modern technology no longer imposes such restrictions. Prepackaged systems put more strains on organizations for change than does customization where the system is altered to fit the organization. Although it is often argued that the latter is preferable, this may mean that organizations needing thorough remodeling may instead revise a system to replicate currently deficient operations. However unsettling it may be, information managers must have systems in need of, and capable of, continuous remodeling as an organization changes. Most challenging of all, this means revamping our theory and practice on a continuing basis as well. Far from simplifying our operations, automation promises ever more complex managerial situations, greater demands on human resources, and staggering financial outlays; but on the brighter side, it holds prospects for demonstrably superior operations that accomplish more, for new constituencies.[45]

INTELLECTUAL ACCESS AND ARCHIVAL CONTROL

In religion, as defined and illustrated by the famous historian A. D. Nock, conversion requires a turn-around and denial, in part at least, of whatever went before; but adherence, a continuity approach, is less traumatic.[46] If one can adhere to old ways and gradually turn to new methods without much conscious denunciation of past practice, the transition seems simpler and easier to most people. The same is true, for example, in the use of historical precedent in managing change.[47] Human behavior is not much different in resisting new technology, or in trying to use a new technology while guarding against its impact on a value system or traditional methodology. This is also why adherence is the initial reaction of many practitioners when automation is first considered: people attempt simply to mechanize what has been done manually and misconstrue this as genuine automation.[48] In both archives and libraries data conversion from manual to machine-readable records has required a massive clean-up of data for machine-handling. Retrospective conversion entails revision in processing; it should result in changes in use as well. This means intellectual accommodations must accompany such automation.

The preliminary stage of conversion to automated systems, standardization in description, was faced first by librarians, but now as well by archivists.[49] When archivists tried to automate conventional finding aids, as in early efforts at the Illinois State Archives, without preliminary standardization and systematization, the results were less than spectacular. Now archivists recognize the need for standards, although consensus has yet to be reached about what these are. They also are beginning to recognize similarities between types of information used for access and control in archival and bibliographic systems, and an equivalency between data elements of such control information in archives and library descriptive practices. Such an intellectual rapproachment was fundamental for the MARC AMC format as an acceptable convention and its assumptions underpinned the work from 1977 to 1982 of the Society of American Archivists' National Information Systems Task Force.[50] Even the once alien idea of authority control is gaining wider acceptance in archival circles.[51] It is less certain, however, if archivists are ready to divorce intellectual access from physical retrieval, or in the design of automated systems understand that an abstraction or theoretical model should be freed from the constraints of a physical archives. Archival control as physical record retrieval, and intellectual access need to be linked and must be compatible, but they are not the same. Intellectual accessibility need not depend on physical retrieval.

Intellectual Challenges

The process of intellectual access in either an archives or a library is based on abstraction and use of a surrogate to retrieve ideas not records, or stated differently, to locate information about information resources. Surrogation in both bibliographic and archival systems can be single-entry precise and terse descriptions as in the former, or narrative description and multi-entry or linked documents in the latter. If librarians ever choose to use machine-readable catalogs to their full potential, to free their description from the artificial limitations once imposed by $3 \times 5''$ catalog cards, they too may resort to narrative description, full-text searching, and indexing as alternatives to AACR2 cataloging conventions. Whereas libraries using manual systems maintain inventory control by the shelf-list, not the catalog, archives have tended to keep description and arrangement more closely aligned and to use inventory control as their dominate form of intellectual access. This is changing, and automation promises to accelerate such change.

Old cornerstones of archival theory and practice, original order, provenance, and *respect des fonds*, need to be reconsidered in automated environments. These principles evolved in manual environments where physical arrangement had to preserve original order to save context and thereby assist evaluation and interpretation.[52] Such concerns apply as well to machine-readable records; they cannot be discounted entirely, but may be modified. Studies comparing access by provenance and by content indexing suggest that the latter cannot replace the former, because each method of retrieval operates differently.[53] Searchers familiar with organizational structures are already familiar with the data structure of an archives, and can search more efficiently by that means than can a searcher unfamiliar with the organization. The latter seem to need indexing alternatives. The two methods together seem to produce the best results in archives; the same might be true in libraries if online catalogs allowed searching by provenance.

In both cases, in library catalogs and archival information systems, intellectual access can entail diverse approaches. An automated system can preserve provenance theoretically, and original order too, as an abstraction mirroring actual housing, without the necessity of having it reflected in the order of the records in a series or books on the shelf or the latter dictating the ordering of retrieval documents in the system. These time-honored conventions in archives were rationalized as an expedient by archivists coping with mass, as much as an intellectual argument that an organic unity characterizes a body of records as a whole, like a book collection, and attests past functions and use.[54] In some ways this rationalization shifted the burden of retrieval from description and arrangement to use, and from archivists to patrons. Now, in current attempts to provide better service, the earlier labor-saving devices only delay the investment of time and energy in the entire process. Reference service in archives has become very labor intensive. While original motivations in libraries and archives for automation includes processing efficiency, now there is increased attention on user services. This may re-intensify labor costs in initial processing.

Archivists could be doctrinaire in their insistence on original order (even when they confuse it with provenance), maintaining that it outweighs considerations of user access. The argument was often unconvincing, especially for users. Now, however, such an argument may also be irrelevant. The idiosyncrasies of a records-creating agency should not dictate forever thereafter information retrieval and the mode of intellectual access to those records. Archivists can artificially document the original state of a file, including its order and condition for preservation purposes, in the preliminary inventory process; and then they can link this document to others which provide alternative, improved accessibility. The intellectual re-ordering of documents in an information system does not require the manual reshuffling of records themselves. It is no longer unthinkable in an automated environment to disband a record series, reconstitute it either in a new physical arrangement with the old order preserved in relevant documentation; or to leave the original order alone and re-arrange the surrogates in the information system. In the latter the archivist could use either pre- or post-coordination of descriptors, documents, or aggregates, to enhance the information system. Although re-arrangement of the abstract documents rather than the physical records seems most preferable to archivists, for uniform storage and improved conservation an argument can be made for the first alternative. Physical re-arrangement and reconstruction in surrogate form could use automation to better advantage in a preservation program. In such a case, format, medium, condition, and physical attributes may be used to classify records in the tradition of the British ''mark and park'' approach to cataloging. Storage consideration, projected frequency of use, as well as intrinsic values assessed in appraisal, and security precautions, might therefore determine archival arrangement and separate this intellectual function from description as commonly practiced.

In traditional archival theory, such thought is heresy!

Changing Processes

Such approaches to archival problems would greatly change the routine in technical services.[55] Physical re-arrangement might be dictated by computerized sorts, whereas in traditional settings arrangement and description go hand-in-hand. Consider the convenience in computer-assisted calendaring a manuscript collection, when a time line could be automatically assembled after random entry of exact dates and proximate chronological termini for periodization. Correspondents would be collated, and name authority control could be aided by the automatic frequency checks and chronological collation. Orthographical variants could be linked to standardized main entries without distorting original usage in the records, thus assuring current users of an archival information system consistency in the assignment of priority access points while leaving the authenticity of the original undisturbed. Sorts and arrangements could be tested theoretically without excess wear on the actual materials, and indexing could proceed at a much higher level of sophistication than is common in archives. Screening for access clearance and security measures, tied to legal controls or conservation measures, might be embedded into the system. In short, managerial control of records might be an easily arranged by-product of intellectual archival control in an automated environment. The premise here, however, is that rather than create intellectual access from physical arrangement and inventory control, the latter might proceed from the former. This would reverse typical processing in archives and manuscript repositories. The real challenge of automation is to rethink almost everything learned about traditional archival operations and procedures.[56]

This does not mean that current developments in automated bibliographic systems in libraries provide the only or the best solutions to archival problems. Indeed, librarians have adhered to old ways in their conservative entry into the computer world, and only slowly in the customization of older software and the development of far more versatile alternatives have libraries begun to experiment with intellectual controls other than those derived from well established cataloging procedures. Even then, rare book curators like their manuscript counterparts and archival colleagues, have had to modify currently streamlined conventions in order to accommodate their special needs. Manuscript curators and rare book librarians, in preserving their respective bias toward archival and bibliographic methodology, have not always cooperated in the evolution of special descriptive standards and approaches to aggregate description.[57] Rare book librarians, for example, often champion the item approach even though they so often deal with collections as much as individual books. One might have expected more of an alliance and greater consensus building between rare book librarians, manuscript curators, and archivists in approaching historical materials, except that the former work more under the umbrella of library organizations, particularly the Rare Book and Manuscript Section of the Association of College and Research Libraries; while the latter work within the Society of American Archivists; manuscripts people are often torn between the two. Consequently, these supposedly allied professions have yet to synthesize their divergent approaches into a system which can accommodate layered, multi-level descriptive standards or combinations of cataloging methods with other forms of intellectual access such as indexing subsystems.[58] Few Special Collections have developed subsystems to create special access to their book collections; often only the archives and manuscript collections are seen as "special" in this regard.

This curious adherence to cataloging standards, sometimes at the most general levels, for special collections and the lack of attention to subsystem development, may be explained by the natural conservatism of professionals working with antiquarian materials and their relative lack of technical interest or expertise, but also by their administrative problems in overcoming the obstacles in library technical services which regard cataloging backlogs in special collections as natural and tolerable. It may also be a result of the development of library automation from circulation applications rather than from the central conceptualization of a unified catalog or institution-wide intellectual control. Consequently, libraries have relatively little software for specific applications to control collections other than circulating books: manuscripts, rare books, instructional media, and artifact holdings have had to rely on modifications of MARC formats for each particular medium. This proliferation of MARC formats and tedious differentiation of data placement in tags, is less than satisfactory. Indeed, the new MARC AMC format is far more adaptable to the cataloging of rare books, especially those which are binder's editions encompassing multiple, diverse titles, than older conventions for rare book cataloging. It would not be unrealistic for a Special Collection's operation to adopt archival approaches to description and arrangement of its book collections at the same time that its archival component finds itself moving closer to certain library approaches. Will the crossover be noticed?

Not only have libraries not used MARC formats for multi-level descriptive control of phased cataloging, they ordinarily do not take advantage of modern computer technology to create subsidiary systems and genuinely relational data bases. Nor have they used automation as a tool in preservation program development. Hierarchical information structures still dominate library mentalities and approaches to bibliographic control. Increasingly libraries are dressing up their online systems with bulletin boards, news services, streamlined help and user instruction aids, and supplementary indexes. It is in the development of such customized accessories that archivists and librarians should be collaborating.

Alternative Approaches

What kinds of options are available to archivists to use automation for more direct user access than through the labyrinth of referrals from guides and catalog entries at the collection level, to inventories and series descriptions, and then to the physical records where users must rely on arrangement descriptors such as folder headings to locate relevant material? There have been several experiments in cutting through this maze by indexing folder headings, although archivists have not been very successful in using taxonomies to organize their master indexes. A variety of methods exist to go beyond such linear and hierarchical reference systems as either the traditional referral sequence or the single-file index, as supplements and alternatives rather than replacements to recognized archival methodology, and still avoid the entrapment of library item-level approaches where documents are linked primarily by classification schema and subject headings based on very general content analysis and a preconceived schedule. These include, but are not limited to:

1. Record sampling and spot quotation of narrative cuttings either keyboarded into a data base or more optimally entered by optical-character recognition (OCR) input, which preserves natural language in context for free-text searching without prolonged, extensive searching and expensive storage if all records were machine-readable and searchable. Such extracts can be assigned to designated sublevels under main entries, to link them and yet distinguish them from upper levels of description and generalized surrogates, so that one could search across documents at any given level of specificity or generalization as well as to move vertically in a relational data base or matrix-designed system. Such retrieval would be especially useful in language studies, direct access to changing placenames, colloquial terms and archaisms, which are more commonly subordinated to standardized forms, and for conceptual searches rather than those aimed at persons, places, or things whose names are known to current users. Diverse techniques such as split windows and the use of superimposed templates to associate various levels of information in a multilevel document about actual records, can create multidimensional displays for users.

2. Abstracting allows a system to retain original vocabularies but not a record's syntax, and condensation can cover more volume per entry. Abstracts can be linked to catalog-like entries and form a sub-system of description for keyword retrieval, with or without the supra-imposition of a synonym or reference system to a controlled vocabulary or thesaurus. Or to invert this common approach, one might create a separate

file to preserve the orginal language with cross-references to abstracts which use only a preferred vocabulary. Machine-translation capabilities are improving rapidly, so that computer-controlled term substitution in abstracts might be considered.

3. Abstracts may also be standardized paraphrases with unilateral correspondence to records, section by section or line by line if one could afford to be so specific, which could co-exist with original machine-readable text in a system so that retrieval could be either free-text scanning or by selective term access. Forementioned multiple display techniques could collate abstracts and extracts, and the addition of a third window or template could collate these with a controlled vocabulary and index as easily as with a boiler-plate catalog entry of the type used for the MARC AMC format. It is theoretically possible to design a system which would allow one to search vertically in any of the three parallel data sets and automatically to retrieve a collated abstract, extract, and catalog description simultaneously. Such a system would preserve original text and context, provide condensed versions suitable for more rapid browsing, and link these to corresponding terms for access to bibliographic records.

4. Indexing can be used either to enhance catalog entries or MARC-formatted descriptions, or to form separate files of indexes with controls operating therein quite apart from governance of higher levels of control. As in the use of the AMC format, formal subject headings may be assigned to create a correspondence to the parent bibliographic system (tagged separately for sorting efficiency and record linkage through preferred subject terms) without purging alternatives. Key-word searching in- and out-of-context (KWIC/KWOC) can supplement single-term retrieval, especially for conceptual searching. Index arrays may consist of single terms arranged alphabetically (least desirable, unless post-coordination is possible), hierarchically with controlled subordination and pre-coordination of terms, or in strings controlled by a prescribed syntax, rotation, or permutation of terms.

5. Indexing by associative terms, derived from relational words in a text, can be arranged in syntax-

controlled phrases (i.e., PRECIS) for access to records rich in conceptual information but which lack concrete, distinctive terms.[59]

6. Name authority control could be used more creatively in archival description than it ordinarily is, if indeed archivists use authority control at all other than through provenance tracings. Max Evans has suggested to archivists that authority control is an alternative to the much-attacked concept of the records group.[60] Authorized standard entries can be superimposed on variants and original versions without writing over them; they can be masked for backup display, or shoved into parenthetical clauses. Such accommodations are especially helpful in retaining provenance data and linking newer online documentation to older manual descriptions.

7. Classification can include a variety of taxonomies, not only library classification schedules. Moreover, any schedule can be exploded to accommodate a specialized schedule within it, as in the case of libraries using the Lynn-Peterson schedules to expand the B section (Religion) for Roman Catholic institutions otherwise using the Library of Congress classification.[61] An archives can adopt a classification schedule from specialized libraries for such purposes, or design one for the particular indepth approach it wants to take to a major collection, as easily as using a thesaurus prepared elsewhere for similar materials. Often thesauri have taxonomies in them which lend themselves nicely to classification. Standard library cataloging practices allow for such diversity, but such customization is labor intensive and expensive.

These are only a few alternative strategies to be deployed in designing information systems which provide access to unique resources. There are several obstacles to their implementation, mostly political and financial rather than technical, as components of a parent bibliographic system.[62] Moreover, bibliographic networks are unable to transfer such specialized documentation beyond MARC formatted information.

If, as maintained here, the relationship between description, intellectual access, and physical arrangement in an automated archival information system is more theoretical than real, documentation can be rearranged as often as need be without touching the records. Or the records themselves can be arranged without preservation of original order, to enhance access through improved conservation and storage measures.

Automation can provide a flexibility and a relativity, therefore, which makes most archivists and library catalogers alike, rather uncomfortable. In such systems there can be no such principle as definitive arrangement and description, no absolute correspondence between arrangement and description as one integral process, and no assurance that any processing is adequate for all time and for every purpose.[63] Information generated by users, for example, can be used as feedback in the periodical revision of index terms, preferred vocabulary, and the creation of associations not evident in the records themselves. It is more sensible to impose minimal rather than maximum standards for description in an automated system, and to make sure that the system can handle greater amounts and more sophisticated data structures than those which an operation is currently using. The maximum may be determined by the hardware's capacity for memory and storage costs, and by personnel limitations, more than intellectual considerations.

MARC AMC Usage

By limiting standardization to control elements and leaving in an archival document free-text and note fields, and by appending sublevels of description, standards need not suppress the individuality of archival records or the creativity of archivists in designing their own subsystems within library or bibliographic networks. One can accommodate house rules and styles even when modeled after bibliographic formats, and still adhere to archival conventions and norms without creating incongruence in an information system. The polarity of past archives vs. library approaches is no longer necessary. The MARC AMC format could be used for no more than a "boiler plate" mechanism to link bibliographic and archival documentation, but it has greater potential than that. If the skeletal AMC document is perceived by archivists to present an ideal maximum for descriptive access, they are mistaken. They would then be like librarians, who also fail to take advantage of computer technology when MARC records are the only form of descriptive access their systems will support.

Use of the AMC format and data entry according to supplemental guides for special materials circumvent the grave limitations of manuscript cataloging *à la* NUCMC and AACR2. These revisions coupled with the sanction to use descriptors derived from sources other than the Library of Congress *Subject Headings* or the Sear's list, promise closer cooperation between archives and libraries in large-scale information exchange. Software vendors, however, are not willing to maintain customized systems which allow an institution to provide the alternative strategies discussed here. Moreover, the opening of bibliographic systems for archives must be considered with the impact of developments of micro- and mini-computers for small-scale environments.[64] Software such as MARCHON II is also providing options such as MARC packaging, so that small archival workstations can be networked to larger bibliographic systems.[65]

While the MARC AMC format option and developments in both RLIN and OCLC beckon archivists to participate in library-dominated networks, inhouse computer systems allow the archivists greater personal freedom to do the kinds of systems development previously suggested; it also gives them greater control over their documentation, independence from vendor and utility pressures and fees, and an intellectual independence even when an archives is politically and administratively under a library. Both alternatives, independent systems development and OCLC/RLG cooperation, have their rewards and limitations. Together, however, they provide interesting options never before explored by archivists. It is the combination of inhouse systems and cooperation through multi-type networking that points to future scenarios which depict a radically different archives from those relatively isolated operations now so prevalent. Such changes have potential for libraries as well. The direction of future automation development is a matter of policy, and hence politics, as much as one of technology and intellectual concerns.

Policy Formulation

Archivists now face a critical decision: how to automate and use modern computer technology to greatest advantage, to maximize linkage in archives, between archives, and between archival and bibliographic holdings, and to provide the greatest possible access to public information resources. Librarians face a related decision about what kind of partnership and opportunity they will afford archivists within library-dominated networks. Will they foster cooperation with archivists or foster the latter's latent tendency toward isolationism? This depends on one's regard for genuinely integrated information systems and attitude toward cooperation and resource sharing (i.e., sharing financial resources to share information sources).

Archivists can:

1. Develop inhouse self-contained systems sufficient to serve their own institutions only, currently defined clienteles, and their immediate managerial needs, without identifying strategies for extra-institutional information exchange. This would be a natural development for private organizations and those archives without public records, but an unfortunate situation were public repositories to take this option.

2. Design inhouse systems on small, immediately

affordable computers, which aim toward compatibility and are meant to be integrated into larger information systems at some future date. This is a viable option for small, independent archives and manuscripts repositories which cannot afford large systems.

3. Develop systems which resist the temptation to work within the still considerable limitations of mini-computers, perhaps by using combinations of personal computers as smart work stations and backup support from clusters of micro-computers or a mainframe, using vendor/utility sponsored solutions, and tapping into library-dominated bibliographic systems while pursuing customization to build archival subsystems meeting local needs.[66]

The first introspective approach is viable only for archives which cannot share their information outside the parent organization. The misapplication of this option to other situations may guarantee archival obsolescence. The second alternative is the most attractive to archivists who are still enamored with their personal computers, but who have not had the technical and mainframe support they need from their institutions. It may also be a default option for archivists lacking the political and administrative authority to make larger systems work for them. The danger is that the goal of future integration remains dreamlike and illusive in such situations; it may not materialize because of an inability to keep pace with large-scale computer technology when daily focii are constantly confined to small-scale environs. The kind of data manipulation and systems development advocated for improved intellectual access to archives outstrips the ability of mini-computers despite their rapidly expanding capabilities. Yet, the third alternative seems to be beyond the technical competence, political clout, and patronage of most archives.

The library model for networking does not appeal to archives which cannot reap the economic benefits from copy cataloging, and it instills fear because within such structures archives are overshadowed by library giants. Although libraries often see themselves as powerless and dwarfed creatures within today's mega-universities, archivists have the same perspective and paranoia regarding their station within multi-million volume super-libraries. Perspectives are relative to vantage points. The barriers retarding intra-archives cooperation are the same for library-archives cooperation. The motivation for information resource sharing between the two must be more altruistic than it has been. Moreover, archivists must realize that old arguments that they cannot share information resources because most of them are non-lending institutions, have been made largely irrelevant by modern reprographics, facsimile transmission, and potential digitization. Although archives cannot now share their recorded information readily and must be content to share documents about their records, the day is coming when the "electronic library" may be quite indistinguishable from the machine-readable archives. Why not prepare for that day now?

Authority Control

While authority control usually means an intellectual construct for imposing preferred entries over variants in a data base, there is a dimension of this activity which deserves more attention than it gets in the literature. The question is who controls intellectual authority over a system? That is a proposition different than asking who has administrative control over the organization. Authority for quality control needs to be clearly delineated not only for the procedures for input and how a program accepts data, but in human components of the system. Which committees, for example, are purely advisory and which ones are decision-making bodies?

Libraries have had to face difficult problems in localizing authority control over records in their bibliographic systems. That problem is compounded in archives-library cooperation where archivists fear that such authority ultimately will reside with librarians who know very little about an archival subsystem. The following are some of the more critical questions raised in library technical services; they pertain as well to archives:

1. Who is authorized to make changes within the system's records?
2. How are such changes to be made (rules and regulations i.e., globally or one by one editing in context)?
3. Where are such changes to be triggered (subsystem or system levels, or externally by a vendor or host system)?
4. To what extent are changes to be made (partial or whole, selective or universal, by purging or masking old data, etc.)?
5. How does one record change influence others, so that one can establish a system archives and biographic history for administrative purposes and ease in making future decisions about modifications which follow logically from one to another, and from pattern to pattern?

To avoid redundancy and managerial chaos, it is ideal to control quality at the onset, with controls on input by field assignments, tags, differentiation between fixed and open fields, definition of data elements, agreement on form of entry and syntax or the ordered structure of data within fields, etc., but this must be accomplished without shifting workloads back to manual operations. Intellectual determinations include: (1) what to record; (2) at what level of detail or generalization must it be recorded; (3) where to place it in an overall document design; (4) in what form of entry; (5) how to file entries; and (6) how to differentiate between data storage formats and flexible displays.

The implications of such decisions on an organizational structure, for personnel and the traditional hierarchical distribution of authority in libraries, are substantial. One need not discuss the MARC format in detail to realize that the open-ended use of the AMC format allows a variety of approaches to be taken if the institution allows maximum flexibility in archival entries without the imposition of library administrative authority on an archives as a means of intellectual authority control. In other words, some organizational structures may not allow archivists to use the AMC format creatively and may lodge all of the discretionary authority over data base design and quality control outside an archives in cataloging or systems and operations units. That assuredly will be distasteful to archivists.

The use of at least one L.C. subject heading per AMC-MARC record, as suggested by RLG, serves to tie archival records to published material on the same subject. This frees term selection and control of descriptors for archives where the subject matter is best known, and where content-analytic and provenance control methods can be balanced. In either case, the need for authority control over description obviously remains. In the recent past archivists passed the flaws of their manual finding aids to their first automated systems without necessary standardization and retrospective data editing. It was often in automation that the inconsistencies and incongruence of manual policies and procedures first became apparent. The feeling that archival retrieval lacked the precision achieved in bibliographic systems also underlays the reluctance of library catalogers to accommodate archival modes of control and description as components of library-hosted information systems. Whether by persuasion or threatened exclusion, archivists have adopted many procedures long identified as library-oriented, including authority control and main entry standard, but not always AACR2 or LSCH in derivation. Adopting library conventions for a minimal number of headings, however, has given archivists a credibility on the part of librarians. The point is that despite valid criticism of the L.C. terms and the inadequacy of the strings they form, the common utility of LCSH provides them with an authority greater than their intrinsic goodness and a usefulness not always related to anything more than convenience in narrowing a search and a commonality for retrieval.

It is ironic that in employing authority control and a preferred, and sometimes a prescribed vocabulary, access is restricted to enhance a search's efficiency by giving it direction. An illustrative analogy would be driving rules to stay on the road, so that in confining free movement to one direction one speeds along in a chosen path to a pre-selected destination. The computer is merely the vehicle. The searcher may be the driver, but the archivist is the engineer and planner who lays out the route. In complex terrain, a map is needed with focal points, agreed-upon names, and directions. Those advocating free-text searching need to understand the meaning of "free" is not the Libertarian sense, i.e., almost a rambling or its equivalent in library use, browsing; the Augustinian sense means that man has free choice to follow rules because rationally they make sense and are self-enhancing. In information systems constraints ironically can be seen as enhancements to information access as much as in theology where such freedom results in the promotion of the common good. Flexibility, not unbridled freedom, is the goal in information systems design and control.

EDUCATION AND EXPECTATIONS

Automation not only challenges fundamental archival thinking, it has broad implications for organization structure and behavior. In libraries automation has meant that staff members oriented around public services, at circulation desks for example, suddenly find themselves in technical services even though they remain at their work stations. Automation transports tasks from one place to another instead of moving people; it redistributes previously centralized functions and operations while concentrating others which once diffused; and it changes interpersonal relationships within an organization. As job roles change, so do performance evaluations and supervisory expectations; new partnerships are formed while others are split; and relationships with the public may also be altered. Indeed, a new public may be created.

Trends in computer-assisted retrieval and their impact on library reference services illustrate many of these changes. Online reference service in libraries is one aspect of these changes; the use in archives of automatic text processing to compose customized reference letters by collating prefabricated paragraphs, is another. Innovations where such reference applications are linked to the institution's retrieval system are rare. Yet, as users become better acquainted with online retrieval systems in business and industry, in law and government, and in progressive libraries, they are becoming more accustomed to helping themselves. Although the advent of the self-sufficient user seems unlikely, certainly the traditional mandatory imposition of the reference librarian or archivist between a patron and information sources is likely to come under increased criticism.

User studies are needed in every library and archives as well, but they are comparatively rare in the latter. The question of "how" in automation cannot be answered without "for whom?" Research and development must go together. Effective automation in archives may be retarded by the lack of high quality user studies and the preponderance of managerial studies in the literature which rest on a consensus of opinion rather than empirical research. Market segmentation to identify specific clients and potential clienteles, and to differentiate their information needs, is an example of needed research. Others include efficiency studies, rating the relevance in retrieval, correlation with published sources, query analysis for the design of reference tools, comparison of indexing strategies, and advances in classification theory by examining types of records (i.e., a modern diplomatics) as well as in appraisal where specific values need clarification for prioritization in designing retrieval systems.

The human dimension of automation is highlighted by these mentions of changing reference services and the impact of computerization on personnel and organizational structures. Automation is likely to modify the behavior of both the user and the provider of information. Consequently, acceptance and the creative exploitation of a new system often depends on whether such change is forced or is self-motivated. In the former case, authority dominates; in the latter, a subtle education process creates a wholesome climate for change. Organizational change tends to be more lasting and thorough when it is supported throughout the whole human system that parallels the technical, electronic system being implemented. There are at least three perspectives to consider when orchestrating the social change, indeed the belief structure of an organization, when implementing an automation system: the vendor or system supplier; the archivist as client; and the user.

Vendor Perspectives

Frustration with vendors, or inhouse developers, can be minimized only if systems analysis of the kind recommended by Richard Kesner precedes the drafting of specifications, a written prospectus, and the establishment of time-tables and a mode of communication between the supplier and implementor.[67] Information provided to a prospective vendor should include an outline of project management concerns, the division of the project into phases with a realistic time-line, and a scenario speculating about the subsequent directions in which an archives might develop. These are more important than an attempt, as has been the case in many evaluations tried by libraries, of trying to isolate every procedure and workflow or stratagem in manual processing, in order to dictate to a vendor exactly what a system must do. That approach seems naive because it does not recognize that the process of automation itself should change such processes, and that most systems are undergoing very rapid development and have accommodations for local variation already in place.[68]

The problem for archivists is the same as it was for librarians a few years ago: few vendors have had sufficient experience adopting their hardware and software to archival applications. Operations managers in libraries accustomed only to bibliographic systems often use their technical competence to persuade the archives to change rather than to work with archivists to modify a system for archival processes. Both operators and developers, however, should be familiar with parallel procedures in office automation, business applications, and library systems. Planning must include preparing for problems, including system failure.[69]

A healthy client-vendor relationship is fundamental for smooth, effective implementation. A manager who does not orchestrate internal change to prepare for automation, and then creates a climate of distrust by destructive criticism of a vendor or system, sets up in the organization a belief that will impede effective automation. Vendors can rightfully expect precise criticism in writing so that problems and hence resolutions, can be identified before frustration buildup. A track record of performance, problem identification, solutions, and communication should be maintained. Finally, vendors who supply systems design and support specification refinement, all of which might normally be expected of the organization, can also expect compensation for services beyond their sales and maintenance obligations. Free consulting and custom programs are not ordinarily part of a sales package, although good follow-up through the implementation period by the account representative is warranted. Archives who rely on libraries or computer centers for support must ascertain what their relationship is to the supplier, i.e., as a vendor, utility, or host, and behave accordingly.

Archivists Perspectives

The archivist as client has a different perspective from the vendor or library host, but not necessarily one of opposition. If a system has multiple clients the host like a utility needs to provide a forum for arbitration of conflicting interests. This is especially important in distinguishing between a utility- and vendor-sponsored network, and in situations where archives are subsystems of library controlled bibliographic systems but are funded separately from the library. Vendors are not directly responsible to users, co-owners, and stockholders as is a utility, but they are for-profit enterprises kept in check only if there is a free market, alternatives, and competition. The relationship is contractual between seller and buyer. The archivist as consumer must develop a records management system to track, prompt, and even legally enforce compliance as necessary, and in turn is subject to like pressure from a vendor regarding payment, implementation, and maintenance. As in all partnerships, each party has rights and obligations. Without being too cynical, remember that vendors are likely to respond in proportion to the profit involved in maintaining an account, and that archives by themselves are not profitable customers. This is one reason why smaller units must ally with larger ones, i.e., archives with libraries, and in turn, libraries with university computer centers and utilities, etc. In each case advantages are offset by a layering of indirect managerial control and what may appear superficially to be a technical issue, is readily made into management and political activity. Such alliances are fragile concerns when it comes to dominance, balance, and internal accord.

The relatively small-scale environment of archives for computer applications and the uneasy alliance between archives and libraries, makes it easier managerially for both archivists and librarians to go their separate ways and let archives rely on micro- and mini-computer applications and conventions of their own device. In such cases archives have been and still are disadvantaged by being dissociated from larger systems and mainstream development. They are denied the corporate expertise accessible through a vendor, utility, or host system. They lack guarantees beyond the immediate installation of the hardware and software, and they are not afforded the reassurance and comfort in sharing risks in automation. The archivist who opts for such independence with risk unshared and without proper contextual support, must recognize the costs involved. Often these are subtle, as the archivist must become more of a computer specialist than archivist, as a by-product of over-reliance on the uneven and volatile advice from the local electronics store. It is easier for archives to use a personal computer than a larger system, and likewise it is easier for a library not to care about archival information sharing, but the ease in both cases has a terrible long-range cost. Yet, it has become common knowledge, or at least a universal perception among archivists, that archives within libraries cannot expect high prioritization from their parent organization for any special attention, unless it is secured, if not by contract, then by written policy. It is odd that archivists therefore regard libraries as reluctant hosts and vendors rather than as utilities.

User Perspectives

A third perspective is that of the patron who ordinarily will have no regard whatsoever for the myriad complications in automation mentioned in this essay.[70] An automated system for an archives will be compared "automatically" to other systems in a similar or parallel context. An archives which stays manual or at best upgrades operations to off-line batch systems, in a library which goes online for bibliographic control, will suffer from such comparisons as inferior, antiquated, backwards, or worse, unuseable.[71] Pressure on archivists to automate may come more from external sources than perceptions of their own needs. Library automation, therefore, is itself a primary motivation for archives to automate. A library's disregard for simultaneous archives automation consequently is more harmful than simple devaluation of archival information services.

Libraries have discovered that once introduced, automation spawns demands for increased services; it has a spiralling effect. Patrons expect that automation is part of continuous development and often want, all at once, more than is deliverable. This is partially because of exposure to automation through entertainment media where computer capabilities need not conform to the real world, and certainly not to the reality of budgetary restrictions. However, these comparative phenomena which set up great expectations for automation in all modern information services are also promoted by our education system's recent advocation of "computer literacy" without clear definition but often an amateurish dilettantism, instead of a more meaningful subordination of computers to the objective of "information literacy." The latter would mean building a self-sufficiency in information retrieval regardless of medium and a focus on the structure and utility of data as information to balance the former's preponderant concern for the machine. In any case, when the personal computer balances checkbooks at home, assists lessons at school, is a playmate in the arcade, etc., the user of tomorrow will hardly be impressed with today's efforts at archival automation and especially not with those which rely on mini-systems alone.

People with such expectations behave differently in information gathering than do patrons who are accustomed only to manual searching.[72] Several academic libraries in institutions with stable enrollments have experienced dramatic increases in use after automation. This is an increase not in users, but of uses. Usage therefore can become more intensive and extensive simultaneously as a result of automation. Libraries have experienced increased pressure to bring collections under automated bibliographic control immediately, all at once, to cut backlogs, and to enlarge collection size in proportion to enrollments. Once patrons are concerted to using online systems, a noted reaction has been the heightened frustration that accompanies any return to manual procedures when, for example, a system is down. At New York University's Bobst Library, while its online catalog or Bobcat was up, alongside the still operational card catalog, librarians observed patrons standing in line to wait for an open terminal rather than revert to a manual search even though the total time spent in waiting exceeded that required for the search. Similar reactions can be expected to be transferable to archives as patrons accustomed to online catalogs and circulation systems in libraries are forced to adjust to manually operated archives. Such archival services will be regarded as throw-backs.

Archives use for non-genealogical research may continue to decline in an indirect ratio to the total research being done, if archives fail to automate effectively. Resistance to archives use will intensify as archivists attempt to provide services for new clienteles who are already addicted to automated retrieval systems. In most cases potential users will not understand, nor really care, why the installation of an automated archival information system is so complicated, or why archives are lagging behind libraries in adopting modern technology. Criticism is not the threat; an attitude of apathy and disregard for archives will prove catastrophic.

Some false patron expectations need to be dispelled immediately. This includes the notion that somehow once an automated system is up, it can produce access immediately to all holdings. Few archives can afford retrospective conversion for any but their most valued collections; if the library recon-experience is studied, the enormity of the task and cost makes this a mute issue. Most library automated systems and online catalogs have yet to gain control over government documents, media collections, and special collections, to say nothing of archives. Overall operations have had to cope with multiple filing and classifications systems in place simultaneously for prolonged periods of conversion from Dewey to L.C., from AACR1 to AACR2, from ALA filing rules to ASCII and EPCDIC files, and from manual to automated functions.

Staff members sometimes expect equally absurd things, such as the total replacement of manual routines by automatic functions. Computers do not provide fool-proof systems when operated by fools; the general public is still rather naive about believing that if a computer says something, it must be so. Error checks, edition work, backup systems, and data security control, all entail safeguard operations and require healthy skepticism. Nor can the manager ameliorate all of the psychological factors in the resistance to technological change. At one extreme patrons and staff alike will want full and immediate automation of all functions and holdings; at the other they will lament the passing of old ways. At best, the manager can prepare a climate of opinion and an anticipation of change and guard against false expectations.

The forementioned impact of automation on the delivery of reference services illustrates how pervasive is the change wrought by computers in organizational structure and behavior.[73] Whereas vendors have stressed the development of "user-friendly" menu-driven programs for patrons to use themselves in hope of capturing large markets with a maximum redundancy and distribution of service points, libraries have favored economizing by consolidating service points into clusters of terminals supported by reference personnel. Reference librarians tending online catalogs, for example, have had to change their style and methods of delivering service. They have had to develop ways to let skilled online searchers conduct their own explorations of data bases, and in the case of online catalogs to devise unobtrusive methods of monitoring use and offering assistance. Professional-client interaction often changes, and new means must be found for evaluating the effectiveness of reference services and retrieval efficiency. Formal surveys, testing, and tracing researchers' interaction with a system by monitoring a tracking record, are all being employed by librarians in automated environments, to replace former search counts, informal observation, and subjective reporting. Components of traditionally direct, unilateral reference service are thus becoming indirect and more reliant on information delivery in prepackaged units matched to segmented user groups.

Archivists, like librarians, may have to replace informal reference with more formal instruction, technical writing in user manuals and guides, professional signage, and formal testing and evaluation. However, archivists still prefer systems copied closely from their manual operations wherein the archivist interposes as an intermediary in most searches. Too many systems seem designed for archivists, not end users. As in the case of libraries which are highly automated, archivists might expect increased pressure for direct patron access to online data bases and resistance to intervention by professionals. Archivists maintain that their collections are too vast, varied, and complicated, for users to negotiate their access tools and system on their own, without the guidance of the archivist. They seldom think, in saying this, what they are also telling users about archival information systems which may be idiosyncratic rather than systematic. How long will such excuses be accepted by an increasingly sophisticated public?

The impact of automation, therefore, will reverberate from the information-delivery setting in two directions at once:

> 1. into courses and classrooms filled by users of automated information systems, who will be indoctrinated and trained as habitual users of computer technology; and

> 2. into curricula for the training of archivists and librarians who have to respond to new clienteles, clients whose information seeking behavior is undergoing rapid modification, and new uses of information resources.[74]

CONCLUSION:
AN ADMINISTRATIVE PERSPECTIVE

Apart from common concerns about funding and technical expertise, administrators must wonder if the investment in automation can be justified by an extension of services to more users, an intensity of usage, information quality control, and savings within the organization of human resources and labor costs. It is so much easier for managers to justify automation on the basis of quantifiable data than on more subjective, qualitative standards. Archives have grave difficulties justifying such investments except on the basis of volume of holdings; their uses and users are small in comparison to libraries. The argument really has to be made on the qualitative side, for research, access to primary documentation, and the emergence of new technologies in information production and dissemination which promise to elevate the standing of archival records in comparison to traditional reliance on printed sources. Book- and record-centered technologies are converging as much as computer and communication technologies. Might one not expect a convergence as well of archivists and librarians in their professional development to cope with new forms of information sources and automated retrieval?

Such professional convergence, as suggested throughout this essay, might be expected to include:

1. a reconsideration of basic principles, assumptions, and methods in archival and bibliographic control, with a rethinking of the traditional cleavage and simultaneous separation between libraries and archives;
2. a shared focus on language and conceptual problems in information storage and retrieval, with less preoccupation about the technology itself;
3. a balanced approach to the human dimension of automation as well as to the mechanical; and
4. a cooperation in basic professional and life-long, continuing education for archivists and librarians which is not mutually exclusive as it has been.

Let us plan for integration through partnership rather than conquest, exchange rather than one-way transfer, and cooperation rather than internecine rivalry with the information profession. Let us hope that automation is more than a means to these higher goals than just satisfaction of immediate self-interests in individual archives and libraries.

REFERENCES

1. This is a revised, shortened and updated version of a keynote address, "The Human Touch: Automation for Archives and Users," Midwest Archives Conference, University of Illinois, spring 1984.

2. For the broad context see the case studies in the U.S. Congress Office of Technology Assessment, *Informational Technology and its Impact on American Education* (Washington, D.C.: GPO, 1982); for libraries, cf.: Richard W. Boss, "Technology and the modern library," *Library*

Journal 109 no. 11 (1984): 1183–9, and his *The Library Manager's Guide to Automation*, 2nd ed. (White Plains, NY: Knowledge Industry Publications, Inc., 1984); John Corbin, *Managing the Library Automation Project* (Phoenix, AZ: Oryx Press, 1985); H. F. Cline and L. T. Sinnott *The Electronic Library: The Impact of Automation on Academic Libraries* (Lexington, MA: D.C. Heath & Co., 1983); D. Reynolds, *Library Automation: Issues and Applications* (NY: R.R. Bowker Co., 1985); James Rice, *Introduction to Library Automation* (Littleton, CO: Libraries Unlimited, 1984); and for archives cf. Lawrence J. McCrank, ed., *Automating the Archives: Issues and Problems in Computer Applications* (White Plains, NY: Knowledge Industry Publications, Inc., 1981); Michael Cook, *Archives and the Computer* (London: Butterworths, 1980); H. Thomas Hickerson, *Archives and Manuscripts: An Introduction to Automated Access* (Chicago: SAA, 1981); and Richard Kesner, *Automation for Archivists and Records Managers: Planning and Implementation Strategies* (Chicago, IL: ALA, 1984). For a British comparison, see R. Bartle and Michael Cook, *Computer Applications in Archives: A Survey* (London: British Public Records Office, 1983).

3. Cf. Nancy Sahli, *MARC for Archives and Manuscripts: The AMC Format* (Chicago, IL: SAA, 1985); Max J. Evans and Lisa B. Weber, *MARC for Archives and Manuscripts: A compendium of Practice* (Madison, WI: State Historical Society of Wisconsin, 1985).

4. Susan K. Martin, *Library Networks*, 4th ed. (White Plains, NY: Knowledge Industry Publications Inc., 1982); Barbara Markuson, "Cooperation and Library Network Development," *College and Research Libraries* 40 (1979): 125–35, and "Computer Based Library Networks," *Midwestern Archivist* 6 no. 2 (1982): 207–22; Richard De Gennaro, "Library automation and networking: Perspectives on three decades," *Library Journal* 108 (1983): 629–35.

5. Ray Denenberg, *et al.*, "Implementation of the Linked Systems Project," *Library Hi-Tech* 33 (1985): 87–107.

6. Frank G. Burke, "Archival Cooperation," *American Archivist* 46 no. 3 (1983): 293–305.

7. Ward Shaw, "Resource Sharing and the Network Approach," ed. Thomas Galvin and Beverly Lynch, *Priorities for Academic Libraries*, no. 39, *New Directions for Higher Education* (San Francisco, CA: Jossey-Bass, 1982).

8. D. Gregor, ed., *Retrospective Conversion: Report of a Conference sponsored by the Council of Library Resources*, Wazata, MN, July 1984 (Washington, D.C.: CLR, 1984); Jutta Reed-Scott, *et al.*, *Issues in Retrospective Conversion* (Washington, D.C.: CLR, 1984) available as ERIC: ED 24759.

9. As a recent case in point, note William Maher's review, *American Archivist* 48 no. 2 (1985): 223–4 of the Association of Research Libraries Spec. kit 107, *University Archives in ARL Libraries* (Washington, D.C.: ARL office of Management Studies, 1984), in contrast to Nicholas C. Burckel and J. Frank Cook, "Profile of College and University Archives in the U.S.," *American Archivist* 45 (1982): 410–28.

10. "Human factors engineering" is now a common component of systems implementation, as advocated in standard texts like R. M. Dougherty and F. J. Heinritz, *Scientific Management of Library Operations* (Metuchen, NJ: Scarecrow, 1982).

11. Administrators and automation experts remark repeatedly in the literature that there is an overwhelming tendency in planning automation simply to repeat past performance without proper analysis of work flow, functions, and organization so that computer applications produce a more efficient organization. Pre-automation preparation and advance education programs must be a conscious component of the overall plan. See J. Becker, "How to integrate and manage new technology in the library," *Readings in Technology* (N.Y.: Special Libraries Assn., 1984), pp. 36–41.

12. C. Edward Wall, "In Quest of Automation," editorial in *Library Hi-Tech* 3 no. 3 (1985): pp. 5, 72, lists five factors in bringing the potential for automation to reality: professional commitment, self-education, planning, opportunity, and resources. See also D. E. Riggs, "Strategic Planning and Library Technology; *Journal of Educational Media Science* 21 no. 1 (1983): 1–14.

13. This is discernible in academic libraries with changing ratios of paraprofessionals to librarians, expectations of more educational credentials for librarians, and an increased management function for professionals. This problem is not confined to libraries, but pervades offices everywhere. For two perspectives, the philosophical and the practical, cf. V. Stibic, *Tools of the Mind: Techniques and Methods for Intellectual Work* (Amsterdam: North Holland, 1983), and A. F. Westin, *The Office Automation Controversy: Technology, People, and Social Policy* (White Plains, NY: Knowledge Industry Publications Inc., 1984).

14. Advice literature abounds. For a sample see J. Drabenstott, "Automation Planning and Organizational Change: A Functional Model for Developing a Systems Plan," *Library Hi-Tech* 3 no. 3 (1985): 15–24 and in the same issue, Charles Lowry, "Technology in Libraries: Six Rules for Management," pp. 27–9, who stresses capital, discriminating choice in technology, organization, personnel, and information resources as crucial; and A. Wolpert, "Strategic planning: A key to successful automation," *Microcomputers in Libraries* (N.Y.: Neal-Schuman Publ., 1984), pp. 171–85.

15. See the SAA model statement by Ann Morgan Campbell, "Archives (Functions of the Archivist)," *ALA Yearbook of Library and Information Services* 9 (1984): 60.

16. See, for example, Hugh Taylor, *Archival Services and the Concept of the User* (Paris: UNESCO, 1984), 98 pp.

17. For a comparison of controlled vocabulary and free text approaches, see C. P. Dubois, "The Use of Thesauri in Online Retrieval," *Journal of Information Science Principles and Practices* 8 no. 2 (1984): 63–6. Archivists should note the interest by the Assn. for the Bibliography of History in a thesaurus for History as well as the extension of the Art and Architecture Thesaurus project to the anthropological and archeological realm of artifact description. The Soviets are also experimenting with controlled vocabularies for historical documentation: G. G. Vasil'eva, "Thesauri of historicisms, archaisms, literary and rarely used terms," *Nauchno-Technicheskaya Informatsiya* ser. 2 no. 5 (1982): 20–3 (Information Institute of the USSR Academy of Sciences).

18. W. Nedobity, "Terminology and its Application to Classification, Indexing, and Abstracting," *UNESCO Journal of Information Science, Librarianship, and Archives Administration* 5 no. 4 (1983): 227–34.

19. Charles M. Dollar, "Appraising Machine-Readable Records," *American Archivist* 41 no. 4 (1978): 423–30, and note the larger discussion ed. by Carolyn Geda, Erick W. Austin, and Francis X. Blouin, *Archives and Machine-Readable Records* (Chicago, IL: SAA, 1980). See also Margaret Hedstrom, *Archives and Manuscripts: Machine Readable Archives*, SAA Basic Manual Series (Chicago, IL: SAA, 1983).

20. L. Hesslager, "Fringe or grey literature in the national library. On 'papryolatry' and the growing similarity between the materials in libraries and archives," *American Archivist*, 47 no. 3 (1984): 255–70.

21. For the issue of utility and obsolescence as archival considerations and the questioning of traditional archival criteria, see T. H. Peterson, "Archival Principles and records of the new technology," *American Archivist* 47 no. 4 (1984): 383–93; Frank Boles, "Disrespecting Original Order," *American Archivist* 45 (1983): 26–32.

22. R. Davies, "Documents: information or knowledge? Choice for librarians," *Journal of Librarianship* 15 no. 1 (1983): 47–65, notes the distinction between systems delivering information about information and those disseminating sources of information directly. See also H. B. Becker, *Information integrity: A Structure for its Definition and Management* (Highstown, NJ: McGraw-Hill, 1984) for risk management of information systems, which pertains as well to the problem of authentification and verification.

23. Thomas E. Brown, "The Society of American Archivists confronts the Computer," *American Archivist* 47 no. 4 (1984): 366–383, recalls the activities of the SAA Committee on Automated Records Techniques and the National Information Systems Task Force.

24. Margaret S. Child, "Reflections on cooperation among professions," *American Archivist* 46 no. 3 (1983): 286–92.

25. An exception to these observations is noted by Michael E. Gill, "The library, archive, and information centre network as surrogate national library," *UNESCO Journal of Information Science, Librarianship, and Archives Administration* 5 no. 3 (1983): 149–52, citing a noble experiment in the integration of archival and bibliographic systems.

26. Note that the concept of "multi-type" networking using means many kinds of libraries, but seldom extends itself to include archives and libraries: J. M. Griffith and Donald King, *Multi-type library networking: A framework for decision-making* (Washington, D.C.: King Research, 1983), available from ERIC: ED 241046.

27. Sue Dodd, *Cataloging Machine-Readable Data Files* (Chicago: ALA, 1982).

28. L. J. McCrank, "Integrating Conservation and Collection Management: An Experimental Workshop Report," *Archives and Library Security* 6 no. 1 (1984): 23–48.

29. F. Gerald Ham, "Managing the historical record in an age of abundance," *American Archives* 47 no. 1 (1984): 11–22.

30. Robert M. Mason, "The Challenge of the Micro Revolution," *Library Journal* 109 no. 11 (1984): 1219–20.

31. For a survey of vendor services and products see J. H. Katayana, "Applications of microcomputers in special libraries," *Microcomputers in Libraries* (N.Y.: Neal Schuman Publ. Co., 1982), pp. 127–43; M. M. Ertel, "A Small Revolution: Microcomputers in Libraries," *Special Libraries* 75 no. 2 (1984): 95–101; Alan Guskin, Carloa Stoffle, and Barbara Baruth, "Library Future Shock: The Microcomputer and the New Role of the Library," *College and Research Libraries* 45 (1984): 177–83.

32. I do not share everyone's enthusiasm for the personal computer, as presented in "The Limitations of Microcomputer on Humanistic and Bibliographic Research," ASIS Mid-winter Conference, Indiana University, 1984; in contrast see Richard Kesner, "The Computer and the Library Environment," *Journal of Library Administration* 3 no. 2 (1982): 33–50; and "Microcomputers, Archives, and Records Management Systems: Guidelines for Future Development," *American Archivist* 45 no. 3 (1982): 299–311.

33. For this emerging architecture see Y. Paker, *Multi-microcomputer systems*, APIC Series (London: Academic Press, 1983), on microprocessor aggregation; and Susan B. Epstein on choosing between micro-based and monolithic systems, "Implementation," *Choosing an Automated Library System* (Chicago, IL: ALA, 1983), pp. 164–71.

34. John Naisbsitt, *Megatrends: ten new directions transforming our lives* (N.Y.: Warner, 1982).

35. J. Thompson, "The End of Libraries," *The Electronic Library* 1 no. 4 (1983): 245–56; cf., Kenneth E. Dowlin, *The Electronic Library: The Promise and the Process* (N.Y.: Neal Schuman Publ. Co., 1984).

36. Susan K. Martin, "The New technology of Library Networks," *Library Journal* 109 (1984): 1194–96.

37. F. Gerald Ham, "Archival Strategies for the Post-Custodial Era," *American Archivist* 44 (1981): 207–16.

38. Information storage and retrieval (ISAR) literature is immense, and textbooks are now plentiful, but applications still tend to be treated as special cases, without adequate comparative analysis. For an exemplary text see Gerard Salton and Michael J. McGill, *Introduction to Modern Information Retrieval* (N.Y.: McGraw-Hill Co., 1983).

39. Note the work at the Smithsonian Institution which tries to link its archival, bibliographic and museum systems together; cf. the discussions in this collection of essays by D. Bearman and R. Szary.

40. For the human and management issues facing both professions, see R. M. Landau, J. H. Blair, and J. H. Siegman, eds., *Emerging Office Systems* (Norwood, NJ: Ablex Publ. Co., 1982), esp. T. M. Lodahl, "Designing the Automated Office: Organizational Functions of data and text," pp. 59–72, and J. W. Driscoll, "Office Automation: the Dynamics of a Technological Boondoggle," pp. 259–77.

41. E. B. Brownregg and J. M. Bruer, "Automated Turnkey Systems in the Library: Prospects and Perils," *Choosing an Automated Library System* (Chicago, IL: ALA, 1983), pp. 49–56.

42. Consider J. D. Naumann and S. Palvia, "A Selection Model for Systems Development Tools," *Management Information Systems Quarterly* 6 no. 1 (1982): 39–48.

43. Jacky Young and Jules Zimmerman, "UNICORN: A Unique Online Circulation System," *Southeastern Librarian* (Winter 1982): 85–6; Jacky Young, "The Vendor's Corner: SIRSI's Unicorn System: Answers to Questions about Automation," *Library Software Review* 3 no. 1 (1984): 52–62; and SIRSI Corp., *Unicorn Collection Management System Overview* (Huntsville, AL: SIRSI, 1985). If SIRSI's system is backed up by Burroughs as the latter's library solution, a powerful alliance is made that protects libraries and archives from vendor failure or abandonment.

44. Richard W. Boss, *The Library Manager's Guide to Automation*, 2nd ed. (White Plains, NY: Knowledge Industries Publications Inc., 1983); William Saffady, *Introduction to Automation for Librarians* (Chicago, IL: ALA, 1983); and Richard Kesner's *Automation . . . .*, pp. 32–50.

45. Hugh C. Atkinson and Patricia F. Stinstrom, "Automation in Austerity," ed. J. F. Harvey and Peter Spyers-Duran, *Austerity Management in Academic Libraries* (Metuchen, NJ: Scarecrow Press, 1984).

46. A. D. Nock, *Conversion* (Oxford: University Pr., 1933).

47. Less philosophically, see Robert D. Stueart, "Preparing Libraries for Change," *Library Journal* 109 (1984): 1726.

48. Sarah Fine, "Technology and Libraries: a Behavioral Perspective," in *Communicating Information: Proceedings of the 43rd ASIS Annual Meeting*, ed. A. R. Benenfeld and E. J. Kazlaukas (White Plains, NY: Knowledge Industry Publications Inc., 1980). This tendency to replicate manual systems was noted early by Susan K. Martin, "Technology Sources you never learned in Library School," *American Libraries* 9 (1978): 359.

49. James B. Rhoades, "Standardization for Archives," *UNESCO Journal of Information Science, Librarianship, and Archives Administration*, 3 no. 3 (1981), 165–9.

50. Richard H. Lytle, "An Analysis of the work of the National Information Systems Task Force," *American Archivist* 47 no. 4 (1984): 357–65; cf. earlier plans outlined by Lytle, "A National Information System for Archives and Manuscript Collections," *American Archivist* 43 no. 3 (1980): 423–26; and David Bearman, "Toward a National Information System for Archives and Manuscript Repositories," *American Archivist* 45 no. 1 (1982): 53–6.

51. Max Evans, "Authority Control. An Alternative to the Record Group Concept," and Richard Szary, "Expanding the Role of Authority Files in the Archival Context," papers delivered at the Society of American Archivists annual conference, Austin, TX, Fall 1985.

52. Michel Duchein, "Theoretical Principles and Practical Problems of *Respect des Fonds* in Archival Science," *Archivaria* 16 (1983): 64–82.

53. Richard H. Lytle, "Intellectual Access to Archives, I: Provenance and Content Indexing Methods of Subject Retrieval," *American Archivist* 43 no. 1 (1980): 64–75; pt. II, "Report of an Experiment Comparing Provenance and Current Index Methods of Subject Retrieval," *American Archivist* 43 no. 2 (1980): 191–206; cf. William T. Durr, "Some Thoughts and Designs about Archives and Automation," *American Archivist* 47 no. 3 (1984): 271–89, who argues for the integration of provenance and subject indexing as compatible means of intellectual access.

54. Rare book librarians, like manuscript curators and archivists, share a regard for provenance and orginal order in their attempt to preserve context and evidence of a collection's use and original aesthetic value. Standard library cataloging practices and classification have had to be altered for such "special collections" to save such values, but rare book cataloging can use archival methods as alternatives to Anglo-American Cataloging conventions. See L. J. McCrank, "The Bibliographic Control of Rare Books: Phased Cataloging, Descriptive Standards, and Costs," *Cataloging and Classification Quarterly* 5 no. 1 (1984): 27–52. For related suggestions about using automation for conservation management, see McCrank, "Integrating Conservation and Collection Management: An Experimental Workshop Report," *Archives and Library Security* 6 no. 1 (1984): 23–48.

55. Note parallel changes in library technical services as described by P. F. Micciche, "Trends in Library and Information Service Organizations," *Technical Services Quarterly* 1 no. 1 (1983): 213–20.

56. Archivists are concerned about processing productivity: Terry Abraham, Stephen E. Balzarini and Anne Frantilla, "What is Backlog is Prologue: A Measurement of Archival Processing," *American Archivist* 48 no. 1 (1985): 31–44; cf. Robert J. Kalthoff and Leonard S. Lee, *Productivity & Records Automation* (Englewood Cliffs, NJ: Prentice Hall, 1981) about the design of electronic work flow.

57. L. J. McCrank, "Strategic Planning for Networking of Rare Book and Historical Manuscript Data Resources," ed. R. F. Allen, *The International Conference on Data Bases in the Humanities and Social Sciences, 1983* (Osprey, FL: Paradigm Press, Inc., 1985), pp. 193–208; cf. Library of Congress Office of Descriptive Cataloging, *The Bibliographic Description of Rare Books* (Washington, D.C.: LC, 1981); and Steven Hensen, *Archives, Personal Papers, and Manuscripts: A Cataloging Manual for Archival Repositories, Historical Societies, and Manuscript Libraries* (Washington, D.C.: LC, 1983).

58. McCrank, "Bibliographic Control . . . ," pp. 27–52.

59. For PRECIS see Derek Austin, *PRECIS; A Manual for Concept Analysis and Subject Indexing*, 2nd ed. (London: British Library, 1984; and for other indexing literature, Hans Wellish, *The PRECIS index system: principles, applications and prospects: Proceedings of the International PRECIS workshop, 1976* (N.Y.: Wilson, 1977).

60. See note 51 *supra*.

61. For the "explosion" of catalog fields to accommodate sublevel description such as collation tables for manuscript codices, and the parallel expansion by substitutions of classes in the L.C. tables, see my reports on "The Mt. Angel Abbey Rare Book and Manuscript Project Revisited: A Case Study in Automated Cataloguing and Publishing," *Proceedings of the Sixth International*

Conference on Computers and the Humanities (Washington, D.C.: Computer Science Press, 1983), pp. 415–30.

62. Cost limitations are severe, both for experimentation and implementation, and assuredly for widespread application of these alternative strategies, given the labor-intensity of normal processing: William J. Maher, "Measurement and Analysis of Processing Costs in Academic Archives," *College and Research Libraries*, 43 (1982), 59–67. See Uli Haller, "Processing for Access," *American Archivist*, 48 no. 4 (1985), 400–15, who extends some of the thinking of Richard Berner about containing processing costs and retaining traditional archival descriptive methods for bulk coverage, but to inculcate into these practices greater consistency and systematization for enhanced access. Cf. Berner's *Archival Theory and Practice in the United States: A Historical Analysis* (Seattle, WA: University of Washington Press, 1983), which was anticipated by related articles, such as "Arrangement and Description: Some Historical Observations," American Archivist, 41 (1978), 169–81. Berner's treatment does not extend into the era of potential of archival automation. It does, however, indicate how radical some of the suggestions in this present essay are in contrast to past archival thinking.

63. Helen W. Slotkin and Karen T. Lynch, "An Analysis of Processing Procedure: The Adaptable Approach," *American Archivist* 45 (1982): 155–63.

64. Richard M. Kesner, "Microcomputer Applications in Archives: Towards an International Information Retrieval Network," *ADPA (Automatic Data Processing in Archives)* 4 no. 1 (1983): 57–66, and his "Computers, Archival Administration, and the Challenges of the 1980s," *Georgia Archives* 9 no. 2 (1981): 1–18.

65. See the forthcoming review of MARCHON II by L. J. McCrank and Ed Harris in *Computers and Humanities*.

66. William J. Maher, "Administering archival automation: Development of inhouse systems," *American Archivist* 47 no. 4 (1984): 405–17.

67. Kesner, *Automation for Archivists and Records Managers . . . ,*" pp. 51–109.

68. See Susan B. Epstein, "Procurement without Problem: Preparing the RFP," *Library Journal* 108 no. 11 (1983): 1109–10.

69. See the special focus on "Vendor Abandonment" in an issue dedicated to Information Technology, *Library Journal* 111 no. 2 (1986): 40–57; cf. the earlier warning of S. Michael Malenconico, "Planning for Failure," *Library Journal* 108 no. 8 (1983): 798–800.

70. Speculation about archives users is risky, since so little research has been done. Like Government Documents, a related department, Archives constitute an "unresearched area" as identified by S. S. Lazinger, "Tovin's 'A Study of Library Use Studies': An ERIC update of neglected areas of research," *Government Publications Review* 11 (1984): 165–71.

71. Elsie T. Freeman, "In the eye of the beholder: Archives administration from the user's point of view," *American Archivist*, 47 no. 2 (1984): 111–123; M. Duchein, *Obstacles to the Access, Use and Transfer of Information from Archives*, A RAMP Study (Paris: UNESCO, 1983), 87 pp., available from ERIC: ED 241054.

72. For a broad discussion of these issues, see R. Kaplinsky, *Automation: The Technology and Society* (Essex, England: Longmans Group, Ltd., 1984); cf. C. L. Jones, "Library Patrons in an Age of Discontinuity: Artifacts of Technology," *Journal of Academic Librarianship* 10 no. 3 (1984): 151–4.

73. D. Nitecki, "Document Delivery and the Rise of the Automated Midwife," *Resource Sharing and Information Networks* 1 nos. 3–4 (1984): 83–101; A. M. Buck, "Managing and Marketing the Information Function . . . ," *Managing the Electronic Library* (N.Y.: Special Libraries Assn., 1983), pp. 91–4; and Hugh Atkinson, "The Impact of New Technology on Library Organization," ed. Julia Ehresman, *Bowker Annual of Library and Book Trade Information*, 29th ed. (N.Y.: R. R. Bowker, 1984).

74. M. L. Dosa, *Trends in the Education and Training of Information Professionals* (N.Y.: ERIC Clearinghouse, Sept. 1982), 31 pp.: ED 237111.

Archival and Bibliographic Information Networks

David Bearman

INTRODUCTION

The library bibliographic networks of the 1970s were made possible by a library leadership which agreed on the application of standards and allowed decentralized market forces to define viable networking services. Because bibliographic networks succeeded, their implementation and management rapidly became the fundamental intellectual, organizational and political focus of the profession over the next decade. To appreciate fully the significance of this achievement in library networking, it is necessary to view the development of networks in their initial context. They were seen in the early 1970s, as only one, somewhat minor, element in the application of computer networking to higher education; now they are the only survivors from that ferment. Among the many papers delivered at the EDUCOM conferences of 1972–4,[1] reports by Henriette Avram on MARC at the Library of Congress (whose 80 initial subscribers had shrunk to 64) and by Frederick Kilgour on the experiments of the Ohio College Library Center (which had almost 300,000 records on file and could process 2,000 titles per day!), were indistinguishable from an array of equally premature and ambivalent ventures ranging from the Museum Computer Network, the NSF's National Science Computer Network, and networks for the delivery of instructional materials between colleges such as the Minnesota Educational Computing Consortium (MECC) and CONDUIT. A bibliography of the burgeoning literature of computer networking opportunities from 1970 to 1976 listed among its thousand references only four think pieces: (by Joseph Becker, Carlos Cuadra, Robert Hayes and Frederick Kilgour) indexed under library networks.[2]

Yet library networking became a reality. It now dominates the library community and provides a basis for planning other cultural information exchanges. It is critical to the future of archival networks that archivists understand the phenomenal success of bibliographic networking between 1975 and 1985. Librarians will need to understand better the requirements

David Bearman is deputy director, Office of Information Resource Management, Smithsonian Institution.

of archives and other cultural information networks if information sharing in the library community is to continue to thrive during the next decade.

LIBRARIES AND BIBLIOGRAPHIC INFORMATION NETWORKS

Bibliographic networks were first envisioned as components of bi-directional computer intercommunication systems serving higher education by interchange of library holdings and activity data. It was assumed by library leaders that their planning would determine the shape of the resulting networks. Because such networks did not evolve as projected, but more closely resembled time-sharing hubs on single application, central cataloging databases, one reviewer in 1980 asserted that the "definition of bibliographic networks has become more elusive in recent years rather than more clear cut as might be expected."[3] Bibliographic networking had been shaped not by abstract national plans, but by market forces dominated by a one-way delivery of cataloging data and services relating to the purchase of such data and its use for building machine-readable catalogs, mainly retrospective and thereafter updated.

The successful development of bibliographic networks was made possible by two ironically contradictory facts: (1) librarians successfully developed an application-level standard for interchange of information on magnetic tape (MARC) which was an "open" connection long before the concepts of such open systems connections had been articulated by computer scientists; and (2) they and the computer industry failed to establish a protocol for direct computer-to-computer communication, which afforded other organizations opportunities to engage in the collation and reselling of data. The establishment of common practices for description of bibliographic entities in a tape format built upon the long tradition of cataloging standards in the library community; the failure to construct a computer-to-computer network was more a product of premature technological projections, but it was turned into a positive factor by an agile leadership which accepted the success of decentralized mechanisms despite its having sought to put centralized systems into place.

Like other cultural professions, librarians expected "The Network" to result from top-down planning. When in the fall of 1970, the Conference on Inter-library Communication and Information Networks (CICIN) called upon the three-month-old National Commission on Libraries and Information Sciences "as a matter of policy . . . (to) devise a comprehensive plan to facilitate coordinated development of the nation's libraries, information centers and other knowledge resources," library leaders certainly anticipated recommendations much like those forwarded in August 1974 by the study NCLIS commissioned.[4] This called for the establishment of a "National Library Network" as an independent Federal Agency to manage a formal pyramid of organizations ranging from the Library of Congress and Regional Library Support Centers to state library agencies and individual participating libraries. The goals of the network would be to own at least one copy of everything, provide ease of access to it, and establish successful mechanisms for its delivery to patrons.

This national image is significant both because it mirrors lesser visions of all the failed networking efforts within academia at the same time, and because it so little resembles actual developments between 1975 and 1980 in the library world. How did the library community move from a vision of a central network in 1975, to 1980 when the ALA issued a 475-page list of cooperative library services?[5] How did the libraries avoid the shoals of institutional monopoly upon which other national networking efforts were wrecked?

Much of the credit goes to the influential NCLIS report *Goals for Action* issued in 1976. While calling for the creation of a national library system, this report focussed on providing standards and defining roles which would support access to information rather than on the structure of a new Federal agency. The residual emphasis on centralized organizational solutions was a national periodical center which was explored by other reports throughout the decade and was eventually stripped of its physical and organizational orientation, becoming first the national periodicals system and ultimately a program for standardization of periodical cataloging data, i.e., CONSER.

Goals for Action recognized that time had passed academic, centralized solutions by, both on a national and a local level. The leaders of the library profession had already launched a host of operational, local networks capitalizing on tape interchange between automated systems based on the MARC formats. The general pattern may be seen in a series of reports about Wisconsin library networks, beginning in 1969 with two academic studies by Charles Bunge and James Kriklas which respectively envisioned a regional and a functional organization.[6] The next major study, still a planning and thinking piece, was authored in 1971 by Joseph Becker and Robert Hayes but was issued by a government agency rather than an academic institution.[7] This reflected the political requirement of sharing responsibilities, but not withstanding envisioned centralized solutions. The Wisconsin Department of Public Instruction by 1977 reported that it was "a widely accepted principle of librarianship . . . that cooperation and resource sharing among libraries of all types in an area can contribute substantially to the effectiveness of library services in that area" (p. iii), but it abandoned centralized organizations for patterns of cooperation.[8] The emergence of practical local solutions based on profession-wide standards, rather than fully blown organizations at the national and international level, is an impressive achievement of the library community. This was largely responsible for the success of bibliographic networking in the 1970s just as in the 1980s it has been for the emergence of electronic banking services.

At every critical juncture the library community has turned over the past decade to standards, to create conditions for the networking of new information. In February 1976 the Association for Research Libraries sponsored a discussion of the role which the Library of Congress would play in establishing authorities—for serial titles (CONSER), MARC Names, and MARC Subject Authority files.[9] When a "white paper" was published in 1978 it argued that LC should take leadership in: (1) standards and planning, (2) distributing authority and cataloging (i.e., bibliographic authority) data, maintain an on-line catalog as the authority of last resort, and maintain a national location database.[10] From the first paper issued by the Network Development Office, the Library began to address standards required for new kinds of services and interconnections, services and interconnections to be offered not necessarily by itself, but others as well.[11]

The U.S. library community discussion of bibliographic networking during the 1980s moved from planning change to managing it, from promulgating designs to seeking understanding of evolutionary principles, and from technical standards to norms of behavior. Consensus on the structure and governance of library networks and on the rights and responsibilities of participants has been sought.[12] Increasingly important deliberation has been concerned about the roles of the public and private sectors in the complex of services and databases which comprise the overall library information network.[13]

Although the success of the library community with a standard-based approach has become evident throughout the academic community, it has not been translated elsewhere into practical networks. An NEH-sponsored meeting in 1980 to extend the benefits to the Humanities of bibliographic information interchange on magnetic tapes split over whether MARC or UNISIST should be the standard for the exchange of abstracting and indexing information; and there it rests five years later.[14] The Museum Computer Network in the U.S., the Canadian Museum Inventory Project, and the British Museum Documentation Association, were by the 1980s each taking different routes to centralism, none of which has yet worked.[15] The archives community has been in a quandary as well.

ARCHIVAL INFORMATION NETWORKS

Archivists watched uncomfortably during the 1970s as librarians exploited the benefits of shared cataloging based on common rules and controlled vocabularies, to build information networks which provided visible local productivity improvements and fringe benefits of a national union list. Their discomfort stemmed both from their realization that the economic basis of library information networks was the local savings accrued from shared cataloging, an opportunity archives seemed to lack since almost by definition their holdings were unique, and from their keen desire for a comprehensive national union list. This national listing was seen as even more critical for the increased use of archives holdings than such lists were for libraries.

While archivists were attracted to the success of libraries, they were repelled by library imperialism. Librarians dictated practices which archivists felt were contrary to the character of archives, and seemed not to notice that archives existed.[16] Archivists rejected the library-constructed MARC Format for Manuscripts, with its assumptions about item level cataloging. They shared an intuitive sense that archives could not use subject and name authorities to provide access to holdings which were the products of activities rather than authors, and which contained materials of mixed subject interest. They choked when bridled with the limits which the Library of Congress placed on the *National Union Catalog of Manuscript Collections (NUCMC)* that refused to list archival holdings except when they were deposited in a "archives" other than that of the parent institution!

Fueled by these frustrations, the National Historical Publications and Records Commission attempted to spur the development of a national database of archival materials by providing funding to state survey (union cataloging) efforts conducted under the auspices of State Records Commissions, using a Federally developed software system called SPINDEX.[17] Several states built substantial databases of holdings in SPINDEX by the early 1980s but this centrally funded approach to archival networking failed because it was designed without providing on-going benefits to participating repositories and they required continued infusions of Federal funds to sustain their systems. Ironically, the NHPRC effort depended on the universal adoption of common software but lacked descriptive cataloging standards to assure that the use of such common software would lead to compatible data. There was still little substantive to report at a national conference in 1981 on regional archival networks.[18] The NHPRC staff proposed a more controlled, centrally administered system; a pilot effort to implement it was funded in three contiguous mid-western states in 1981–3, but this collapsed in acrimony over questions of descriptive standards.

The Society of American Archivists fortunately had become sufficiently concerned about the apparent conflict between the NUCMC and the NHPRC approaches to national information systems, that in 1977 it appointed a task force to advise its leadership about which was appropriate.[19] This group, the National Information Systems Task Force (NISTF), advised the profession that neither centralized approach would provide the best basis for future networking. NISTF argued that the profession should put into place technical means for exchange of data, broadly designed to meet the needs of any kinds of exchanges which might have potential benefits, and that this in turn depended upon an analysis of the information requirements of archives.

NISTF received funding early in 1981 from the National Endowment for the Humanities to launch a two-pronged effort to establish the basis for national archival information interchange. The first path led to the development, and co-operative sponsorship with the Library of Congress, of a MARC format for the interchange of information about materials under archival control (MARC-AMC) so that archives could exchange such data if they desired.[20] The second path, taken in parallel, was to publish a series of discussion papers analyzing opportunities for archival information exchange and the implications of these for the design of archival information systems (both in-house and in networks) in order to stimulate experimentation with information exchange.[21]

This author as director of the NISTF, demonstrated to archivists that the benefits of library bibliographic networks derived from the fact that they did *not*, in fact, exchange information about library holdings, but rather that they exchanged authority records about bibliographic entities. At the time this seemed counter-intuitive to many librarians, but it opened the vistas for archival information systems designers to think about the kinds of authority records in archival systems and the economics of their interchange. It also began to liberate archivists from thinking about the "bibliographic" record as having a privileged status in information systems design, surrounded by subservient "authority" records which served only to validate the "headings" in the bibliographic file. Over the past several years, librarians, or rather the sponsors of library biblio-graphic networks, have also discovered that the "counter-intuitive" explanation of bibliographic systems is useful. One consequence has been the development of a separate "holdings" format in MARC to segregate the "non-authority" bibliographic data from the "authority" biblio-graphic data.

The MARC AMC Format, however, went far beyond simply intro-ducing some new fields; a number of its departures open the way for extension of the MARC format vehicle for information exchange to the broader arena of cultural institutions. First, MARC AMC is not a format to describe a particular form of material or medium (book, journal, film etc.), but rather a formation in which to describe anything managed collectively and from a perspective of provenance, i.e., the way archi-vists manage their holdings. Because the assumptions of librarians about how holdings are managed were relatively homogenous, the MARC family of formats had distinguished between different materials which were all managed by a single set of cataloging conventions (AACR2:).

From the perspective of outsiders, there was a fundamental similarity between the approaches taken by librarians to all of these source types of information packages, which was, in turn, different from that taken by archivists. Hence, archivists argued that the cataloging convention being employed should be explicitly referenced in the MARC AMC format and other formats could, in time, be merged into a MARC Format for Library Control. The structure of the record reflects the uses to which it may be put (which dictate the cataloging standards), not the particular type of information container it describes. Librarians had already discovered this result in their applying different formats to microform or machine-readable versions of an item, simply because the recording medium changed while the information remained constant.

Second, archivists with MARC AMC also departed from LC-centrism of the formats, in which the assumption was that the Library of Congress generated record permeated the data structure. The MARC-AMC was thereby providing for peer networks as they had been imagined originally by the higher education computer-network enthusiasts of the early 1970s, which was being made increasingly likely by the success of the LSP (Linked-Systems Project). Third, the AMC format represents an extension of concept of MARC as the vehicle for "cataloging" data by providing for inclusion of extensive processing, and control history information concerning all aspects of collections management activities. Finally, although not explicitly made in the proposals to MARBI, an entirely new idea of authority control and its function, made possible by the AMC format, is becoming evident with practice.[22]

ARCHIVAL AND BIBLIOGRAPHIC DISTINCTIONS

Had I been asked three or four years ago to write about "Archival and Bibliographic Information Networks," I would have used the title to argue for political reasons within the archival profession, that the library and archival community could use the same MARC formats and network systems. This is, of course, demonstrably true now that it is operational within the Research Libraries Information Network (RLIN). The more important question today is whether archival and bibliographic networks *should* merge. This depends on a realistic appreciation by both communities of the differences between their two approaches. Illustrating these differences, in the hopes of developing more suitable networks in the future, is more important now than encouraging archivists to take part in bibliographic utilities. The marketplace is now providing on its own incentives for such cooperation.[23]

Libraries collect, largely by purchase, mostly non-unique works on various subjects which are commercially available. The authors and editors of such works write them to communicate specific ideas in a structured fashion (i.e., they intend for the works to be on some subject); thus, cataloging merely places them in the context into which they were intended to fall. There is no logical or necessary connection between the holdings of different libraries; hence library administrators may use union lists and inter-library lending statistics from networks to determine what to acquire, and to use standardized authority cataloging for retrieval from their individual catalogs.

Archives accession documentation generated by the activity of their parent organizations. These records are the very consequences of the activity, not merely reports about the activity as a subject; and the records have not been structured except to support day-to-day use. As the repository of significant documentation of an organization's activity, archives will accession the materials if they provide valuable evidence of a significant function. Processing such materials, after their role in supporting the function which generated them has diminished or ceased, is a complex undertaking currently conducted over many years. The materials are "unique" so they will not have been catalogued by others, and they are associated only with one archive.

Archivists have long known that if archival networks could assist archivists and the records managers through whom they work, to develop schedules for the timely destruction of records of certain functions and the accessioning of records of other functions, such cooperation would have the same leveraging impact on archival processing costs as bibliographic authorities have for libraries. There are regularities between types of activities or functions, across time and jurisdictions, which make "function" a valuable proxy for accessing the information content of the resulting materials. Moreover, types of records which are generated by any activity are culturally dependent and these "forms of material" are also strong indicators of intellectual content. Form of material can be used to distinguish within specific functions the appropriate scheduling for documentation. In addition, because archivists do not describe each item in the large bodies of records they accession, form of material and function continue to serve in place of content description of the materials for retrieval purposes.[24]

The development of controlled vocabularies for forms of material and functions is consequently a focus of professional activity in the archival community. The Research Libraries Group is presently attempting to implement national archival information exchanges which can be economically attractive to participants. RLG is attaching significance to the two forementioned "authority" files which, as earlier hypothesized, would be valuable for archival information exchange and incorporated into the MARC Archival and Manuscript Control Format: (1) Form of Material, and (2) Function. These two access points will provide archival information systems the same control over headings which name authority and subject provide for librarians. They should, for the first time, permit the co-location of information across archival information systems, and progress toward a national "union list" of archival records with a structure that reveals not only what is held by the nation's archives but also what is missing.

What implications do such emerging archival practices hold for library systems? One is that archival "authority" files are of such interest independent of the associated bibliographic records, that the privileged position of the "bibliographic" record is thereby challenged. In an archival network one would ask not only "where are records for the function of licensing hospitals?" but also, "are there any states which do not license hospitals, and in which states is the function assigned to the Secretary of State rather than to the Department of Health?" This is akin to asking the library catalog for the birthplaces of German novelists of the nineteenth century by searching name-authority files, or seeking to establish the strength of the collection by requesting a comparative count of the volumes indexed under the facet "country name—economic conditions" and those under "country name—population." Both name-and subject-authority files as presently distributed in the library community would not support this kind of extension of the bibliographic database for research. The extension of authority control beyond the conventions of librarianship will create pressure for multiple, independent authorities containing searchable primary information. How can we move towards networks which support these capabilities?

TOWARDS SCHOLARLY REFERENCE NETWORKS

In the process for the past three years of designing museum information systems, it has become evident that there is a significant conceptual difference between the way in which a secondary reference system like a bibliographic database and a scholarly reference system, such as databases of primary information regarding paintings or volcanoes, must treat authority control. Scholarly databases must support conflicting authority records pointing to the same entity, each with its own authority source, because the nature of scholarship is not served by the assertion of a single authority source. Scholarly databases in addition must provide for different disciplines to index information according their own approaches—art historians being more concerned with geo-cultural entities like Flemish painters than geo-political entities like Dutch painters, while vulcanologists are more inclined to see geo-morphological entities like fault zones or river valleys. The approach pioneered by MARC-AMC, which does not assert the privileged position of any given set of standards or authorities, but requires the "cataloging" organization to identify its approach, permits the construction of scholarly databases rather than just bibliographic databases. Improved capabilities are required actually to support such distinctive view-points.

In looking at museum information systems, we find ourselves returning to fundamental discussions of the information science literature of fifty years ago, to identify facets of knowledge such as time, place, actors, etc., and to develop concepts of scholarly reference systems in which geo-political, geo-cultural, geo-morphological, geo-ecological, and other like vocabularies can be mapped, one to another, so as not to require catalogers within a given discipline to adopt what are to them artificial concepts in the description of the objects of their scholarship. As we do, the limitations of current library schema of subject headings are increasingly apparent and burdensome. Not only are LC subjects multi-facet phrases which conflate such chrono-terms as "pre-1960" for one heading with "ante-bellum" for the next, but there are no firm rules of facet ordering or independent vocabulary control over facets.

In the next phase of the evolution of bibliographic networks, the problem can be stated simply: If we accommodate new types of secondary references, from abstracts and archives to objects and specimen, in order to build more robust information systems, how can we incorporate these as multiple independent files, each pointing to any or all of the others, and to relate the intellectual structures of one profession or discipline to those of others?

The challenge is to create and sustain a multi-disciplinary, cross-professional focus on standards by a leadership which articulates a vision of integrated scholarly reference services but permits the market to provide those services which are required. It is too early yet to know whether archival networking needs simply crossed the path of bibliographic utilities during the mid-1980s and will go its own way, or whether bibliographic utilities will expand to accommodate the needs of other cultural information exchanges because the library is quintessentially a reference resource. What can be said for sure is that further extension of the bibliographic utility will require the leadership of communities responsible for the curation of cultural evidence—books, archives, museum objects, historical properties, and the like, to adopt flexible standards and develop common practices to sustain them.

REFERENCES

1. EDUCOM, *Networks for Higher Education*, spring conference proceedings, 1972; *Planning for National Networking*, spring conference proceedings, 1973; *Networks and Disciplines*, fall conference proceedings, 1973; *Computing and the Decision Makers*, spring conference proceedings, 1974.

2. U.S. National Bureau of Standards, *Annotated Bibliography of the Literature on Resource Sharing Computer Networks* (Washington, D.C.: GPO for the U.S. Dept. of Commerce, 1976).

3. Donald Simpson, "Bibliographic Networks," *ALA World Encyclopedia of Library and Information Services* (Chicago, IL: ALA, 1980), pp. 80–83; see the same for Alice Wilcox, "Resource Sharing," pp. 479–482.

4. Vernon Palmour, Marcia Bellassai, & Nancy Roderer, *Resources and Bibliographic Support for a National Library Program*, NCLIS Report (Washington, D.C.: NCLIS, August 1974).

5. Association of Specialized and Cooperative Library Agencies, *Library Cooperation*, 3rd edition (Chicago, IL: ALA, 1980).

6. Charles Bunge, *Library Cooperation for the Madison Area: A Survey a Recommendations* (Madison, WI: University of Wisconsin Library School, 1969); James Kriklas, *Centralized Technical Processing for Public Libraries in Wisconsin: Report of a Statewide Study* (Madison, WI: University of Wisconsin Library School, 1969).

7. Wisconsin Dept. of Public Instruction, *A plan for a Wisconsin Library and Information Network: Knowledge Network for Wisconsin* (Madison, WI, 1971).

8. Wisconsin Department of Public Instruction, Task Force on Interlibrary Cooperation and Resource Sharing, *Interlibrary Cooperation: A Wisconsin Plan*, Bulletin 7069 (Madison, WI, 1977). None of the Wisconsin studies mention any primary materials, despite the fact that the Wisconsin State Historical Society is not only a library and one of the best state archives in the Midwest, but was by 1977 also the national leader in archival automation.

9. Association for Research Libraries, *Conference on The Library of Congress as the National Bibliographic Center* (Washington, D.C.: ALR, February 1976).

10. Lawrence Buckland and William Basinski, *Role of the Library of Congress in the Evolving National Network* (Washington, D.C.: Library of Congress, Network Development Office, 1978).

11. Brett Butler, *Nationwide Location Database & Service*, Planning Paper No. 1, Dec. 1977 (Washington, D.C.: Library of Congress, Network Development Office, 1978); NCLIS, Task Force on Computer Network Protocols, *Computer Network Protocol for Library and Information Science Applications* (Washington, D.C.: NCLIS, Dec. 1977); Battelle Laboratories, *Linking the Bibliographic Utilities: Benefits and Costs*, Report to Council of Library Resources (Washington, D.C.: Sept. 15, 1980); C. Lee Jones, *Linking Bibliographic Databases: A Discussion of the Battelle Technical Report*, CLR-BSDP (Washington, D.C.: CRL, October 15, 1980).

12. Allen Kent and Tom Galvin, eds., *The Structure and Governance of Library Networks* (NY: Marcel-Dekker, 1979). Library of Congress, Network Advisory Committee, *A Nationwide Network: Development, Governance, Support*, discussion paper resulting from the October 1–2, 1980 meeting of LC-NAC; revised, May 1981: 15 p.; Duane E. Webster and Lenore Maruyama, *Ownership and Distribution of Bibliographic Data*, Highlights of a Meeting of LC-NAC March 4–5, 1980: revised, May 1981; Norman Stevens and James E. Rush, *Issues Relative to the Role of State and Multi-state Networks in the Evolving Nationwide Bibliographic Network*, (Washington, D.C.: Council on Library Resources, April 27, 1981).

13. Library of Congress, *Network Development Office*, Network Planning Paper No. 8 *Public/Private Sector Interactions: The Implications for Networking*, Network Planning Paper No. 8 (Washington, D.C.: LC, 1983).

14. National Endowment for the Humanities, *The Interchange of Bibliographic Information on Magnetic Tape in the Humanities* RT-0163-79-1213 (Washington, D.C.: NEH, 1980).

15. An excellent account of the state of museum networking is to be found in D. Andrew Roberts, *Planning the Documentation of Museum Collections* (Duxford, Cambridge: Museum Documentation Association, 1985), 568 p.

16. Typical of library studies at the time was an NCLIS-issued report, *The Problems in Bibliographic Access to Non-Print Materials* (Washington, D.C.: NCLIS, 1979), in which charts, dioramas, flashcards, games, machine-readable data files, and many other forms of published, non-print materials were discussed, but which entirely ignored the existence of manuscripts or archives! Indeed, the report contained an article by Lenore Maruyama on "Non-print media databases at the Library of Congress," which neglected to mention manuscripts even though all other MARC formats were discussed.

17. For an account of the software and the expectations of its authors, see H. Thomas Hickerson, *Spindex Users Conference*, proceedings of a meeting held at Cornell University, March 31 and April 1, 1978 (Ithaca, NY: Dept. of Manuscripts & Archives, Cornell University, Libraries, 1979). Perhaps the best summary of where archivists were (or were not) in 1981, is to be found in Hickerson's

Archives and Manuscripts: An Introduction to Automated Access, SAA Basic Manual Series (Chicago, IL: SAA 1981).

18. The proceedings of the National Conference on Regional Archival Networks, held in Madison, WI on July 14–17, 1981, ed. John Fleckner, *Midwestern Archivist,* vol. 6, 2 (1982). Its contents reveal that archivists had not yet developed any "information" networks (as opposed to cooperative efforts not involving regularized exchange of bibliographic data) and that some of the "networks" or cooperatives which did exist were little more than branch offices of a single entity (i.e., the Presidential Libraries, all administered by a single office within the National Archives) or local repositories of a State Archives.

19. Richard H. Lytle, "A National Information System for Archives and Manuscript Collections," *American Archivist,* 43 (198), 423–426, announces the formation and mission of NISTF.

20. Nancy Sahli, *MARC for Archives and Manuscripts: The AMC Format* (Chicago, IL: SAA, 1985); Max J. Evans and Lisa B. Weber, *MARC for Archives and Manuscripts: A Compendium of Practice* (Madison, WI: State Historical Society of Wisconsin, 1985), distributed by the SAA. Steven L. Hensen gave archivists something like a descriptive standard in his *Archives, Personal Papers, and Manuscripts: A Cataloging Manual for Archival Repositories, Historical Societies and Manuscript Libraries,* (Washington, D.C., Library of Congress, 1983).

21. David Bearman, *Towards National Information Systems for Archives and Manuscript Repositories: Alternative Models,* NISTF Report (Washington, D.C.: NISTF, August 1981); *Towards National Information Systems for Archives and Manuscript Repositories: Opportunities and Requirements,* (Washington, D.C.: NISTF, September 1982); *Towards National Information Systems for Archives and Manuscript Repositories: Problems, Policies and Prospects,* (Washington, D.C.: NISTF, March 1983).

22. David Bearman and Richard Szary, "Beyond Authorized Headings: Authorities as reference files in a multi-disciplinary setting," *Proceedings of ARLIS/NA Conference on Authority Control,* February 10, 1986 (forthcoming).

23. The differences noted in this discussion are simply those which relate to the subsequent argument, for a more balanced view of the similarities and differences between archives and libraries, see: Robert L. Clark, Jr., ed. *Archive-Library Relations,* (NY: R.R. Bowker, 1976).

24. David Bearman, "Who about What or from Whence, Why and How: Establishing Intellectual Control Standards to Provide for Access to Archival Materials" in *Conference on Archives, Automation and Access,* (University of British Columbia, Victoria, B.C., 1986); and David Bearman and Richard H. Lytle, "The Power of Provenance Based Retrieval in Archives," *Archivaria* (Winter 1985, in press).

COOPERATIVE PROGRAM DEVELOPMENT AT INSTITUTIONAL AND NATIONAL LEVEL

Government Publications as Archives: A Case for Cooperation Between Archivists and Librarians

Richard J. Cox

INTRODUCTION

Archivists have stronger professional ties to historians than to librarians because of the deep roots of the first and most influential archival institutions, the State Archives and the National Archives, in the professional historical community. Without "scientific" history and such proponents as J. Franklin Jameson, the emergence of the archival profession would have taken much longer.[1] During the past decade, however, there has been a shift by archivists toward the adoption of library principles and practices accompanied by vigorous expressions of need for cooperation between the two professions. This trend has been fueled by the development of more vibrant professional archival associations and a stronger national focus in planning and development.[2] Although Robert Clark's *Archive-Library Relations*, the "first comprehensive book" on the subject, is now a decade old,[3] there are many signs suggesting that archivists and librarians continue to be interested in working energetically together.[4]

Richard J. Cox is Associate Archivist for External Programs, New York State Archives, Albany, NY.

Despite progress in archives-library cooperation, such association is still in an embryonic stage. Past collaboration between the two professions has been minimal compared to unrealized potential. Librarians have shown little interest in acknowledging and building upon the contributions of archivists to the modern information society. Conversely, archivists have failed, especially because of their educational standards, to develop a theory that supports such cooperation.[5] Instead, both professions are making unilateral efforts in areas of overlapping interest with only minimal coordination of action or cross-fertilization of ideas, resulting in weaker products than could be achieved by both disciplines working together. The management of government publications is a classic example of this problem.

THE IMPORTANCE OF GOVERNMENT PUBLICATIONS

The transition from an oral to a written and from a scribal to a print society wrought tremendous cultural change. Modern information technology is causing change of similar magnitude in the late twentieth century.[6] Government, so interested in order and administration, quickly acquired printing as a valuable tool. By the time America was settled, government-sponsored printing had become a routine activity. During the colonial era the staple of a printing business was government contracts, which allowed a public printer to branch into commercial publishing.[7] Although publishing by the Federal government did not really take off until the establishment in 1861 of the Government Printing Office, official printing was long beforehand an important part of its work.[8] Most governments, from the Federal to the smallest local level, began publishing during their earliest days. The press publicized and legitimized their work.

The importance of government publications is evident in that so few aspects of the political realm are not documented through printing. Government printing has become essential for information about public administration, both for government's own use and by its citizens. Governments publish to document the legislative process, assist in administration, report completed projects or progress of work, provide information about the activities and condition of its citizenry, generate findings of research undertaken by governmental bodies, and provide general information about the nature and labors of government. A wide variety of government publications support these important functions—maps, research findings, guides, checklists and directories, committee and commission reports, periodicals, decisions and opinions, and audio-visual resources. These publications leave few other types of documents that are unique information sources with different perspectives on governmental operations.[9]

A recent study about the nature and condition of government records derives their six major functions as:

1. Document the history and intent of public policy.
2. Assure accountability to legislatures as well as the public through documentation of government programs.
3. Retain basic data necessary for research on scientific, medical, and economic problems.
4. Assure the effective administration of ongoing public programs....
5. Assure effective administration within government agencies.
6. Form the basis of a national history and an understanding of American government.[10]

Not only are these functions evident in government publications, they could not be performed without the printed records of government.

Government publications are being more highly touted as a preeminent source of information about government activities, past and present. This has been caused partly by the efforts of libraries to be information purveyors to as wide a community as possible and by the discovery, in the past two decades, of the immense wealth of information in publications of Federal, state, and local governments.[11] More of the general public and the research community are endeavoring to gain access to government publications. Even the renaissance of local history and the immense popularity of genealogy have affected the uses of these publications.[12] Nevertheless, recent user studies of government publications reveal that their potential use is very far beyond their actual reference.[13] The introductory comments of a national study on government publications noted that these documents are ''a major source of information in practically every field of endeavor and are crucial to informed public decision-making,'' but they are also ''recognized as probably the most neglected and under-utilized information resource available to the public.''[14] Regardless of such difficulties, most library administrators believe that government publications in their institutions are necessary and very important. In examining these publications in public libraries, one librarian concluded that ''libraries which fail to provide access to these sources will be less able to meet the information needs of their users. . . . If this information is not provided by the public library, they will turn elsewhere and the public library will become less relevant to the information needs of a part of its population.''[15] There is little question or debate about the value of government publications.

THE CONDITION OF GOVERNMENT PUBLICATIONS

Given this acknowledged importance of government publications, the extensive problems one sees in their management in libraries and archives today are surprising. The best management is the national depository system for federal documents supervised by the Government Printing Office, but even its effectiveness is questioned when considering easy access to information.[16] The management of state and local government publications in libraries faces even more difficulties. These are programs generally described as beleaguered, wanting in resources, and indecisive in management.[17] A national evaluation of state publications in depository libraries concluded that the latter programs are hampered because of the notion that each state is unique and the lack of national minimum standards.[18]

Public archives treat government publications no better than libraries. Public archives are supposedly concerned with all information generated by their governments, whatever its recorded form.[14] Unfortunately, government publications have not held a prominent place in the universe of record keeping. The first modern American manual on archival administration mentioned publications but relegated their management to libraries or advocated their being kept, as found, with other records.[20] The result has been a general neglect by archivists of government publications.[21] A recent survey of state archives reveals a sporadic and inconsistent pattern of *interest* in the management of government publications.[22]

The administration of government publications is the victim of the continued lack of systematic coordination and cooperation between libraries and archives. The two professions continue to emphasize, to a considerable degree, their differences rather than similarities. Consider how government publications could be treated ''archivally'' to the benefit of both professions, opening the door to increased cooperation.

AN ARCHIVAL MODEL FOR APPRAISAL AND SELECTION

In recent years librarians and archivists have advanced parallel emphases in the administration of their materials. Librarians now stress collection management, the "systematic, efficient and economic stewardship of library resources."[23] Collection management is a way that librarians (and archivists) can "control the flood of publications and records and . . . cope with the demands of the emerging information society." Collection planning, good selection, evaluation of holdings, and sharing of resources and cooperative collecting are all aspects of collection management.[24] Archivists have developed complementary approaches to library collection management. During the early and mid-1970s archivists pursued the notion of regional networks based on cooperative collecting.[25] More recently archivists, due to a greater awareness of their limited resources and the enormity of the challenge of documenting modern society, have developed stronger definitions of collection policies extending beyond the limits of a single institution.[26] Work is now underway to define "documentation strategies," a collecting regimen that requires a constant focus on all information creators.[27] What are the implications of these approaches for the administration of government publications?

For librarians, "collection management" applied to government publications has stalled on selection. Although librarians have recognized that the volume of government publications is growing at an exponential rate requiring selection, they still retain some fundamental misconceptions in how they should approach selection. The discovery that the use of these sources decrease quickly as they get older has made some build collection management around use.[28] Other librarians have defined the selection and maintenance of government publications more broadly as the public's "present" information needs plus availability of resources to make these sources accessible.[29] The predominant problem with most of these arguments is that they adhere to the concept that *all* government publications are somehow perpetually valuable. Most of the literature on selection of government publications has been written from the perspective of the Federal depository system which provides an "out" for the local librarian if a patron wishes a document that has not been previously selected by that library—the national system may be able to provide a back-up copy.[30] Even guidelines for state government publications depository systems have adopted a concept of "archival" collections as being a comprehensive collection.[31] Moreover, the tremendous difficulty in even identifying and acquiring state and local government publications has made premeditated or planned selectivity almost a moot point.[32] Although librarians acknowledge the necessity of selection of government publications, they have little that approaches a system to enable selection to succeed.

Archivists have placed great emphasis on the selection of records possessing historical and other long-term research or administrative values. The first modern archives manual, written by T. R. Schellenberg three decades ago, defined the ideas that continue to shape appraisal decisions. Schellenberg in examining government records identified two broad values: evidential and informational. The former value is the "evidence" of how a government is organized and how it functions. Schellenberg generalized that "all archivists assume that the minimum record to be kept is the record of organization and functioning and that beyond this minimum values become more debatable." But Schellenberg also recognized the interest of the general public and research community in these records, when he devised the idea of informational value. This latter concept acknowledges that almost any record can be found useful for some reason, although not every public record can be saved. The archivist "must show that a careful selection of the documentation produced by a modern government is necessary if he is not to glut his stacks with insignificant materials that will literally submerge those that are valuable," as well as to use "limited" funds "judiciously."[33] Schellenberg's earlier approach to archival appraisal is very close in principle to the more recently reinvented idea of library collection management.

Unfortunately, archivists have not followed logically the direction they set in appraisal when working with government publications or the publications of any institution. The Society of American Archivists' manual on appraisal states that the "archivist should keep a record set of all publications of his institution," although it does attempt to identify the variety of publications that possess greater value.[34] Thus, in practice at least, archivists have also subscribed to the idea that all government publications have permanent value. The various approaches to appraisal—sampling, records management scheduling and assistance, adequacy of documentation, reappraisal, and evidential and information values—have not been uniformly applied to government publications.[35] Appraisal assumes that not all information has long-term or permanent value, that the varying values of information mandates selection so that the most important information is accessible, that costs of maintaining information in its different forms need to be considered, and that information comes in different physical forms and conditions which might govern what is maintained or discarded. Government publications need to be evaluated according to such criteria, especially the newly formed concept of "documentation strategies."

Documentation strategies, as a form of archival appraisal, have emerged for two reasons. First, other systems of appraisal have been "less effective and less efficient than need be," primarily because they are "highly decentralized," "uncoordinated," "highly reactive," "generally passive," and "highly duplicative."[36] The second rationale, containing in it the reason for the general failure of standard archival appraisal techniques, is that in modern post-World War II society the creation and use of information is spread among a diverse group of records creators from individuals to big government. Archivists are not only concerned with their limited resources, but also the super-abundance of records and information. "What is needed is not a method to eliminate competition, but a strategy to build coherent collections cooperatively, minimizing duplication."[37] To accommodate these needs, several archivists have developed definitions of collecting methodologies: (1) collection or acquisition policy prepared by an individual repository although now in tandem with and respect for what other repositories are collecting; (2) collecting project developed by a group of repositories and individuals to document a specific historic issue or event; and (3) documentation strategy which involves records creators, custodians, and users in a plan to document an ongoing issue or activity such as the operation of a local government or the effort to protect our environment.[38]

The idea of documentation strategy both reveals the reason why government publications have been so difficult to manage and provides a mechanism for dealing with them in the future. First, a documentation strategy draws attention to the fundamental question of what is being documented. In working with government publications, librarians and archivists have been concerned with their information content and not necessary how that content relates to other information sources. F. Gerald Ham, in an article presaging work on documentation strategies, argued for more disciplined appraisal in our age of abundant information, including "an analysis of the extent to which documentation in print has devalued the information in the archival record."[39] Government publications are the prime example of such "documentation in print." If the goal is to document government, then *all* government information sources must be examined carefully as a whole, requiring its publications to be evaluated in relationship to more traditional archival sources.[40] If the goal is to document an ongoing event or process, such as a scientific or technological project, then government publications should be evaluated in tandem with other information sources.[41]

The concept of documentation strategies also invites the involvement of information creators, administrators, and users in cooperative efforts. This approach provides a better mechanism in evaluating the selection and use of government publications than has been proposed previously. Since libraries have been traditionally the repository for government publications and public archivists and records managers generally have had responsibility for appraisal, such strategies depend on their bringing these two disciplines together. The adoption of strategies relating to government publications should not be overly difficult since many public archives are already administratively associated with public libraries,[42] and many communities already support a tremendous diversity of libraries, archives, and public agencies.[43]

Another inherent and important assumption in documentation strategies is that their analysis of existing information will discover areas not adequately documented and, if necessary and possible, recommend the creation of needed information.[44] For governments the best and easiest means of creating such documentation is publication. The preparation of published reports, research studies, and administrative and informational documents are already accepted forms of government publications and are excellent choices for completing documentation.

ACCESS TO GOVERNMENT INFORMATION

Although archival appraisal appears to be an acceptable model for the selection of government publications, the bibliographical control of these documents by archival arrangement and description systems has already been judged by librarians as unsatisfactory. Federal government publications have long been handled through an archival arrangement by issuing agency, type of document, and title—a system with little universal acclaim because of the difficulty in achieving subject access.[44] Servicing the information needs of the public has raised questions about such an archival approach to government publications. As Bernard Fry wrote,

> the archival heritage . . . is a mixed blessing for government publications viewed today as an important informational resource. For many libraries the decision to follow the principle of archival arrangement has provided a practical way of identification, shelving, and servicing large numbers of varied formats of government documents which did not conform to standard library practice and could not be accessed according to traditional library concepts. However, the resulting failure to catalog, list, index, publicize, and distribute government publications on the same basis as conventional library materials raises a formidable . . . problem for both the document specialist and the potential user.[46]

Such a complaint, however, should be weighed against both the validity of library classification schemes and the continuing development of archival arrangement and description methodologies.

Despite whatever disadvantages archival control might possess, librarians have not developed alternative systems that, in practice at least, have proven more efficient to government information users. A recent study about online catalog use noted that "traditionally, sizable government documents collections in libraries have been less likely to be catalogued than have other library materials," adding that librarians "have treated government documents like the journal literature—by providing access through separate indexes. . . ."[47] The result is a system as clumsy as how librarians have viewed archival description. Even federal government publications are not considered readily accessible, even though their bibliographic control is often more developed than for most other government publications.[48] State and local government publications are covered by a myriad of competing bibliographic control systems based both upon subject access and archival description.[49] Basic decisions, such as whether government publications should be separate collections or integrated into the main library holdings, remain unresolved.[50] Some librarians have argued minimally for their intellectual integration so "that government publications have the same levels of physical availability, bibliographic accessibility, professional service, and status as other information resources in the library."[51] Much better administration of government publications seems indicated.

Consider the origins and future prospects of archival arrangement and description for handling government publications. Archival control systems were developed to manage large quantities of records in an efficient and expeditious manner. They open new opportunities for improving other aspects of initial bibliographic control in acquisition.[52] Finally, the archival arrangement and description process is itself undergoing extensive change that will possibly resolve some of the knottier problems of subject access.

Archival arrangement and description is built on several major principles—provenance (maintaining records by the agency of origin), original order (the concept of adherence to original filing schemes), record group (organizationally related records arranged according to provenance with strict attention to hierarchical relationships of the records), and series (records arranged according to a filing system or maintained as a unit because they relate to a particular subject or function or result from the same activity). For the description of public records, the inventory unites all of these principles by incorporating the record group and series as the primary descriptive elements and adding a history and analysis of the functions of the records creator. The justifications for the use of such a system is the maintenance of evidence about the nature of the records creator, protection of the integrity of the records and their information, better consideration of the nature of the records, and allowance for records to be handled efficiently and effectively. The development of such a system of archival arrangement and description was motivated by the need to handle large quantities of documentary material and, quite naturally, emerged primarily from the National Archives and its staff.[53]

Librarians accustomed to subject control, perceive difficulties with archival arrangement and description because of its dependence upon physical arrangement rather than content of the records. However, the archival originators of this system were from the beginning deeply aware of this problem. Early public archivists endeavored to use, with notable failure, library subject classification systems,[54] later firmly adhering to the idea that "while records may pertain to subjects, they ordinarily do so only to the extent that such subjects are the object of action."[55] T. R. Schellenberg, the leading theoretician from the National Archives, suggested that records being held only for informational content could be "maintained in whatever order will best serve the needs of scholars and government officials"[56] and later acknowledged that abiding by provenance, record group, and series would be opposite of what the users desired—subject access.[57] Indeed, over the years a significant body of literature has developed critiquing the archivist's ability to provide adequate reference, i.e., efficient subject access, to their holdings.[58] However, it is also obvious that the vast quantity of modern public records and the limited resources of public archivists will not, for the foreseeable future, allow the adoption of other systems that are more labor-intensive.[59]

Automation offers the break from this dilemma with the hopes of allowing better subject access through existing archival practices of arrangement and description. Not too many years ago, literature on archival automation was sparse. Just within the past few years, however, articles and even book-length studies have appeared rapidly on this subject.[60] Less than a decade ago the literature mainly focused on the prospects of archival automation, both for administration of archival practices and improved access to the information contained in the records.[61] Now case-studies of practice in the use of archival automation are increasingly frequent. The implications for improved subject access are much more obvious today. Automation makes it possible to have both the traditional provenance-based access and subject access, making "debates over which approach is correct unnecessary and misleading."[62]

The key to the prospects for automation is the recent emendations of the U.S. MARC Archival and Manuscripts Control (AMC) format. For years since 1973 when librarians originally adopted a MARC manuscripts format, the archival community avoided its use because of its orientation to the individual item rather than series, collection, or record group. After the work of the National Information Systems Task Force, the AMC format was revised to allow for more customary archival practice. The new format has opened the way for better control over archival sources like government publications. The AMC format includes fields for subject headings and, in addition, provides control over all levels from record group or collection down to item. Government publications could be treated as series or as individual items within record groups (records originators), and researchers could gain better subject access to their information content. The use of the AMC format will allow greater linkage into broader library communication networks, intellectually integrating government publications into the larger collections as many desire.[63]

There are additional distinctive advantages to the control of government publications by the AMC format, primarily in providing increased information about these publications as well as providing a system for more efficient acquisition. The AMC format supports the continued use of the provenance method of archival arrangement and description. For several generations archivists have built a convincing argument that knowledge about records creators and the origins of records is not only essential to appraisal or the selection of archival records, but it is beneficial to their use.[64] As Max Evans has argued recently, "the archival approach to the management of records is based on the assumption that context is the key to understanding" and although one manifestation of this assumption, the record group, "is flawed as an access tool," context still remains important and can be adhered to, with the necessary subject access, through other means. Evans, building on an earlier skepticism about the record group concept, and in approaching automation, advocates the use of authority control that includes information about the records creator and the functions of the creator which with automation allows greater subject access to and administrative control of the records.[65] Thus, government publications would be arranged and described as series and connected to their creating agencies in a way that additional information about their function and purpose is provided and which guarantees more sophisticated subject access.

Adherence to the AMC format and the archival principles of arrangement and description, especially the centrality of series, provides the relief for one of the biggest problems in government information—the acquisition of government publications. The archival scheme allows for building upon records management principles, specifically scheduling records series. Tying acquisition to the established government records management programs provides the opportunity to acquire government publications in a systematic and thorough manner. Records managers survey all the records being produced by a particular agency, evaluate these records' value and use, and recommend disposition either ultimately by destruction or transfer to an archives. Records management is essential for the efficient administration of a government's information and is crucial to the successful operation of a government archives as well.[66] Although government publications are often intermingled with other files, they are as likely to be maintained separately for distribution and other administrative purposes. The operation of a government records management program should provide systematic control by and a steady flow to the repository of all publications being created by the government. The only obstacle is the uneven quality of records management programs available in government today.[67]

RECOMMENDATIONS FOR COOPERATION

Margaret S. Child has emphasized the need for cooperation between the library and archives professions while acknowledging their propensity to work independently.[68] Archivists have much to learn in cooperating with each other; nevertheless, the fact remains that archivists and librarians must cooperate in matters like government publications. Some recommendations for promoting cooperation in the administration and use of government publications follow:

1. *Libraries and archives presently responsible for government publications should seek means to cooperate in the selection and administration of government publications.* The National Archives is a logical place to investigate how government publications could be handled as part of all government information, since it now has responsibility for the "archival collection" of government publications and has long been involved in the management of Federal records.[69] As likely a place, however, is the combination of state libraries and state archives, many of which share administrative structures. There should be few obstacles for the staffs of these institutions to develop better working relationships in regard to such shared information sources as government publications.[70]

2. *Professional associations of archivists and librarians should seek stronger working partnerships to resolve problems facing the selection and administration of government publications.* National and state library associations have long had Government Documents round tables. Archivists should involve themselves in these as well as support keener interest in government publications within their own professional groups. These associations should be crucibles for cooperative projects as well as forums for adopting standards to achieve cooperation in the administration of government publications as the norm.

3. *Both library and archival education should encourage stronger professional development to support cooperative management of government publications.* Although many universities connect archival and library education, a proximity of programs has not been seen always as an opportunity to develop better understanding of such mutual concerns as government publications. The graduate education of librarians and archivists should be used to develop the theory underlying practice in managing government publications.

4. *A literature of case studies needs development, about the appraisal of government records that incorporates both published and original sources materials.* A substantial literature of case studies already

reveals that government publications are not being utilized adequately. However, archivists should produce appraisal analyses that show how and when government publications can be substituted for bulkier archival holdings. Librarians need to study better how information in various types of government publications are used and which ones might have more ephemeral value. Librarians and archivists must become aware of how government publications fit into a broader spectrum of informations.

5. *The U.S. MARC format for Archives and Manuscripts Control (AMC) needs to be evaluated thoroughly for its potential to improve subject access in government publications.* The growing participation by state archives in national networks that employ the AMC format should make this evaluation possible within a reasonable period. The recent funding by the National Historical Publications and Records Commission to the Research Libraries Group to support seven state archives in using RLIN to share appraisal information may be the first step in such an evaluation.

CONCLUSION

The future of rapidly developing information technology and the prospects for the library and archives professions provide a context for considering improved management of government publications. Increasingly government publications are being valued simply for their information and are being moved from traditional paper to machine-readable formats.[71] Modern technology makes it difficult to distinguish between published and unpublished documents.[72] This blurs older distinctions between archives and libraries. The numerous implications of such changes do not ameliorate the need for archivists and librarians to work together in selecting and administering government publications. Archivists have already determined that their present systems of appraisal and arrangement/description can accommodate the transition to society's great reliance on automated information.[73] The possibility exists that the current separation between archivists and librarians could disappear because of such information technology. Richard Kesner has called for archivists to "become information specialists drawing upon a wide array of automated tools and analytical techniques in serving our constituents."[74] Librarians already see themselves this way. Cooperation in managing government information and publications is one way of preparing both professions for potential merger and to serve a more vital role in the modern information age.

NOTES

1. Ernst Posner, *American State Archives* (Chicago: University of Chicago Press, 1964), chapter 1; and Victor Gondos, Jr., *J. Franklin Jameson and the Birth of the National Archives 1906–1926* ([Philadelphia]: University of Pennsylvania Press, 1981).

2. Frank Cook, "The Blessings of Providence on an Association of Archivists," *American Archivist* 46 (1983): 374–99; Philip P. Mason, "The Society of AAs in the Seventies: Report of the Committee for the 70's," *American Archivist* 35 (1972): 193–217; Mason, "Archives in the Seventies: Promises and Fulfillment," *American Archivist* 44 (1981), 199–206; Larry J. Hackman, "The Historical Records Program: The States and the Nation," *American Archivist* 43 (1980): 17–31; and F. Gerald Ham, "NHPRC's Records Program and the Development of Statewide Archival Planning," *American Archivist* (1980): 33–42.

3. Robert L. Clark, Jr., ed. *Archive-Library Relations* (New York: R. R. Bowker Company, 1976).

4. The most prominent example is the adoption of the MARC format for archives and manuscripts; see Richard H. Lytle, "An Analysis of the Work of the National Information Systems Task Force," *American Archivist* 47 (1984): 357–65; and Nancy Sahli, "National Information Systems and Strategies for Research Use," *Midwestern Archivist* 9, no. 1 (1984): 5–13. Additional evidence that such a trend is occurring is a recent reactionary literature that urges archivists to retrench themselves into professional history; see Mattie U. Russell, "The Influence of Historians on the Archival Profession in the United States," *American Archivist* 46 (1983): 277–85; and George Bolotenko, "Archivists and Historians: Keepers of the Well," *Archivaria* 16 (1983): 5–25.

5. The need for stronger archival theory has been well-presented in Frank G. Burke, "The Future Course of Archival Theory in the United States," *American Archivist* 44 (1981): 40–46. For discussions from a variety of perspectives about archival education, see Richard C. Berner, "Archival Education and Training in the United States, 1937 to Present," *Journal of Education for Librarianship* 22 (1981): 3–19; James W. Geary, "A Fading Relationship: Library Schools and Preappointment Archival Education Since 1973," *Journal of Education for Library Education* 20 (1979): 25–35; Lawrence J. McCrank, "Public Historians in the Information Profession: Problems in Education and Credentials," *Public Historian* 7 (1985): 7–22; Frederick J. Stielow, "Continuing Education and Information Management: Or, the Monk's Dilemma," *Provenance* 3 (1985): 13–22; Hugh A. Taylor, "The Discipline of History and the Education of the Archivist," *American Archivist* 10 (1977): 395–402; and Peter J. Wosh, "Creating a Semi-professional Profession: Archivists View Themselves," *Georgia Archive* 10 (1982): 1–13.

6. M. T. Clanchy, *From Memory to Written Record: England, 1066–1307* (Cambridge: Harvard University Press, 1979); Elizabeth L. Eisenstein, *The Printing Press as an Agent of Change: Communications and Cultural Transformations in Early Modern Europe* (New York: Cambridge University Press, 1979); and J. David Bolter, *Turing's Man: Western Culture in the Computer Age* (Chapel Hill: University of North Carolina Press, 1984).

7. Lawrence C. Wroth, *The Colonial Printer* (Charlottesville: Dominion Books, University Press of Virginia, 1964, [org. pub. 1931]).

8. Stephen W. Stathis, "The Evolution of Government Printing and Publishing in America," *Government Publications Review* 7A, no. 5 (1980): 377–90; and Jerrold Zwirn, "Federal Printing Policies, 1789–1861," *Government Publications Review* 7A no. 3 (1980), 177–87.

9. Peter Hernon and Charles R. McClure, *Public Access to Government Information: Issues, Trends, and Strategies* (Norwood, NJ: Ablex Publishing Corporation, 1984), chapters 3 and 17; and Terry L. Weech, "The Characteristics of State Government Publications, 1910–1969," *Government Publications Review* 1 (1973): 29–51.

10. *Committee on the Records of Government: Report* (Washington, D.C.: The Committee, 1985), pp. 13–14.

11. David W. Parish, "Into the 1980s: The Ideal State Document Reference Collection,"

Government Publications Review 10 (1983): 213–19; and Michael O. Shannon, "Collection Development and Local Documents: History and Present Use in the United States," *Government Publications Review* 8A (1981): 59–87.

12. See, for example, Jean Ashton, "Into the Swamp: Government Documents for the Literary Historian," *RQ* 24 (1985): 391–95; Bruce Morton, "U.S. Government Documents as History: The Intersection of Pedagogy and Librarianship," *RQ* 24 (1985): 474–81; and Betty Jean Swartz, "Getting to the Source: Government Documents for the Genealogist," *RQ* 23 (1983): 151–54. Even popular history guides are promoting the potential use of government publications: David E. Kyvig and Myron A. Marty, *Nearby History: Exploring the Past Around You* (Nashville: American Association for State and Local History, 1982), pp. 67–8.

13. Barbara J. Ford, "Reference Use of State Government Information in Academic Libraries," *Government Publications Review* 10 (1983); 189–99; Nancy P. Johnson, "Reference Use of State Government Information in Law Libraries," *ibid*, pp. 201–11; and Peter Hernon's studies: "Information Needs and Gathering Patterns of Academic Social Scientists, With Special Emphasis Given to Historians and Their Use of U.S. Government Publications," *Government Information Quarterly* 1 no. 4 (1984): 401–29; "Infrequent Use and Non-Use of Government Publication by Social Scientists," *Government Publications Review* 6 no. 4 (1979): 359–71; and *Use of Government Publications by Social Scientists* (Norwood, NJ: Ablex Publishing Corporation, 1979). Many researchers have difficulty making effective use of standard information sources, government publications being only one aspect; see Margaret F. Stieg, "The Information of Needs of Historians," *College & Research Libraries* 42 (1981): 549–60.

14. Bernard N. Fry, *Government Publications: Their Role in the National Program for Library and Information Services* (Washington, D.C.: NCLIS [National Commission on Libraries and Information Science], 1978), p. 1.

15. Gary R. Purcell, "Reference Use of State Government Information in Public Libraries," *Government Publications Review* 10 (1983): 184.

16. Hernon and McClure, *Public Access. . . .*

17. Yuri Nakata and Karen Kopec, "State and Local Government Publications," *Drexel Library Quarterly* 16 (1980): 40–59; and Paula Rosenkoetter, "Treatment of State Documents in Libraries," *Government Publications Review* 1 (1973): 117–34.

18. Margaret T. Lane, *State Publications and Depository Libraries: A Reference Handbook* (Westport, CT: Greenwood Press, 1981).

19. For a good introduction to the purpose of public archives, see Posner, *American State Archives.*

20. T. R. Schellenberg, *Modern Archives: Principles and Techniques* (Chicago: University of Chicago Press, 1956), pp. 38, 114, 147–48.

21. Two otherwise fine analyses of local public records ignore the subject: David Levine, "The Management and Preservation of Local Public Records: Report of the State and Local Records Committee," *American Archivist* 40 (1977): 189–99; and H. G. Jones, *Local Government Records: An Introduction to Their Management, Preservation, and Use* (Nashville: American Association for State and Local History, 1980). This problem impedes researchers desiring access to such records; Robert D. Armstrong, "The Beast in the Bathtub, and Other Archival Laments," *American Archivist* 45 (1982): 375–84.

22. Richard J. Cox, "State Government Publications and State Archival Institutions," *NAGARA* (National Association of Government Archivists and Records Administrators) *Clearinghouse* 7 (December 1984): 4–5, 16. That government documents were generally separated from archival materials and treated differently was revealed earlier by Richard C. Berner and M. Gary Bettis, "Dispositions of Non-manuscript Items Found Among Manuscripts," *American Archivist* 33 (1970): 275–81.

23. Paul H. Mosher, "Collection Development to Collection Management: Toward Stewardship of Library Resources," *Collection Management* 4 (1982): 41–48, esp. p. 45; see also Murray S. Martin, "A Future for Collection Management" *Collection Management* 6 (1984): 1–9.

24. Jutta Reed-Scott, "Collection Management Strategies for Archivists," *American Archivist* 47 (1984): 23–29, esp. p. 24.

25. John A. Fleckner, "Cooperation as a Strategy for Archival Institutions," *American Archivist* 39 (1976): 447–59, is the classic statement on this approach. Note also the special issue on archival networks in the *Midwestern Archivist* 6, no. 2 (1982): 91–240.

26. Faye Phillips, "Developing Collecting Policies for Manuscript Collections," *American*

Archivist 47 (1984): 30–42; and Frank G. Burke, "Archival Cooperation," *American Archivist* 46 (1983): 293–305.

27. Helen W. Samuels, "Who Controls the Past?" *American Archivist*, forthcoming; and Larry J. Hackman, "Towards Adequacy of Archival Documentation," draft paper in possession of the author.

28. Kevin L. Cook, "Circulation and In-Library Use of Government Publications," *Journal of Academic Librarianship* 11 (1985): 146–50.

29. Charles R. McClure, "An Integrated Approach to Government Publication Collection Development," *Government Publications Review* 8A, nos. 1–2 (1981): 5–15.

30. Yuri Nakata, *From Press to People: Collecting and Using U.S. Government Publications* (Chicago: ALA, 1979), esp. chapter 4.

31. Lane, *State Publications and Depository Libraries*, 30–31.

32. Nakata and Kopec, "State and Local Government Publications," 44; Yuri Nakata, Susan J. Smith, and William B. Ernst, Jr., *Organizing a Local Government Documents Collection* (Chicago: ALA, 1979).

33. Schellenberg, *Modern Archives*, pp. 140, 152–53.

34. Maynard J. Brichford, *Archives & Manuscripts: Appraisal & Accessioning*, Basic Manual Series (Chicago: SAA, 1977), pp. 4–10. Generally, such practices have been followed in other settings as well; see Nicholas G. Burckel, "Establishing a College Archives: Possibilities and Priorities," in *College and Univesity Archives: Selected Readings* (Chicago: SAA, 1979), p. 43. The retention scheduling of government records tends to schedule publications permanently as in the *Texas Municipal Records Manual* (Austin, Texas State Library, Regional Historical Resource Depositories and Local Records Division, 1985).

35. Julia Marks Young, comp., "Annotated Bibliography on Appraisal," *American Archivist* 48 (1985): 190–216.

36. Hackman, "Towards Adequacy of Archival Documentation."

37. Samuels, "Who Controls the Past?"

38. Hackman, "Towards Adequacy of Archival Documentation," and Samuels, "Who Controls the Past?"

39. F. Gerald Ham, "Archival Choices: Managing the Historical Record in an Age of Abundance," *American Archivist* 47 (1984): 15.

40. Leonard Rapport paved the way for this in his development of reappraisal methodology: "No Grandfather Clause: Reappraising Accessioned Records," *American Archivist* 44 (1981): 143–50, and "In the Valley of Decision: What To do About the Multitude of Files of QuasiCases," *American Archivist* 48 (1985): 173–89.

41. Joan K. Haas, Helen Willa Samuels, and Barbara Trippel Simmons, *Appraising the Records of Modern Science and Technology: A Guide* ([Boston]: Massachusetts Institute of Technology, 1985), pp. 9, 54–55, 63, 74, and 82.

42. State archival repositories fall into a number of different administration patterns, a major one of which is association with or placement in state libraries; see *Directory of State Archives and Records Management Programs* (NAGARA, 1985).

43. This is especially true in urban areas; see Frederic Miller, "Documenting Modern Cities: The Philadelphia Model," *Public Historian* 5 (1983): 75–86.

44. This is a rather new and controversial suggestion, cutting across the grain of traditional archival practice. However, given the increasing use of modern information technology, it will probably be given more serious attention in the near future.

45. Morton, "U.S. Government Documents as History," pp. 476–77. Most researchers generally go for information which is the most accessible and SUDOCS, the Federal government's Superintendent of Public Documents classification scheme, is seen as "too complicated for the scholar [and most researchers] to use on his own;" Stieg, "Information of Needs of Historians," p. 553; and Hernon, "Information needs and Gathering Patterns of Academic Social Scientists," p. 406.

46. *Government Publications*, pp. 9–10.

47. Roseann Bowerman and Susan A. Cady, "Government Publications in an Online Catalog: A Feasibility Study," *Information Technology and Libraries* 3 (1984): 331.

48. Hernon and McClure, *Public Access to Government Information*, p. 11.

49. Nakata and Kopec, "State and Local Government Publications;" Rosenkoetter, "Treatment

of State Documents in Libraries;'' and Russell Castonguay, *A Comparative Guide to Classification Schemes for Local Government Documents Collections* (Westport CT: Greenwood Press, 1984).

50. Nakata and Kopec, "State and Local Government Publications," p. 55; Castonguay, *A Comparative Guide*, p. 18; Susan Folsom Berman, *Municipal Publications in the Public Library: Guidelines for Collection and Organization* (Westerly, RI: South County Interrelated Library System, Westerly Public Library, n.d.), pp. 13–15; and Nakata, Smith, and Ernst, *Organizing a Local Government Documents Collection*, pp. 13–18. Archivists have recommended generally that publications remain with larger archival holdings unless they are "discrete printed items;" see David B. Gracy II, *Archives & Manuscripts: Arrangement & Description*, Basic Manual Series (Chicago: SAA, 1977), pp. 41–42.

51. McClure, "An Integrated Approach to Government Publication Collection Development," p. 6.

52. Hernon (*Public Access*) notes that bibliographical control includes such elements as location, acquisition, recording of publications, and provision of subject access.

53. Richard C. Berner, *Archival Theory and Practice in the United States: A Historical Analysis* (Seattle: University of Washington Press, 1983) is a detailed analysis of archival arrangement and description.

54. Donald R. McCoy, *The National Archives: America's Ministry of Documents, 1934–1968* (Chapel Hill: University of North Carolina Press, 1978), pp. 77–80, 105–09.

55. T. R. Schellenberg, *The Management of Archives* (New York: Columbia University Press, 1965), p. 93.

56. *Modern Archives*, p. 193.

57. *Management of Archives*, p. 91. Schellenberg was vitally concerned with the problem of subject access, especially after his increased acceptance of many library principles and practices. One of his last articles struggled with the need for broad subject control: "A Nationwide System of Controlling Historical Manuscripts in the United States,'' *American Archivist* 28 (1965): 109–12.

58. Peter J. Scott, "The Record Group Concept: A Case for Abandonment," *American Archivist* 29 (1966): 493–504; and Mario D. Fenyo, "The Record Group Concept: A Critique," *American Archivist* 29 (1966): 229–39, are early criticisms of this. More recent complaints include: Mary Jo Pugh, "The Illusion of Omniscience: Subject Access and the Reference Archivist," *American Archivist* 45 (1982): 33–44; and Elsie T. Freeman, "In the Eye of the Beholder: Archives Administration from the User's Point of View," *American Archivist* 47 (1984): 111–23. For related concerns see Frank Boles, "Disrespecting Original Order," *American Archivist* 45 (1982): 26–32. For a recent dissenting opinion see Michel Duchein, "Theoretical Principles and Practical Problems of *Respect des Fonds* in Archival Science," *Archivaria* 16 (1983): 64–82.

59. There is also a growing literature on this subject as well. For a summary of recent reports and studies, see Richard J. Cox, "Our Disappearing Past: The Precarious Condition of America's Historical Records," in the *OAH* (Organization of American Historians) *Newsletter*, forthcoming.

60. For the growth of this literature compare Richard M. Kesner, comp. and ed., *Automation, Machine-Readable Records, and Archival Administration: An Annotated Bibliography* ([Chicago]: SAA, 1980) and his *Information Management, Machine-Readable Records, and Administration: An Annotated Bibliography* (Chicago: SAA, 1983). For examples of fuller studies see H. Thomas Hickerson, *Archives & Manuscripts: An Introduction to Automated Access*, Basic Manual Series (Chicago: SAA, 1981); Lawrence J. McCrank, ed., *Automating the Archives: Issues and Problems in Computer Applications* (New York: Knowledge Industry Publications, Inc. for American Society for Information Science, 1981); and Richard M. Kesner, *Automation for Archivists and Records Managers: Planning and Implementation Strategies* (Chicago: ALA, 1984).

61. Such as Richard M. Kesner, "The Computer's Future in Archival Management: An Evaluation," *Midwestern Archivist* 3, no. 2 (1978): 25–36, and his "Computers, Archival Administration, and the Challenges of the 1980s," *Georgia Archive* 9 (1981): 1–18.

62. W. Theodore Dürr, "Some Thoughts and Designs About Archives and Automation, 1984," *American Archivist* 47 (1984): 271–89.

63. Nancy Sahli, *MARC for Archives and Manuscripts: The AMC Format* (Chicago: SAA, 1985) and Max J. Evans and Lisa B. Weber, *MARC for Archives and Manuscripts: A Compendium of Practice* (Madison: State Historical Society of Wisconsin, 1985).

64. This is evident in archivists' view toward administrative history which has been seen as a unique speciality of the archivist, an outlet for scholarly publication, and a means for appraisal. See Karl L. Trever, "Administrative History in Federal Archives," *American Archivist* 4 (1941):

159–69; Authur D. Larson, "Administrative History: A Proposal for a Re-evaluation of Its Contributions to the Archival Profession," *Midwestern Archivist* 7 (1982): 34–45; Michael A. Lutzker, "Max Weber and the Analysis of Modern Bureaucratic Organization: Notes Toward a Theory of Appraisal," *American Archivist* 45 (1982): 119–30; JoAnne Yates, "Internal Communication Systems in American Business Structures: A Framework to Aid Appraisal," *American Archivist* 48 (1985): 141–58; and David Mycue, "The Archivist as Scholar: A Case for Research by Archivists," *Georgia Archive* 7 (1979): 10–16.

65. Max Evans, "Authority Control: An Alternative to the Record Group Concept," paper presented at the SAA annual meeting, November 1, 1985.

66. Frank B. Evans, "Archivists and Records Managers: Variations on a Theme," *American Archivist* 30 (1967): 45–58; and Richard H. Lytle, "The Relationship Between Archives and Records Management: An Archivist's View," *Records Management Quarterly* 2 (1968): 5–8.

67. Unfortunately, records management in practice has not worked as well as in principle. See a Canadian perspective which is not far afield from government in the United States: Bryan Corbett and Eldon Frost, "The Acquisition of Federal Government Records: A Report on Records Management and Archival Practices," *Archivaria* 17 (1983–84): 201–32.

68. Margaret S. Child, "Reflections on Cooperation Among Professions," *American Archivist* 46 (1983): 286–92; and her "Statewide Functions and Services," in *Documenting America: Assessing the Condition of Historical Records in the States*, ed. Lisa B. Weber ([Albany]: National Association of State Archives and Records Administrators [NASARA] in cooperation with the National Historical Publications and Records Commission [NHPRC] [1984]), pp. 47–57.

69. LeRoy C. Schwarzkopf, "The Proposed National Depository Agency and Transfer of the Public Documents Library to the National Archives," *Government Information Quarterly* 1, no. 1 (1984): 27–47. Unfortunately the separation of the National Archives from the General Services Administration has changed NARA's records management function, although no one is sure of its implications; see Linda Vee Pruitt, "Archives and Records Management in the Federal Government: The Post-GSA Content," *Provenance* 3 (1985): 87–93.

70. For example, legislation has been introduced recently that would tie together the Alabama Department of Archives and History and the Alabama Public Library Service into a cooperative regional depository system for state government publications. The state archives would be responsible for the archival collection of these publications and the state library would administer the depository system.

71. Margaret T. Lane, "Distribution of State Government Publications and Information," *Government Publications Review* 10 (1983): 159–72; and Peter Hernon, ed., *New Technology and Documents Librarianship: Proceedings of the Third Annual Library Government Documents and Information Conference* (Westport, CT: Meckler Publishing, 1983).

72. Lise Hesselager, "Fringe or Grey Literature in the National Library: On 'Papyrolatry' and the Growing Similarity Between the Materials in Libraries and Archives," *American Archivist* 47 (1984): 255–70.

73. Carolyn L. Geda, Erik W. Austin, and Francis X. Blouin, Jr., eds., *Archivists and Machine-Readable Records* (Chicago: SAA, 1980); Margaret L. Hedstrom, *Archives & Manuscripts: Machine-Readable Records*, Basic Manual Series (Chicago: SAA, 1984); and Trudy Huskamp Peterson, "Archival Principles and Records of the New Technology," *American Archivist* 47 (1984): 383–93.

74. Richard Kesner, "Automated Information Management: Is There a Role for the Archivist in the Office of the Future?" *Archivaria* 19 (1984–85): 162–72.

Conservation and Collection Management

John F. Dean

The importance to the research library of coherent collection development policies and of a working conservation program, has been expressed
with increasing regularity and vigor by library literature over the last
several years. While the literature of collection development has, in the
past, been concerned mainly with the selection process, there has been an
increasing emphasis of late, on managerial strategies applied to the
existing collections. This change of emphasis may be attributed to many
factors, from budgetary constraints to librarian enlightenment, but
increasing collection size and diminishing shelf space seems to be the
chief motivating factor. There is a growing realization that the policies of
the past, which assumed unlimited collection growth and extolled sheer
collection size as a desirable virtue, can be sustained no longer. There is
a clear evidence that continual and unrestricted growth causes logistical
and financial problems for space and processing costs, and leads to
inconvenience and intellectual problems for readers.[1]

Conservation literature has also undergone a change. In 1946, Pelham
Barr lamented that: "Silence, rarely broken, seems to surround the
subject of book conservation,"[2] while in 1970, James Henderson noted
that, despite " . . . almost a quarter century in which the need for
administrative attention to conservation has been recognized, few libraries in the nation today have anything resembling a total conservation
program or a conservation unit of significance."[3] Jesse Shera observed in
1972, in referring to the modern librarian's view of both conservation and
librarianship, that over time

> . . . the purpose of conservation became blurred and indistinct,
> when it was not actually discredited and even ridiculed, until today
> the most damning charge which one can bring against the library is
> to call it a "storehouse" and the librarian its "keeper".[4]

After a period of "crisis" literature, in which the nation was alerted to
the impending demise of its books and archives, a more pragmatic

John F. Dean is the conservation librarian directing the preservation programs for Cornell
University Libraries, Ithaca, NY.

approach seems to have emerged, and some useful works on the managerial aspects of conservation have appeared.[5]

The changes in emphasis to which both collection development and conservation seem gradually to be subject, have brought about corresponding changes in terminology. Collection development is, to many librarians, too narrow a term as it has been generally applied specifically to the activities normally associated with selection and fund allocation, whereas the newer term, collection management, incorporates these activities and those associated with evaluation, weeding, storage, and conservation. Similarly, the terms "preservation" and "conservation" have each undergone changes in meaning to the point where differentiation now seems pedantic.

In the case of collection development, the increasing use in research libraries of formal statements of collecting intent has tended to obscure the management aspects, but such statements are nevertheless essential to development/management/conservation procedures.

OBJECTIVES AND POLICIES

The most basic issues concerning all academic library planning relate directly to the objectives of the institution itself; but these objectives, while generally assumed in mission statements of sweeping ambiguity, are rarely available in any useful form, and must be assembled somehow from: statements of the administration and academic departments; press releases; reports; program announcements; etc. The difficulty librarians often experience in extracting this vital information from the institution, suggests that some coherent, continuing, formal joint planning mechanism should be developed in order to communicate: projections on possible changes in the size and constitution of the student body (undergraduate to graduate ratio); number and type of interdisciplinary programs planned; future changes in faculty appointments; number and types of new programs; number and types of old programs to be discontinued; new directions in organization; changes in relationships to other institutions; physical changes (new building construction, etc.). Such a joint planning mechanism can provide the library with the means to develop a strategy for the establishing of its own objectives, help it to determine courses of action, allocate resources, and evaluate progress.[6]

The collection development policy is usually the most tangible statement of intent on the part of the library, and should incorporate all that has been learned from the institution and from the library's efforts to evaluate its success or failure in meeting the institution's needs. Collection evaluation should, ideally, be a constant activity and substantial evaluation of the collection is best done before the formulation of collection development policies. This seems rarely the case however, yet evaluation would seem to offer the most concrete definition of the strengths and weaknesses of the collection, and by extension, to identify areas of needed collecting intensity. Collection evaluation is crucial to all the necessary subsidiary policies deriving from the collection development policy: weeding; storage; and conservation. While several methods of evaluation have been used in libraries,[7] a recent set of questions posed by Rose Mary Magrill seems to demonstrate the essential nature of the process. She notes that: "Questions such as the following might trigger a collection evaluation:

> What percentage of the collection is held in a particular format? How is the collection divided among the subjects (expressed in either broad or narrow terms) for which the library is responsible? How do selected subsets of the collection compare with the total number of works published or distributed in that subject or format? How old is the collection? Are some parts of the collection older than others? How many items in the collection can be identified as appropriate for any particular group of users? How well does the collection match (in terms of percentages of the whole) the teaching or research program(s) to be supported by the library?[8]

All these questions, and those relating to the collection's quantity and quality, are pertinent to collection management activities leading to the formulation of policies and procedures. A systematic program of collection evaluation and review seems an essential tool if the collection is to fulfill its purpose. Unfortunately, librarians seem to suffer from a particularly uncomfortable form of schizophrenia when the results of evaluation have to be translated into action. As William McGrath observes, "We have a very difficult time overcoming the notion that a collection is its own reason for existence." No matter how we amass the collection, McGrath continues, whether by idiosyncratic or systematic means, it is a collection " . . . and that is what the profession of librarianship takes for granted as one of its basic and inviolate responsibilities."[9] This difficulty, which librarians have in their proprietary and somewhat static view of the collection for its own sake, is clearly at odds with the basic principles of collection management. Hugh Cline and Loraine Sinnot, as part of a larger study, interviewed several bibliographers who regarded it as their duty to " . . . maintain comprehensive collections despite the fact that the university no longer maintained any degree programs or research institutes whose faculty or students would use the materials."[10] There seems to be general, but rather vague and largely unstated agreement amongst librarians in research libraries that any library charged with universality must have large numbers of books which are unused and not related to current programs.

REVIEW AND WEEDING

The process of collection evaluation can be extremely labor-intensive and dispiriting if the chief motivating factor involves the identification of materials which are inappropriate to the main thrust of the collection. Yet this review process is essential if librarians are to bring any coherence to their collections, despite the highly sensitive nature of some of the subsequent necessary actions. In particular, the notion of weeding seems to raise objections which, while understandable, are, in the final analysis, not fully supportable. These objections often involve the concept of immediate and undifferentiated access to works of all periods, topics, and scope, and the notion that, as no one can predict the future, all library materials should remain available for serendipitous discovery by future scholars. Margit Kraft points out the inconsistency in this latter argument, as selectors who plead our inability to predict the future, nevertheless tend to purchase books on the basis of their potential use, and adds that " . . . a large amount of the material accumulated for future use has never been used and may never be used."[11] Objections to weeding, while sometimes valid, become less realistic as collections grow in size and unmanageability.

The term "weeding" is applied generally to the activity of separating less useful books from the collection in order to enhance its effectiveness and to create space for newer, more appropriate and useful books. Research library collections, particularly those in older institutions, have usually developed in ways which are idiosyncratic rather than systematic; involving the acceptance of inappropriate gifts, entire collection purchases, and staff and faculty purchases reflecting personal interests and eccentricities instead of adherence to institutional objectives. Weeding, designed to identify and clarify a prime use collection, seems a necessary activity under these circumstances.

The disposition of weeded books depends upon the resources of the library, and the strength and vociferousness of the arguments against weeding. Generally, the options consist of storage (for lesser used, but appropriate books), and discard (by exchange, sale, or disposal). A further consequence of weeding activity is the identification of books which need to be replaced, because of their deteriorated condition, and books which need conservation treatment.

STORAGE AND STABILITY

Books identified as storage candidates, are generally those which seem appropriate to the collections, but whose levels of past use do not justify a location in any prime use library space. The rationale for weeding books by the frequency and patterns of past use, is that past use is a good indicator of future use. In possibly the most complete study of use patterns, Herman Fussler and Julian Simon concluded that, with certain qualifications, future use *can* be predicted on the basis of past use for groups of books with defined characteristics. Fussler, while noting that the average frequency of use in a large research library may be as low as once in fifty years, cautions that use alone should not be the sole criterion of appropriateness, but that it is " . . . relevant to any alternative system of access that might provide several different levels of accessibility to research related materials."[12] The differentiation of levels of access based upon use makes possible the creation of space in a prime use area for the addition of new books, while protecting by storage the cumulation of "knowledge" represented by appropriate, but little-used books.

From the standpoint of conservation, the storage of books in a facility designed expressly for the purpose, provides an extemely attractive strategy. By stabilizing less-used books in an acceptable environment, conservators are able to establish priorities based upon use by concentrating their efforts on the prime use collection. An acceptable storage environment would include: a low fire/flood risk building with optimum security systems; low temperature and stable humidity controls (60–65°F and 40–50% humidity); staff access only for shelving and retrieval purposes; compact or size-classification book shelving. Unfortunately, such conditions are rarely available, and too often on- or off-campus storage involves the use of outdated library facilities or industrial warehouses designed for other uses. As relegation to storage under these circumstances often condemns books to slow incineration because of high temperatures, and/or possible mold damage because of high levels of relative humidity, it is understandable that the storage concept is met with some resistance and skepticism by faculty and selectors. Often, the response to the availability of storage space is to use storage as a device for avoiding discard decisions, and to indulge in crisis weeding by the transfer of any bulky, long-run materials to create space in a prime use area. In this case, the long-term effect is to place long serial runs into storage because they consume large amounts of shelf space, and to gradually reduce the effectiveness of the prime use collection by leaving untouched, large numbers of unused and/or inappropriate monographs. In practical terms, the ability to review the collection, particularly for storage, is conditioned by a library's ability to effect the necessary bibliographic record changes. Recent studies by Grace Agnew, Christina Landram, and Jane Richards present a dismal future for rational review and weeding by demonstrating by their survey significant cataloging arrearages in many research libraries. Of 88 respondent research libraries, 68 reported arrearages of up to 150,000 titles; in some cases, up to ten percent of the collection. While noting that some libraries had titles which had been in the arrearage for ten years, it was reported that four libraries stated that " . . . some or all of the backlog would probably never be catalogued."[13] In citing "inadequate levels of staff and staff expertise" and "acquisition levels and the ratio that results from these two factors," as the chief causes, the authors reveal a situation in many libraries which would seem to render the possibility of weeding record-changing unlikely. Nevertheless, for those libraries able to confront the challenges of evaluation and weeding, some opportunities for limited action can result from an active and viable conservation program and the survey and decision-making components deriving from it.

CONSERVATION PRIORITIES

The chief concerns of a conservation program can be summarized as follows:

1. The need to maintain the collections responsibly by the institution of satisfactory environmental controls, thereby reducing damage and deterioration.
2. The need to replace materials too damaged or deteriorated for normal use.
3. The need to safeguard new book and periodical purchases by the design of appropriate contractual binding standards and specifications, and the development of efficient management systems to implement them.
4. The need to preserve and restore to satisfactory condition, materials where retention in original format is important.

The rationale for these actions is elegantly and succinctly stated in the *RLG Preservation Manual*:

RLG libraries have a special obligation to each other and to scholars nationwide to preserve their collections. Member libraries depend on each other to provide or lend titles held and listed in the *National Union Catalog* as well as those that are unique resources. . . . A strong collection will remain so only if it receives continual preservation attention. . . . The goal of [preservation programs] should be the maintenance of all library materials in good condition either in their original format or in reproduction, to allow the researcher continued access.[14]

The responsibility to provide an environment conducive to the prolongation of the life of library materials, is the most basic and important of the concerns noted. If a library were able to implement only this single aspect of a conservation program, particularly if optimum temperature and humidity levels were in place for a long period of time, the need for remedial conservation actions would be greatly reduced. Other actions concerned with collection stability, such as: good housekeeping, good building design and maintenance, shelving, handling and facilities control, are inexpensive and uncomplicated when compared to the high costs and complexities of conservation treatment. Yet, few libraries seem able to provide satisfactory conditions for their collections, including many with active conservation programs. The reasons for this are probably many and varied, but a plausible one might be the apparent inability of librarians to affect institutional priorities in planning, funding, and maintaining library facilities. Too often, it seems, librarians are willing to accept *any* additional space whether new or renovated, to house obese collections which, if slimmed down, might be accommodated in smaller facilities with enhanced environmental controls.

The replacement of materials too damaged, and often too deteriorated for normal use, is an activity similarly fraught with problems of ill-distinguished priorities, and as such, is at the heart of the collection management/conservation interface. The crisis literature, previously referred to, has tended to be simplistic, focusing attention on the "millions of valuable books deteriorating in nation's libraries."[15] and the "Damage in the Stacks (Research libraries foresee 'terrific crisis' as rate of book deterioration speeds up)."[16] There is little doubt that, purely from the standpoint of conservation, the situation is desperate and probably irretrievable at the national level. There are, however, certain assumptions which can be challenged at the local level. For example, collection surveys in various libraries have indicated that from thirty to sixty percent of collections are embrittled (i.e. paper that will not withstand a double corner fold) or on the edge of embrittlement. It could be implied that: (a) each of the libraries whose collections were surveyed must act to replace all of the brittle items or to stabilize all items approaching embrittlement (for example, "the Columbia University Library indicates that it will cost $34 million to preserve the 30 percent of its collection already in danger of irreversible deterioration");[17] (b) each item is important to the institution and to scholarship at large and thus worthy of replacement; (c) the actual percentage of a collection identified as brittle has direct relevance to a library's conservation priorities; (d) the brittle items are actually used. From the standpoint of collection management, the assumptions are not entirely valid, as it is likely that a number of brittle items is irrelevant to research needs. Moreover, it is possible that a larger percentage of the books mass-produced on groundwood paper are of less permanent value than other books in the collection. Relevance is not the only issue. Christinger

Tomer points out that " . . . many of the documents that Barrow and others have presumed to be unusable have remained intact for far longer than 50–60 years . . . [they] are intact and usable because their availability has not been a matter of interest to library users in many years."[18]

The most sensible approach to replacement is through cooperation amongst libraries; the RLG Cooperative Preservation Microfilming Project is an example of a project rooted in sound collection management principles. The stated initial intent of the project is the microfilming of U.S. monographic imprints and Americana published between 1876 and 1900. Because the subject and period are defined, based upon "retrospective strengths at member institutions," and the entire project coordinated through the RLIN system, the project has a sound philosophical and management base. Participant libraries are urged to " . . . survey their collections systematically, to evaluate every U.S. imprint published within the period, and, if curatorial judgment deems the volume worthy of preservation and no other film is located, to film it."[19] The success and viability of this project thus far seems to indicate its value as a model to other consortia.[20]

The activity that almost all libraries have in common as a conservation measure, is the binding of books and periodicals through commercial binders. Large sums of money are devoted to this, and, while there seems to be greater awareness by librarians of some of the issues involved, it is still approached generally in an uncritical and unsystematic fashion. Some of the difficulties stem from what Mr. Cline and Miss Sinnot describe as librarians having " . . . substantial reliance on traditional grounds for authority . . . " and, in particular, a reluctance to cancel serial subscriptions when appropriate. "Thus," they point out, "significant portions of materials budgets are expended to maintain complete runs of serials with little or no concern for their utility to support research or instructional programs."[21] This "reliance on traditional grounds for authority" is clearly evident in any analysis of a library's binding program. Poor selection decisions are compounded by inappropriate binding decisions, and vast numbers of books which may never be used are bound in a fashion designed for high use. Selectors frequently confuse utility with importance, thus a suggestion that documented low levels of use do not indicate the need for binding is taken to be a criticism of the overall value of a particular work, and by extension, an attack upon the selector. As many forms of binding are destructive, in some cases the decision not to bind as a consequence of low use is in itself a sound conservation measure.

The most relevant data in deciding on the most appropriate forms of periodical binding should be derived from a study of patterns of use after binding. Many studies indicate that, for most titles, the levels of use are quite low; in fact, during the period of the most intensive use (i.e. when current) the periodical is not protected by a binding. It seems somewhat paradoxical to provide binding structures which are high in cost, have poor flexibility, and which reduce the useful life of the work, merely to satisfy some desire for traditional uniformity. There are now available, through reputable commercial binders, alternative structures and methods of leaf attachment which librarians can apply according to observations of patterns of use and possible retention schedules.[22]

The first-time commercial binding of new paperbacks is another area in which libraries have unquestioningly expended large sums on binding. In this case, however, the librarian is faced with an understandable dilemma, as, unlike a periodical run in which use over time may be observed, a new paperback acquisition is an unknown quantity. One solution to the problem is to provide all new paperbacks with a simple minimal binding for shelf protection, and to base more remedial forms of binding on use, monitored at the point of circulation. A 1981 study of this technique, after seven years of processing, noted that "less than one half of one per cent have needed a more robust binding as a result of heavy use."[23]

An area in which librarians have generally applied the incidence of use to commercial binding decisions, is that of rebinding, as in most cases, binding damage resulting from use is identified at the point of use. Unfortunately, books so identified are often sent off for binding without proper regard for the actual needs of individual problems. Thus, books which have intact text blocks and sewing are routinely oversewn or adhesive-bound by the binder when a systematic in-house repair or binder recase would be more appropriate. As a cost containment *and* conservation strategy, in-house repair has much to commend it: the original size and leaf affixment methods are preserved, and the book can be processed quickly and with a minimum of record-keeping and decision-making.

The need to preserve and restore materials in original format can best be addressed by the establishment of a conservation facility within the library. Conservation by an outside agency can provide an excellent standard of work, but it is invariably high in cost, and the library loses an element of essential control. The most important considerations, however, lie in the recognition that: (a) conservation programs must be consistent and sustained, and should not rely upon the fortuitous availability of special funds in order to treat a few favored items; (b) research libraries have large numbers of library materials which must be preserved in original format, as the format is in itself an important element for research; (c) the existence of conservation staff and facilities within the institution tends to "drive" the entire conservation enterprise.

A library conservation operation is also high in cost, and for this reason as much as any other, selection of materials for conservation is of crucial importance. The criteria for conservation treatment are little different than for other aspects of collection management review. An item in need of conservation treatment is usually older and likely to be irreplaceable; it should be relevant to the library's research programs; and, in terms of priority for treatment, it should have some evidence of use. As the identification of the appropriate treatment candidates and the decision on the appropriateness of treatment are matters requiring both bibliographic knowledge and familiarity with conservation techniques, a vital link between the selector/curator and the conservators must be established by the development of a conservation liaison unit.

Headed by a suitable librarian, a conservation liaison unit must operate on a number of levels, dealing with all aspects of conservation, from simple book repair to major conservation treatment. A typical task of this unit is the monitoring of materials identified as damaged after use. If an item has brittle paper, it should be marked as a "replacement candidate" and the necessary preliminary searching done to help the selector decide on a course of action. If the paper and the sewing is sound, and the book is not appropriate for full conservation treatment, it should be marked "repair candidate" and sent for a sound in-house repair. If the sewing is broken, the book should be reviewed for commercial rebinding. If the book conforms to the criteria for full conservation treatment, it should similarly be searched to determine relevance, and, if appropriate, treated by the conservation staff. Furbishing and surveys to identify candidates for conservation action, are also the responsibility of this liaison unit, as is the monitoring of the library environment. The Johns Hopkins University was the first institution to establish the position of Conservation Liaison Officer, but as the need to coordinate collection management, curatorial responsibilities, and conservation action, becomes more apparent, conservation liasson will become a common organizational element in research libraries.

ARCHIVES

The management and conservation of archives involve most of the features described for research libraries, the basic differences being largely in terms of emphasis and scale. The collection and management of historical records pose intellectual problems which are less concerned with current scholarly activity and use, than they are with the responsibility to safeguard archival materials and information for posterity. Because archivists are no better equipped to predict the future than librarians, some of the same arguments are advanced in defence of ambiguous, or often, non-existent collection policies. The arguments generally take the form of "as we cannot predict what will be of value to researchers in the future, then everything is fair game for accumulation.'' Clearly, archivists must attempt to articulate the bounds of their acquisitions criteria in some systematic way, and having done so, should apply them to the collections on hand as well as to the selection process. The act of producing a collection policy is similar to the library system for the drafting of collection development policies, in that the objectives and needs of the institution must first be identified, followed by some evaluation of the collection. Unfortunately, archivists do not have the bibliographical controls available to librarians for published materials, and many archives lack adequate descriptions and inventory statements. While the larger institutions have helped to develop methods of collection analysis and disposition procedures, many archives are quite small, underfunded, with enthusiastic but generally untrained staff, and, more often than not, housed in wretched conditions. Paradoxically, it is these archives in particular which must begin to examine systematically collections and try to identify those items which can best be preserved by reprographic means, those which must be preserved in original format, and those which should be transferred to some other institution better able to care for them.

The most important conservation concerns for archives are similar to those stated for libraries:

1. The need to stabilize collections by the institution of satisfactory environmental controls, by maintenance of sanitary conditions, and by proper housing.
2. The need to preserve the information contained in deteriorated materials by reprographic means.
3. The need to educate archivists and the general public in conservation fundamentals and handling procedures.
4. The need to preserve, by conservation treatment, materials where retention in original format is important.

As all these needs seem beyond the capability of many archives on an individual basis, the need for cooperative action is indicated. By addressing the issues of standardization and philosophy on a group basis, archives can join together in appropriate consortia and begin to address the pressing problems of day-to-day management. An archives consortium can offer: increased funding for group members by the development of professional fund-raising systems; central information systems benefitting both archives and users; educational and technical training programs; central conservation expertise and services. The latter point in particular is of great importance given the high capital costs of most of the conservation services appropriate to archives, such as: preservation microfilming; mass deacidification; fumigation; conservation treatment, including ultrasonic mylar encapsulation. At this point, it is difficult to predict where the leadership thrust for cooperation will be based; in some cases, the initiative seems to be developing at the state level, particularly in terms of inventory gathering. However, in the absence of state or federal encouragement, archivists must begin to cooperate on any appropriate bases, regional or topical, and work to construct mechanisms which achieve effective collection management and conservation systems.

CONCLUSION

The need for effective collection management and conservation programs is gaining more recognition, but real progress will be elusive if librarians and archivists regard both activities as "extra" burdens, rather than integral parts of the enterprise. The collection management problem is beginning to be recognized because of increasing collection unmanageability due to growth and lack of space. The conservation problem has been stated bluntly and accurately by Decherd Turner of the Humanities Research Center of the University of Texas:

> If I could have a 100 more people for a 100 years, perhaps I could hurl back the tide of deterioration threatening to engulf the . . . Center. . . . But 100 people and 100 years is hopelessly unrealistic. Decisions on how dollars are to be applied become rather simplistic in the light of this crisis. The bottom lines read: use every dollar you can to forward the conservation process; use every salary dollar you can to hire conservation personnel; use every supplies dollar you can for conservation supplies, equipment, laboratories.[24]

In estimating that in a few years "one half of all personnel budgets will be applied to the conservation enterprise," Mr. Turner urges that "the larger libraries must all become training centers for the aid and benefit of smaller collections" as "the new aristocracy in the library personnel structure will be the conservation specialists."[25] As Decherd Turner's predictions come true, the present actions of research libraries and archives in establishing collection management priorities and dealing with the conservation consequences will become more evident.

REFERENCES

1. B. J. Enright, "Biblioclothanasia: Library Hygiene and the Librarian," *Essays on Information and Libraries* (London: Bingley, 1975), p. 20, quotes Lord Bowden's remarks on the cyclotron as applying to research libraries, " . . . the united efforts of all the staff are only sufficient to keep the machine on the verge of operation."

2. Pelham Barr, "Book Conservation and University Administration," *College and Research Libraries* 7 (1946): 214.

3. James W. Henderson and Robert G. Krupp, "The Librarian as Conservator," *Library Quarterly* 40 (1970): 182.

4. Jesse H. Shera, *The Foundation of Education for Librarianship* (New York: Becker and Hayes, 1972), p. 139.

5. Carolyn Clark Morrow, ed., *The Preservation Challenge* (White Plains, NY: Knowledge Industry Books, 1982), is an example.

6. John Dean, "Growth Control in the Research Library," *Steady-State, Zero Growth and the Academic Library*, Colin Steele, ed., (London: Bingley, 1978), 85–6.

7. See particularly George S. Bonn, "Evaluation of the Collection," *Library Trends* 22 (1974): 265–304.

8. Rose Mary Magrill, "Evaluation by Type of Library," *Library Trends* 22 (1985): 268.

9. William McGrath, "Collection Evaluation: Theory and the Search for Structure," *Library Trends* 22 (1985): 242–3.

10. Hugh F. Cline and Loraine T. Sinnot, *Building Library Collections: Policies and Practices in Academic Libraries* (Lexington, Mass.: Lexington Books, 1981), p. 137.

11. Margit Kraft, "An Argument for Selectivity in the Acquisitions of Materials for Research Libraries," *Library Quarterly* 37 (1967): 290.

12. In the seventeen years since the publication of this study, increases in the sizes of research library collections would probably reduce Fussler's "once in fifty years use" even more: Herman H. Fussler and Julian Simon, *Patterns in the Use of Books in Large Research Libraries* (Chicago: University of Chicago Press, 1969).

13. Grace Agnew, Christina Landram, and Jane Richards, "Monograph Arrearages in Research Libraries," *Library Resources and Technical Services* 29, no. 4 (1985): 347.

14. The Research Libraries Group, *RLG Preservation Manual* (Stanford, CA: RLG, 1983), p. 52.

15. Quoted from the *National Enquirer* of February 14, 1978, by Pamela Darling, "Creativity vs. Despair: The Challenge of Preservation Administration," *Library Trends* 30 (1981): 179.

16. Jack Magarrel, "Damage in the Stacks . . . ," *Chronicle of Higher Education*, 30 May 1978, p. 2.

17. "The Preservation Crisis," *Journal of Academic Librarianship* (November 1980): 290.

18. Christinger Tomer, "Selecting Library Materials for Preservation," *Library and Archival Security*, 7 (1985): 2–3.

19. *RLG Preservation Manual*, p. 11.

20. Richard W. McCoy in "The Electronic Scholar . . . ," *Library Journal* 110, no. 6 (1985): 39, issues a timely warning against possibly destructive network competition in this area, particularly between OCLC and RLIN. "Valuable and unique services of each group are sometimes closed off to members of the other. National programs in preservation, special resources, and retrospective conversion of catalog data are bifurcated, and, in some cases we overcome this only by expensive data entry. Costly preservation microfilms are produced redundantly when one institution does not know that another has already filmed the item."

21. Cline and Sinnot, *Building Library Collections* . . . p. 137.

22. John Dean, "The Binding and Preparation of Periodicals: Alternative Structures and Procedures," *Serials Review* 6, no. 3 (1980): 87–90, describes a successful alternative structure now available from many binders.

23. _____, "The In-House Processing of Paperbacks and Pamphlets," *Serials Review* 7, no. 4 (1981): 82.

24. Decherd Turner, "The Self-Destructing Book . . . ," *Discovery* (Spring 1982), p. 28.

25. *Ibid.*

Funding Resources
and Priorities for Cooperation:
Toward a National Records Program

George L. Vogt

Writing in today's climate on funding resources and priorities for cooperation is risky. The story of a harried Ivy League political scientist comes uneasily to mind. The professor, an authority on Latin America, was late for class. Rushing into his office, he grabbed what he thought were his lecture notes on Latin American federalism, and sprinted to class. When he arrived at the lectern, he opened the folder and found it empty. Unfazed, he gave his students a piercing look and said, "Gentlemen, there *is* no federalism in Latin America," and walked out. Ladies and gentlemen, there may soon be no federal funding resources for libraries and archives in America. It now seems at least possible that balancing the federal budget will wreak havoc on all programs that librarians and archivists have labored so hard to establish, leaving a void that state, local, and private sources cannot possibly fill. Under these circumstances, planning, goal and priority setting, and cooperative ventures become all the more important.

Consider the lessons of the Bicentennial. For years there was no perceptible progress toward a coordinated, nationwide attack on this country's records problems. Many hoped to see a renewed interest in historical records as the Bicentennial era approached. Those hopes were dashed as an assortment of Bicentennial celebrations unfolded. One is hard-pressed to name a single major and lasting archives- or library-related program that owes its existence to Bicentennial fever. Instead, the funding focus has been and continues to be on ceremony rather than substance, on transitory events (exhibitions, lectures, mock conventions) rather than permanent programs. Not that these highly visible events are bad—they do bring glamor, interest, and a public dimension to otherwise musty-seeming programs. No, the real disaster is that, even in circumstances that should have fostered joint planning and cooperative effort, there has been virtually none. In the absence of an overarching design and

George L. Vogt is the director of the National Historical Publications and Records Commission (NHPR) Records Program, Washington, D.C. The views expressed in this article are those of the author, not necessarily the policies of NHPRC or NARA.

pattern of cooperation, there is little chance of bringing the stellar resources of federal programs, private foundations, and research institutions into cosmic conjunction.

MOVEMENT TOWARD COOPERATION

Archives and manuscript libraries have revelled for too long in their individuality; occasionally devising highly specialized accessioning and cataloging systems; and often measuring their holdings and program accomplishments in idiosyncratic terms. The uniqueness of manuscripts has seemingly reinforced this mindset among their keepers. Fortunately, the growing appreciation of shared preservation problems and the rapid adoption of computerized systems for describing archival and manuscript collections are forcing serious thought about standardization, shared conservation facilities, research projects of wide applicability, information networks and clearinghouses, shared appraisal techniques, and other common concerns.

There has been desultory interest in systematic data collection, development of reasoned goals and priorities, strong national leadership, and coordinated effort among funders and advisory bodies. Now there is a growing demand for a national approach to historical records problems. The implications for manuscript libraries and archives are potentially great, for a coordinated program may well be the best means of doing more with less, of reshaping (and thus preserving) key federal resources, and of winning support from the public, from private funders, and from state and local governments.

The impetus for a national program comes mainly from a few senior archivists who have never given up hope for a truly national program and a new generation of talented and reflective recordkeepers, many of them trained as both historians and archivists, who have moved the subjects of planning and cooperation to the forefront of archival discussions. These new leaders, including state archivists and state historical society administrators, believe that manuscript librarians and archivists need new tools, methodologies, and strategies if they are to fulfill their mandate to preserve and make available to future generations this nation's records. They argue persuasively that the enormity of their present problems— paper mountains, diverse electronic information systems, an uninformed and unenthusiastic public, and inadequate physical, fiscal, and personnel resources—precludes effective individual action and requires collective strength. For this reason they place a high priority on networking (both personal and electronic), gathering and disseminating information, and developing replicable models and benchmark program standards.

The movement toward a coordinated national program proceeded in fits and starts through most of the 1960s and 70s, as efforts to establish a national Historical Records Commission eventually resulted through congressional splicework, in the creation of a new grant program under the renamed National Historical Publications *and Records* Commission.[1] The old NHPC had maintained a grant program for documentary editions, receiving administrative support and staff through the National Archives and an annual appropriation for grants from the Congress. The new Records Program, with inadequate funding and a somewhat inactive system of state advisory boards, was slow to develop a viable national program.

The change came, instructively enough, in Fiscal Year 1982 at a time of greatly reduced funding. Facing the possible demise of the records grant program, the Commission decided to concentrate its remaining Records Program money on a series of state assessments of records conditions and programs. Forty-three states eventually undertook the projects and produced reports addressing needs in four areas: state government records, local government records, other records (e.g., those in universities and historical societies), and statewide programs and services. As the reports mounted, reviewers found the needs and recommendations strikingly similar from state to state, a conclusion which lent further support to the idea of cooperative, coordinated solutions.[2] Particularly in the areas of information and training, there seemed little reason to duplicate locally what could be better produced centrally. Similarly, why build a multitude of conservation laboratories when a few regional facilities would suffice?

In the course of the assessment projects, an interesting change occurred. Vigorous new leaders in a number of states energized the once somnolent state boards by encouraging them to supervise the statewide studies and move beyond the confines of grant review. Several boards undertook additional statewide projects. The Kentucky board launched a regrant program to assist city and county governments in establishing local archives, microfilming key records, and preparing finding aids. The New York board helped develop two major projects, one devoted to the state's judicial records and another to build public awareness of historical records problems. Fearing that the assessment reports might fade into the unremembered past, many state coordinators agitated for effective follow-up, particularly where the reports indicated the wisdom of collective action. To provide leadership and communicate with the Commission, the coordinators chose a six-member Steering Committee which was mainly composed of heads of state archival agencies. In the context of a ten-year review of the Records Program, the committee proposed to the Commission a major shift in emphasis; namely, the subordination of the grant program to a new leadership and planning role for the Commission and its state boards. At the October 1985 meeting, the Commission endorsed the ideas with enthusiasm and began discussing how to implement the various proposals.

KEY ELEMENTS IN A NATIONAL PROGRAM

In August 1985 the Steering Committee published a brief but important checklist of suggested elements for a national historical records program, consisting of things that do not now exist except in fragments.[3] As constituted the elements would serve the entire spectrum of recordkeepers and record creators, public and private, large and small, manuscript librarians as well as archivists. The most recent version of the proposed elements suggests the scope and ambition of its creators.

1. *A process that accurately describes current historical record conditions in the nation.* One of the legacies of rugged individualism in archivy is confusion of terminology. One institution's "record box" may not be the same as another's "manuscript file." Among the entries in the *Directory of Archives and Manuscript Repositories in the United States*, holdings are described in linear feet, cubic feet, volumes, envelopes, file drawers, pages, items, and "safes."[4] Nor is there agreement among archivists and librarians on condition descriptions. Is "bad" worse than "crumbling" but better than "deteriorating"?

There is little consensus on preferred ways of monitoring and reporting collection usage. As a result, all efforts to survey and quantify are doomed to some degree of frustration and inexactitude because the Babel of archival languages reduces data to unintelligibility. To remedy the problem in part, the Society of American Archivists and the Association of Research Libraries are developing uniform reporting standards for their institutions. In addition, the National Association of Government Archives and Records Administrators (NAGARA) is developing similar standards for use by any government records program. The assumption underlying these projects is that a standard and comprehensive reporting format for similar types of institutions will produce reasonably accurate statistics, which in turn will serve as planning and educational tools.

2. *A consultative mechanism that regularly specifies principal historical records needs and priorities*

and suggests how they might be addressed most effectively. The word "mechanism" refers to a variety of activities, one of which is the important work begun by the Society of American Archivists' Task Force on Goals and Priorities. The forthcoming task force report is a remarkably thorough and logically organized compendium of needs (specific activities, special studies, etc.) pertaining to historical records, their creation, management, care, and custody.[5] The task force, which included historians, records managers, and other non-archivists, managed to elevate discussion of record problems well above narrow professional interests.

Other likely components of a "consultative mechanism" are continuing state-based projects to assess records needs (similar to those funded through the NHPRC's State Historical Records Advisory Boards), periodic meetings to review needs and priorities, and greater involvement of non-archival groups (e.g., public officials and politicians) in strategy discussions. The purpose of these efforts is to insure continuing consensus about goals and priorities, to engender participation by a broad range of archival, historical, and other groups, and to produce, ultimately, better educated and more influential advocates of action.

3. *An active program to communicate these needs, and the reasons for addressing them, to the general public and to the wide variety of specific publics that must be informed about and involved in these issues.* Such efforts must be both direct and indirect. Direct methods could include the creation of a national public information office to provide timely news of broad public interest and a dramatic annual report on the condition of this country's historical records. Indirect methods could include special media productions; for example, a public television series on the transformation of historical records and information systems, special training programs in techniques of developing public information programs in the local setting, and so forth. The goal is to educate the general public, convince record creators and funders of the need for action, and (not incidentally) increase the public accountability of the archival community, which now

"enjoys" a low profile and commensurate public expectations.

4. *Work to influence key parties (the Congress, governors, legislators, national programs and associations, major interest groups, etc.) to act on these principal needs.* These actions include organized lobbying for funds, administrative changes, and targeted projects; intensive salesmanship to record creators of the financial and administrative benefits of good records programs; and an organized campaign to provide appropriate expertise to key players. Most important, lobbying successfully for more funds, staff, or bigger programs is not in itself sufficient to solve records problems. Many problems are best addressed early in the process of records creation (for example, adopting the use of durable papers for important documents). To make that point, one must convince the appropriate persons that early and vigorous action means less cost and trouble in years to come.

5. *Advice to and coordination with the National Archives and Records Administration (NARA), especially in respect to NARA activities affecting non-federal historical records or non-federal archival programs.* The National Archives does not now play a role fully comparable to that of the Smithsonian Institution for non-federal museums or the Library of Congress for the nation's libraries; however, its new status as an independent government agency is provoking much discussion of its responsibilities to the archival profession. With fourteen regional facilities spread across the country, NARA is alone among the "Big Three" Washington cultural institutions in being quite literally "national." Already, the Archives is undertaking research and development work of broad interest and applicability to all recordkeepers, holding basic archival training programs open to all, and developing cooperative research programs with others, including the Public Archives of Canada. New roles could include developing more specialized training programs, publishing manuals of recommended practices on different subjects, promoting public awareness through creative use of the regional NARA archives and records centers, and assisting in the birth

of a national clearinghouse for records information. As many have noted, the National Archives' budget, staff, and holdings exceed the combined resources of all the state archives. NARA could, if it chose, focus great attention on problems of not only federal records but those of the entire nation.

6. *Major efforts to increase funding for historical records programs in the United States.* Most state, local, and private record programs are underfunded if they exist at all. Governments are sometimes slow to realize the financial and administrative benefits of sound public record programs; private institutions often fail to develop adequate funding bases for their ambitious programs. Without minimizing the importance of reaching and convincing public funders of the validity of program needs, most proponents of aggressive funding campaigns agree that the private sector has been too long neglected. Many corporate and private foundations now support the preservation of historic buildings, but few have been educated to the comparable need for records preservation. True, it is easier to place a plaque on a building than on an acid-free storage carton, but there are many different kinds of possible public notice and acclaim.

Other conspicuous problems include the absence of a national membership organization for our documentary heritage akin to the National Trust for Historic Preservation and of a clearinghouse of information about successful fundraising and publicity techniques. The nation's archives, particularly the National Archives, have been slow to present themselves to foundations and corporations for promotion in ways that many museums and some libraries have mastered.

7. *A program to establish and promulgate canons of good practice for historical records programs.* "Good practice" means not only standards for individual tasks and procedures (e.g., encapsulating manuscripts) but also attention to appropriately designed programs. What components, for example, must a city government include in its records program to meet minimum standards for preserving documents and making them available to users? Are reference rooms, full-time staff, forty hours of public access per week, and various items of equipment *sine qua non* of ac-

ceptability? What elements make the difference between a so-so records program and an outstanding one? What kinds of resources and administrative support are minimal? good? outstanding? What is considered "good practice" in developing institutional collecting policies, in finding appropriate homes for congressional collections, or in deaccessioning inappropriate materials? Professional organizations need encouragement and guidance in addressing these issues.

8. *Provision for research and exchange of information needed to identify, preserve, and make available historical records.* Given the technical problems posed by deteriorating paper and the bewildering variety of new documentary media, the need for continuing research is obvious. The list of urgent research questions is far longer than any list of completed archival studies. Among the needs are studies of sampling techniques as they might be applied to large collections and case files, specialized appraisal studies of problematical collections (congressional papers, scientific research project records, etc.), testing programs for "archival" materials, and research into the characteristics and longevity of numerous information media. A national program could identify and publicize the most important needs and help match researchers with funders.

In addition to attacking existing problems, a national program could also draw archivists and librarians into the early stages of design for new information systems. A recurring problem is the creation of ephemeral storage systems that satisfy secretaries but not historians and archivists. Even the vaunted disks of digital information read by lasers are of uncertain durability. (One salesman recently floored a roomful of archivists by stating proudly that the disks would last "at least ten years." Manufacturers need to take into account management and archival concerns that transcend short-term business interests.[6] In the world of the "paperless office," the term "to archive" means to protect from accidental erasure, not (as an archivist would argue) to insure permanent retention. Most modern office information systems, including the largest computers, seem to have been designed by persons who think a decade is a long time.

9. *Coordination of existing federal grant and advisory programs pertaining to historical records.* Pundits may argue about the existence of federalism in Washington—as well as Latin America—but among government granting agencies, cultural institutions, and advisory bodies concerned with this nation's documentary heritage, confederalism is the rule. Each goes its separate way with a minimum of intercourse. There is a startling absence of coordination and consultation among these bodies, in part because there is neither a nationwide program to link and coordinate their movements nor an existing mechanism to force "feds" to talk to each other.

Particularly in a time of retrenchment, it is vital that government programs not duplicate functions and services. Even in an area as fundamental as preservation research, there is now poor coordination of effort among the numerous groups directly concerned with the problem. In other areas as well, programs and special initiatives come and go with little attempt to distribute responsibilities among federal interests. As a result, we find overlapping programs and no little confusion among grant applicants. Do we really need two programs funding historical records surveys, and several funding technical research? We need a formal or more realistically an informal study group composed of key persons from appropriate federal grant and advisory programs, representatives of non-federal funding agencies such as the Council on Library Resources and major foundations, and vocal delegates from key professional organizations. This advisory group could give central focus to discussion in Washington that now takes place piecemeal, if at all, and could encourage concerted action on important issues, including joint funding. Almost every grant and research program now tries to protect existing turf while identifying additional areas of "vital concern" for itself. Federal programs need streamlining, and the public needs a candid and thorough information guide to funding sources.

10. *A strong partnership between the national historical records program and the states to deal with key needs that are best approached within a state framework.* We need a guidance and support system

that bolsters local efforts to improve records legislation, public records facilities and programs, and statewide and regional services to both public and private
institutions. Implicit in such a program is a greater role
for the National Archives as a truly "national," as
distinguished from "federal," institution. Most states
now have active, broadly constituted State Historical
Records Advisory Boards. There is strong potential in
these gubernatorially appointed boards for effective
local action.

FURTHER DISCUSSIONS

In January 1986 a small group met in Washington at the invitation of
the NHPRC to discuss these ideas. The group included the state archivists
of New York, Minnesota, and Kentucky; the City of San Diego records
manager; the director of the Rhode Island Historical Society; the special
collections librarian from the University of North Carolina; the chairman
of the newly composed Society of American Archivists' Committee on
Goals and Priorities; the Washington coordinator of the National Coordinating Committee for the Promotion of History; and representatives of
the National Archives and NHPRC.

While there was broad agreement on the validity of individual elements
and even about the need for an "overall, coordinating body" for a
national program, there was no consensus about the nature and compo-
sition of that body. The group debated the merits of: (1) an expanded
NHPRC; (2) a U.S. version of the Canadian Council of Archives; (3) a
private organization modeled after the National Trust for Historic
Preservation; (4) a board composed of state archivists and/or state
historical society directors; and more than a dozen others, including
(briefly) a Ministry of Culture. The discussions will undoubtedly continue because there is little likelihood of records problems going away.
More importantly, there is now heightened interest in moving aggressively and collectively to solve these problems.

Often in meetings such as these, people are torn between the desire to
plan wisely and fully (and constantly), and the urge to "quit talking and
do something." The need many feel to articulate a full-blown policy
apparat is sometimes at odds with others' belief that form should evolve
from, and adapt to, function. Regardless of disagreement over larger
plans and strategy, there remains a strong consensus about certain basic
and immediate needs. These include: (1) data and information collection;
(2) creation of a central clearinghouse for all kinds of records information; (3) research into already identified questions of collection manage-

ment (including appraisal techniques, preservation issues); (4) study of the various problems and promises of new technology; (5) better continuing education for recordkeepers; and (6) aggressive programs to stimulate public awareness of the value of historical records, the benefits of free access to them, and the need for legislative and administrative support for records programs.

In that short list, there is nothing that does not touch librarians, records managers, county and municipal clerks, and historical society officials, as well as persons formally employed as archivists. A successful assault on most of the problems means in most cases some sort of cooperative approach. One example is the Joint Committee established by the American Association for State and Local History (AASLH) to monitor its local government records project. The committee is one of the few continuing forums in which historians, archivists, records managers, and local officials meet to discuss common concerns and joint solutions. If Washington sometimes seems unduly compartmentalized to outsiders, it is a hotbed of collegiality compared to the unfortunate tendency of professional organizations to speak to their own and not to each other. Cooperative ventures begin with dialogue—lots of it.

CONCLUSION

A few years ago, funding issues loomed less importantly in discussions of goals and priorities than they now do. The impending budget cuts in Washington have lent unwelcome immediacy to efforts to promote public awareness of records programs and to tap other public and private funders. These other resources are likely to figure large in the aspirations of administrators in coming years. Public resources (appropriations, budget lines, or special funds made available by state and local governments) are unlikely to increase dramatically in most jurisdictions and, in any case, will probably not rise fast enough to make up for absent federal dollars. There may be no increases, just cuts, for those institutions and programs unable to demonstrate convincingly their needs and to mobilize strong public support. Public support, especially for something less tangible than a building, is hard to win. Libraries will probably always have an easier time than archives simply because they benefit from greater visibility and public support. However, archives, especially those linked to strong institutional records management and information services, may ultimately be the greater beneficiaries of increased reliance on electronic data communications and machine-readable records. It has not escaped notice that in private corporations, the persons who control information flow and provide the raw materials for decision making are being accorded larger and larger slices of the pie.

Whether the blade is called Gramm-Rudman-Hollings or something else, the budgetary axe is likely to rise and fall many times during the next three years. Within federal agencies, particularly those dealing in discretionary services and grants, civil servants are already battening hatches and breaking out the foul-weather gear. More than one cultural agency ended 1985 and began 1986 with rounds of planning and budget meetings to prepare for serious retrenchment, including major personnel losses and program casualties. Though some argue that only now is Washington experiencing what many state and local institutions have felt over the past four or five years, it is still true that the traumas of Washington will shake the library and archival communities anew and make the subjects of funding resources and cooperative programs and strategies high priorities for discussion. To wait for the axe is to risk all.

REFERENCES

1. For a brief history of the origins of the Records Program, see National Historical Publications and Records Commission, *Annual Report for 1984* (Washington, D.C.: NHPRC, 1985). The report is available upon request form the Commission office, National Archives Building, Washington, D.C. 20408.

2. Consultant reports discussing each of the four assessment areas are printed in Lisa B. Weber, editor, *Documenting America: Assessing the Condition of Historical Records in the States*, (Atlanta, GA: National Association of State Archives and Records Administrators, 1984). The publication is available upon request from the Commission office, or from the Executive Secretariat, National Association of Government Archives and Records Administrators, Room 10A75, New York State Archives, Cultural Education Center, Albany, NY 12230. This organization changed its name in 1985 to reflect a broadened membership.

3. *NAGARA Clearinghouse: News and Reports on Government Records* 1 (1985): 16. The original list of nine elements has remained essentially the same, except for the addition of one concerning coordination of federal programs.

4. *Directory of Archives and Manuscript Repositories in the United States*, (Washington, D.C.: National Historical Publications and Records Commission, 1978). The second edition, scheduled to appear in late 1986, will show a similar diversity of terminology.

5. Printed copies of the task force report will be available in spring 1986 from the Society of American Archivists, 600 S. Federal, Suite 504, Chicago, ILL 60605.

6. Constant innovation and intense competition in some areas are hindering the development of industry-wide standards and creating severe problems of equipment compatibility and transfer of data. Clifford A. Lynch writes, "Today there are no standards for formatting data on any kind of optical disk at any level. In fact, there is not even much standardization of the interface to an optical disk at the hardware level. . . . " See Lynch's "Optical Storage Media, Standards and Technology Life-Cycle Management," *ARMA* [American Records Management Association] *Quarterly* 20 (1986): 44–54. He also notes that experts are predicting a new generation of optical storage systems every two to three years.

EDUCATION AND PROFESSIONAL DEVELOPMENT

The Relevance of Archival Theory and Practice for Library Education: An Argument for a Broader Vision

Francis X. Blouin, Jr.

Formal education for archivists over the past ten years has been subjected to considerable study. While archives administrators have been educated people, it is only within recent memory that an array of formal programs have been developed to acquaint students with the issues, problems, and procedures relevant to managing archival collections. This effort has been fueled by the appearance of ever more vexing problems facing those who deal with modern archives. The increasingly complex problems of selection, arrangement, preservation, bulk, legal considerations, and new technology, have formed the basis of curricula established for the training of archivists. Such the efforts for formal education of archivists lies at a crossroads. On the one hand, archives and archivists can envision a separate discipline and separate identity based on a set of issues unique to their collections and institutions; on the other, in the wake of rapidly developing technology and new conceptual models of interactive information systems, many issues and problems once thought unique to archives now have wider applications. From an information perspective, much of what was once the exclusive concern of archivists constitutes methods or organization of information with a multitude of uses.

Curricula designed for the education and training of archivists need to

Francis Blouin is director of the Bentley Historical Library, University of Michigan, Ann Arbor, MI.

look beyond traditional archives problems and toward developments in post-graduate education geared for information professionals. In this period of new and large-scale developments in the strorage, retrieval, and transfer of information, programs tailored exclusively to archives or to libraries in the traditional sense will not be competitive with the more vigorous, aggressive, and integrated programs predicated on a larger vision of what constitutes the world of information.

Archives as institutions rest on principles, concepts, and practices which have a long history and which have specific applications. However, the environment in which these activities occur is changing. Library and other information activities characterized by principles, concepts and practices different from archives may blend together to address problems posed by this changing environment. Education geared to prepare individuals for life-long careers should anticipate the future. To do so requires a vision of what might be. In the case of developments and possibilities in the information world, this vision should be broad gauged, seeking to bring together diverse disciplines rather than encouraging separateness and exclusivity. There are conceptual reasons for speculating on what might constitute this vision, and there are practical reasons which might argue for specific strategies for organizing educational programs predicated on a broad view of the so-called information age.

A committee of distinguished citizens was called together in 1985 to "identify and propose means by which governments at all levels might rid themselves of needless and wasteful records while ensuring the preservation of that fraction deserving to be kept."[1] That simply stated charge belies the complexity of the task and the problem studied. The final report of this Committee on the Records of Government, issued in 1985, addressed several aspects of the government records problem. A central theme of the report focused on the impact of new technology on the way government kept records, thus requiring new procedures for those charged with their preservation in an archival context. For archivists as well as for all those who select, organize, preserve and make available information, this report was yet another important signal that the traditional contexts of information, whether book, file folder, or photograph, are rapidly changing. It is by now a cliché to point to a new world of information or the technological revolution in communications.

The often heard words "information" and "technology," whether used together or apart, seem to elude any precise definition. Nevertheless, these words serve as a point of departure to discuss a strategy for preparing a new generation to meet the challenges they pose. "Information" is useful because it is not format specific; it blends the notion of a book, manuscript, map, disk, etc., into a single category. It also suggests a fluidity among those formats; for example, a text in book form today may appear on disk tomorrow. A record or manuscript may appear originally both as hard copy and in electronic media posing a choice as to what form may best be retained. Information as a concept needs to be kept quite separate from its format.

Technology, of course, is the force driving and pushing the rethinking of what information is. New technology and its rapidly developing capacity to hold textual information is having an impact not felt since the invention of printing.[2] For those in the information field, technology means not simply new machines, but a whole array of conceptual approaches to the selection, organization, preservation, and use of information. New technology means data bases, electronic records, communication, and a whole host of dazzling developments and possibilities.

Meeting the challenges posed by this new world of information technology is a frequently discussed topic in library and archives circles. Dealing with new information products and by-products challenges traditional notions of our selection, organization, preservation, and use of information. The traditional disciplines have been primarily format oriented. Library Science concerns books, maps, media; that is, single items. Archives Administration deals with manuscript collections and record groups. Data Management treats machine-readable forms. Each has a separate set of principles and perspectives critical in confronting the larger issues of information technology. Yet the information problem has become multi-disciplinary, requiring an integration and in some cases, a blending of these traditional disciplines.

Library science as a discipline traditionally oriented toward the book, has begun to reach out aggressively to other formats. The cataloging of special materials, the management of media, the design, acquisition, and management of data bases, have all entered the better library school curricula. Moreover, there has been movement toward broader conceptualization of the problems associated with those new formats. There is increasing interest in the organization of information and general questions regarding access to information. Problems in the transfer and storage of information loom particularly large. As these issues are explored by research and are discussed apart from specific format concerns, then library science will define a new intellectual core. The concepts which form this core will be the basis of a more information-oriented discipline.

Archives and concepts of archival organization are central to this process and most germane to any efforts at defining a new conceptual core for programs designed to educate information management professionals. There are three basic reasons for this centrality. First, archives and libraries as institutions are essentially quite different. They deal with different kinds of material and cope with distinct problems. Second, archives and libraries have much in common. This commonality has become increasingly significant in the context of information technology-based changes. Third, there are a series of practical realities underlying the efforts to establish a broadly based discipline to address the problems posed by information technology.

Archives and traditional libraries are essentially different because they evolved with two very different approaches to the organization of material. Thus archival methodology raises a specific conceptual framework relating to the organization of archives and manuscripts. Moving beyond any consideration of format, this methodology offers conceptual approaches to whole, broad questions about the organization of information.

Archives differ from libraries in fundamental principles. In the purest sense of the term, an archives is a record or group of records generated in an organized or personal activity which may be institutionalized and on-going, as for government, an association, or a corporation. Persons connected with such organized activity do not necessarily author the entire records. Rather, they generate the records in the process of work; material is both incoming and outgoing. Individual activity similarly generates personal records. Personal papers or personal records too, are archives in this sense. Since archives are generated by personal or organized activity during the lifetime of an individual or organization, they have an organic relationship to that individual or organization. It is this relationship between records and the activity generating them which gives archival practice its particular identity. This basic principle of provenance is the essential and fundamental aspect of the definition of archives. It is the undissoluble relationship of an activity to its records.

This notion of the organic relationship between generators of records and the words themselves suggests a longstanding holistic approach to the organization of and access to information. In practice archivists work to maintain the relationship between the records and the activity which has generated the record. Excavations in the ancient world point to a sense of this principle of organization among the keepers of records for the earliest empires. For large organizations this means today that departmental records are kept in series appropriate to each division, wherever possible and practical, in their original order. The original order of the records, a corollary to the concept of provenance, is the way individuals and organizations who generated the records perceived the relationship of each item to the other, which often can be as important as the information contained in them. This approach also indicates gaps in a continuing record, where the lack of information can be as important as its presence. Original order preserves context which often enhances the content of an archives.

This provenance-based ordering of the record requires a different approach to the problem of access. It is, of course, possible to index the material, to point out particular named or subject strengths of a particular body of records. It is also possible to gain access to such records through a search strategy based on provenance. The relative merits of these two approaches, subject and provenance retrieval, are explored in detail by Richard Lytle.[3] He demonstrates the relative effectiveness of the two approaches, and in the process provides an important statement regarding the significance of provenance as a conceptual framework for developing information systems.

Another aspect of an archival system pertains to the placement of records. An organization might choose to keep its records at hand to serve administrative or legal needs. The archives therefore might be distributed among the rooms or buildings which house the organization, or the organization might choose to estabish a records repository to house records centrally. Although older organizations occasionally set aside a separate area for historical records and called that the "archives," all records of an organization, whether in file cabinets, records centers, or these "archives," constitute its total archives. Companies in the United States such as Coca-Cola in Atlanta, Navistar International in Chicago, and International Business Machines Company in New York, all maintain their own archives which include an historical archives facility and a records management program. Other types of organizations maintain their own records as well, including federal, state and local governments, universities, churches, and others ranging from the Ford Foundation to the 92nd Street Young Men's Association in New York City. Some corporations have chosen to retain their current administrative records but deposit early archives of historical research value elsewhere, usually in an historical library or museum. The early records of the J.P. Stevens Company are housed in the Merrimack Valley Textile Museum Library in Andover, Massachusetts. The early records of the DePont Company are kept at the Eleutherian Mills Historical Library in Greenville, Delaware. Early Dun & Bradstreet credit reports are at Baker Library, Harvard University. These collections remain part of the archives of their respective companies, but are housed in institutions not necessarily a part of the company generating the record. An archives is, therefore, a more fluid concept transcending the notions of a fixed collection, in a specific space, with rigid administrative frameworks.

The term "library" does not always indicate the concepts used to shape a particular collection. The Merrimack Valley Museum Library, Eleutherian Mills Historical Library, and Baker Library are libraries, for example, which house in their manuscripts division a number of archives. Baker Library, for example, houses the extant archives of over five hundred business firms dating back to the time of the Medici, most of which are from firms and organizations that have gone out of business. Similarly a number of libraries in the United States exist which are essentially collections of archives of many people and organizations. The Bentley Historical Library at the University of Michigan has over 4,500 separate archives of people, ranging from farm families to governors and senators of the state, and archives of organizations, ranging from the Detroit Urban League to the records of the University of Michigan. The Bentley Library is one of many important research libraries whose collections consist primarily of an assortment of archives rather than of published material. These libraries provide systematic access to a variety of archives brought together under a collecting theme for purposes of research.

Even though these collections of archives are frequently called libraries, they differ in fundamental ways because of the nature of their material from libraries housing published works. Archives, to be accessible to a researcher, require a degree and form of attention quite distinct from that given to published materials in traditional libraries. The latter are generally concerned with individual items, produced in multiple copy, relatively uniform in size, and created by an author. Libraries consisting of archives are, on the other hand, concerned with unique material, clustered in record groups which can vary enormously in bulk and size, created by an activity. These basic differences require that a library treat archives quite differently from books and other individual items.[4]

Cataloging and classification schemes in libraries have been devised to assist users in locating books, records, tapes and films associated with whatever question is at hand. Each item has predictable attributes such as author, title, date of publication. Because books are complete entities unto themselves, individual subject attributes can be assigned and a library can cross-reference headings within a card or on-line catalog. This bibliographic-based system has been attempted for unpublished materials as well. Many of the early historical manuscript repositories in the United States began to view manuscripts as printed material and each distinct item in a miscellaneous collection, an organized personal or institutional archives, as if it were a book. Author was noted along with subject information, as well as date. Then in some cases items were rearranged according to these subject categories. Because of the bulk and size of archives, these early systems very quickly became unworkable. The variety of subjects covered in unpublished material makes subject classification virtually impossible on a large scale. More importantly, however, schemes which tended to break down archives and focus on individual items destroyed the most important feature of archives that each item is related to the other and the research value of each is thereby enhanced.

Archival material is not cataloged and classified; instead, it is first ordered, then arranged and described according to certain principles and procedures. The advantage of these principles in organization is the preservation of the organic relationship between the activity generating the record and the record itself. The activity and its complexity are reflected in the record itself. One must therefore understand the nature of the activity which generates the record in order to best interpret the content of the record itself. It is this principle which governs the organization of archives in manuscript libraries and is the fundamental distinction between archives and libraries.

The basic thrust of an archivist's work is to arrange and describe the order of a collection. Arrangement involves preserving or restoring the original order of the material or imposing an appropriate order on the collection. After the material is boxed, foldered, and labelled, an inventory is prepared. Inventories first describe the nature of the activity that generated the particular archives or record group. This is followed by a box by box contents list which frequently includes a list of folder headings. These inventories are not designed to present the researcher with a sense of all potential uses of the material or subjects covered, but it provides the researcher with a detailed sense of the relationship of the existing record to the activity which generated that record. Through the inventory and a well-developed sense of the nature of the activity which generated the record, in theory the researcher, through imaginative use of inventories, should be able to locate material of relevance to the particular question at hand. As importantly, the researcher should be able to detect gaps in the record, actions or periods of time not documented. This system requires considerable preparation on the part of the user to be effective and/or an experienced reference staff. When information exists in a specific archives which might not be readily apparent to a researcher, this can be highlighted through secondary name or subject indexes at the end of the inventory.

The provenance-based approach to the organization of information has been the fundamental intellectual contribution of archivists to individuals, organizations, and even whole societies concerned with effectively maintaining an adequate record of their past. It is this approach to information which has given archivists their particular identity and defines the archives discipline. This fundamental difference in approach to the organization of information and to the type of information with which the archivist is concerned, has implications for other areas of information-related activities. There is a host of information-related problems within the context of modern archival practice that further distinguishes archives and libraries.

Archivists have been working in the area of selection to identify and define strategies and procedures to deal with the enormous bulk of records produced in recent decades. This problem is multi-dimensional. It involves development of satisfactory approaches to select that small portion of records worthy of retention. This critical question raised by the Committee on the Records of Government, the problem of appraisal, has a corollary problem of adequacy of documentation. This concept pushes archivists toward better understanding of the nature of organizations which generate records and the uses to which these records are put. This points to the traditional link between archives and history, suggesting that the selection and appraisal of the records of the past cannot be accomplished without some deeply rooted sense of historical study and broadly conceived trends.

Archivists have for a long time wrestled with the problems of access and confidentiality, balancing the needs of the user against the wishes of the creator. Libraries who also cope with problems of effective access, have been traditionally open institutions facilitating access without restriction. Archives, at times, however, have found it necessary to be more cautious in the release of information. Acceptance of some restriction in the short run can lead to a more complete and candid historical record. The application of restrictions to access requires procedures rather specific to archival institutions and repositories.

Differences between libraries and archives in the United States are also apparent in the applicability of the law. New copyright legislation enacted has raised complicated issues for archivists in whose collections are contained the literary property of thousands of individuals, not all of whom have given consent that their writing might be made public. This problem is also a gray area in current privacy legislation and under the libel laws. Archivists must interpret the basic issues raised by this legislation to their users. In addition, the issues of replevin and the ownership of papers of public officials, while of less concern to the library profession at large are other undefined areas of the law which affect those who work with archives.

The most critical area looming on the future for archivists is the electronic record, which has implications for all organizational records, whether federal, state, local or private. This new format for archival records will pull archivists and their discipline away from manuscript dependence and push them toward a more abstract sense of the principles or organization and arrangements.[5] Of necessity, this new format will require new solutions. The multiplicity of reports and activities which emphasize this issue are evidence enough that these technical developments are shaking the foundations of traditional archival activity. The Society of American Archivists' Committee on Goals and Priorities (GAP) has identified this as a key problem for the archival profession.

Archivists as professionals are unique; their discipline, the administration of archives, rests on a small body of theory, principles, and techniques which are distinct from any other field. In order for archives to function properly and serve society, the fact of these unique principles must be acknowledged and preserved. Those archivists whose major responsibilities involve the practical application of these theories and principles in archives, whether active within an on-going organization or inactive and deposited in a manuscript library, must be perceived as having a unique set of problems within the larger world of information. However, librarians and archivists can profit by learning the theory and practice of each other. Each offers a very different perspective on the organization of information that is appropriate within a given context or situation. Most important, each must be recognized not simply as a variation of a theme, but rather fundamentally different.

The differences between archivists and librarians are emphasized in part because they are so fundamental, but also because they may not readily be perceived beyond the bounds of the archival discipline. Moreover, this particular discipline and its corresponding record of experience has much to contribute to emerging programs in information studies. The thrust of this contribution rests on archives as an alternative model for the organization of information. The further one moves from a format-based notion of what constitutes information to a more abstract notion, the more relevant the archival model becomes. As traditional library education moves away from a book- and catalog-oriented curriculum, the more important alternative models become to the process of shaping the intellectual core of a more ambitious discipline. It is at this point that the common concerns of archivists and librarians emerge in three areas: (1) organization of information, (2) problem solving, and (3) questions of policy.

In the area of organization of information, the fundamental approach in library education has rested on a bibliographic orientation based on, but not limited to a core course focused on the principles of cataloging and classification. With good reasons, this course has been and will continue to be fundamental to all who wish to work with books housed in traditional settings. However, in this information age there is every likelihood that most new students in either archives or library studies will have to wrestle larger information problems in fairly undefined or at least non-traditional formats. The question will then arise as to how this material should be organized. Individuals charged with the responsibility will need to think creatively and draw from a variety of existing frameworks, or indeed create a new approach.

The archival approach to organization offers a contrasting model to the bibliographic. The introduction of these concepts into basic courses on the organization of information has several advantages. First, it will acquaint students with an alternative. Second, and more important, it will permit students to step outside the bibliographic mode and to analyze it more critically. Similarly, the bibliographic perspective will encourage a more critical appreciation of the archival. Third, it will contribute toward a broader definition of essential components or intellectual core of what constitutes information studies.

Problem solving, an ubiquitous term, certainly has pertinence to the information world. There are great problems to be solved. The problem of selection of material to be permanently preserved, whether the item is a manuscript tax report, a brittle book, an electronic blip, or a magnetic tape, is a critical one. The bulk of information in this proverbial explosion, facing all those in information-related institutions, is in need of systematic attention and creative solutions. Archivists and librarians approach the problem of selection with different methodologies. Students sent to encounter these problems should be as well equipped as possible to meet the challenges that such continuing problems represent. The increasing appearance of records in electronic form exacerbates the need for developing new approaches for this selection process.

A third area, policy, can also be enriched in the library curriculum by the introduction of an archival perspective. Discussions about information, its power and potential, naturally cross nearly all disciplines. Librarians and archivists have a particular stake in defining what policy rightly should be determined by their own professional concerns. These include questions of access, privacy, cost, and service. In any case, traditional archivists and librarians have much to offer from their wealth of experience and expertise. Because the issues of the future seem less specifically format-based, they will require a blending of knowledge of a variety of disciplines within the field of information studies.

Although archives and libraries are distinctly different in origin, in theoretical base, and in the nature of the work required, there are great similarities. A more serious blending of the two disciplines within an information studies curriculum is urged because major concerns will converge. The most important information issues straddle the two disciplines and ultimately will require joint efforts if progress is to be made. The forementioned problems of selection and organization of information are two critical areas where the interests and experience of the disciplines intersect. There are many others. The impact of the electronic record as a source of information and permanent record has yet to be fully understood. Clearly there will be issues relating to access, preservation, system design, and periodic reviews which will raise questions calling for a multi-disciplinary response. An integration of traditional bibliographic principles and archival principles will place archivists and librarians in a better position to build the intellectual and conceptual foundations for solutions to these many new problems.

There is also a set of practical realities facing the educational establishment which further argue for this integration of disciplines. These lie in three areas: (1) numbers, (2) institutional infra-structure, and (3) the nature and reality of a guiding vision. These more practical factors are particularly relevant to archivists because of the current interest on their part to expand programs geared specifically toward those planning to enter the profession. Archivists want to define the boundaries of the archival profession more explicitly through specific degree programs exclusively designed for the preparation of archivists. This is short-sighted and does not anticipate the kinds of changes likely to occur in the environment in which archivists learn and work. The future growth of the archival profession lies in integration with currently allied professions rather than in taking further steps toward separateness and exclusiveness.

First, there are simply not sufficient numbers of archivists or employment opportunities to justify an exclusive definition of the archival discipline. While those fully educated and comfortably employed as archivists may take some satisfaction in the attempt to separate the archival profession, the reality of the numbers can only deflate high expectations. The growth of archival consciousness in the private sector and the expansion of select state programs, are encouraging. Yet, given the slow growth in the public sector and the history of uncertainty in the private sector, archivists would be wise to proceed on this separate route with caution.

A second problem very much related to the first is the institutional infrastructure in which archivists have been educated. There are programs in history departments and in schools of library science. There are records management programs. Naturally, the variety of approaches has led many to argue the need for a separate, clearly defined program. Because of the numbers problem, however, institutions of higher education are unlikely to respond with significant resources specifically for the education of archivists in a separate curriculum. There is simply not the demand, equated to tuition income, to justify such an expense when other disciplines can mount far more impressive statistics.

The case for more vigorous archival education can best be made within the current institutional framework for library education. There are several reasons for this. First, library education is now already housed in separate schools within major universities and thus has the budgetary strength and flexibility to entertain the notion of a broader-based curriculum to include archives. Second, library school curricula are now in a state of vigorous re-examination, searching for new methods and models to educate students for this new world of changing information/technology. This means a more receptive environment for the development of specific courses relating to archives and records management. More importantly, the schools offer a more receptive environment toward the integration of basic archival theory and principles into the core curriculum of emerging information-oriented programs. Archives in Library Science schools could be seen as similar to incorporating tax studies in law schools or neurology in medical schools as part of a large, integrated effort toward a single professional service.[6] Third, archivists would do well to engage the ferment over library vs. information education, and not shun it. Archivists should take advantage of an existing infrastructure, mindful of the terrible obstacles likely to arise in the pursuit of a parallel or separate structure.

A third practical dimension which relates to the nature and reality of a guiding vision for archivists as educational and pedagogical questions are pursued, takes this discussion full-circle. Because of the developments in information technology, there are likely to be many changes in the total information environment. The electronic textual record is probably at the core of these changes. The problems posed by these new systems will be large and immediate. Many outside library and archives are interested in obtaining a piece of this very lucrative expanding field. Information management programs are well established in schools of engineering and business. Librarians and archivists are in a very strategic position to address these issues and, in fact, to dominate the endeavor to organize and structure these new systems. This profession, however, will have to compete intellectually, conceptually, and with the strength of all their numbers. It is this guiding vision of a critical role in information technology and service which argues strongly for further integration of these two separate but related disciplines.

Archivists will always be mindful of their ties to History and traditional practices. This important aspect of archival training will remain and will be cultivated within the broader context of technological change. But this guiding vision should be located on the cutting edge to insure that archivists trained in their youth will be prepared to engage rather than to avoid critical issues raised by new conceptual and technological approaches to the organization and use of information.

Archives and libraries are indeed separate—institutionally, intellectually, and conceptually. But they are related in so many concerns and problems posed by new developments in information technology.

REFERENCES

1. Committee on the Records of Government, *Report.* (Washington, D.C.: GPO, 1985), 10.

2. Elizabeth Eisenstein, *The Printing Press as An Agent of Change*, Cambridge: University Press, 1979), 2 vols.

3. Richard Lytle, "Intellectual Access to Archives: I Provenance and Content Indexing Methods of Subject Retrieval," American Archivist 43 no. 1 (1980), 64–76; and "Intellectual Access to Archives: II Report of an Experiment Comparing Provenance and Content Indexing Methods of Subject Retrieval," American Archivist 43 no. 2 (1980): 191–208.

4. I am indebted to Mary Jo Pugh, formerly of the Bentley Library, who suggested this framework for the distinction.

5. Trudy Huskamp Peterson, "Archival Principles and Records of the New Technology," American Archivist 47 no. 4 (1984): 383–393.

6. Manfred Kochen, "Information Science Research: The Search for the Nature of Information," *Journal of the American Society for Information Science* 35 no. 3 (1984): 195.

Librarians and Archivists: Organizational Agenda for the Future

Robert M. Warner

HISTORICAL BACKGROUND

Librarians and archivists, historically dissimilar in their training, outlook, methodology, and philosophy, are today facing very similar problems and challenges. The library and archival professions are in a period of transition. Technology is changing the way these professionals do their jobs. Never wealthy, both professions are seeking ways to make maximum use of the limited resources allotted to them by a society which is increasingly imposing new demands on them. Both professions seek more influence and status. Both seek new ways to shape society's values. How these two professions relate to each other in facing their common challenges and meeting their common problems is an important consideration for the future of both. American librarians and archivists evolved from different backgrounds to meet different needs. That fact is important to help us understand present attitudes and help project a different set of conditions for the future.

Librarianship, the older of the two professions, established its identity earlier. It is fair to say that it is much the stronger of the two, better identified (though not as positively as it would wish) in the public's mind, and with a better educational system to reproduce itself.

Professional librarianship evolved after the Civil War as the U.S. rapidly emerged from its "book poor" status. It is estimated that the number of volumes in significant public libraries rose from 3 million in 1860 to 12.3 million by the time America celebrated its Centennial in 1876—an increase of 310%.[1] From that point on the production of books accelerated, and with the tremendous influx of books came the problem of how to care for them and how to train those who would care for them. One author described the typical librarian of this period as: " . . . usually a decayed gentlewoman with the virtues and foibles of her class! . . . The office was apt to be bestowed upon a local poet, a prominent represen-

Robert M. Warner is Dean, School of Library and Information Science, University of Michigan, Ann Arbor MI.

tative of the Grand Army of the Republic, a retired minister or teacher who was short of funds, or anyone who was known to like books—whether he or she actually read them or not. The ultimate was found in Chatfield, Minnesota, where the matron of a restroom doubled as a librarian.''[2]

With a rapidly growing problem and no effective means of coping with it, it is not surprising that Melville Dewey and like-minded persons called for a formal library training program in 1876, a call which led to the creation of the first formal instruction in librarianship, the centennial of which will be observed this year. Though Dewey deserves recognition for his pioneering action, his curriculum was itself something of a limitation in the advancement of the profession. It made only modest demands on students' minds but covered minutiae, including in explicit detail how to perform janitorial work. One of Dewey's early students noted that ''what Dewey taught was not the love of books . . . but how to administer a library and how to care for the needs of those who would know and use books. . . . He was not a great student or scholar nor a great bibliographer, but he was what might be called a great mechanician.[3] But the librarians at least had the beginning of a formal education, and with the founding of the American Library Association they had a professional forum to address their problems and encourage the development of their own literature—all necessary components in establishing a professional identity.

By contrast, the archival profession was considerably later in taking these steps. Though the collecting of historical manuscripts of the U.S. goes back at least to Jeremy Belknap who founded the Massachusetts Historical Society in 1791, there were no true archives before 1900, and certainly no National Archives. To be sure, the problem of caring for records increased after the Civil War, as the pension legislation which followed the conflict created huge new paper work burdens. The late-nineteenth century also saw the historical profession demanding access to documents to meet the requirements of the new German-inspired scientific history. Finally, to meet these and other pressures the American Historical Association brought about the first appropriation for a National Archives Building in 1926 and in 1934 secured legislation creating a National Archives. The archivists' first professional organization, the Society of American Archivists, came along two years later. As far as formal education is concerned, that came still later and for that matter its pattern and development are still undefined.

From the beginning, then, archivists were not librarians, or vice versa, and both were quick to point out their differences. To be sure, the differences were real. The most obvious, of course, was that archivists were concerned mainly with records or manuscripts, unique, non-printed material, while librarians dealt with books or publications.

The philosophies of the two were also different; librarians began with a pragmatic, "how to" orientation, with no models to follow, whereas archivists were trained largely as historians who were preoccupied with the content of their records and role of aiding fellow historians in research. If they were active professionally it was as members of historical organizations.

The impact of their institutions on society most clearly defined and divided the two professions. The great and immediate demand for the services of the librarian at all levels of society, for all age groups, and in all places, caused the profession to establish standards and practices, to develop a high degree of proficiency, and to pass its accumulated knowledge along to the next generation of practitioners. On the other hand, archives, until relatively recently, were little known and little used by the general public. Archivists felt slight need for self analysis and definition.

There was little formal interaction on a professional level between archivists and librarians; polite co-existence was the usual order, broken occasionally by flashes of hostility. Differences in interests and philosophy were further emphasized by differences in methodology. Both professions were concerned with access and both sought to make materials available for use, but they accomplished their similar goals in very dissimilar ways. Their different methods of approach were largely determined by the volume and nature of the material and the clientele who used the material.

When the production of books threatened to overwhelm them, librarians devised cataloging schemes. When the volume of records produced during World War I and the New Deal presented a similar threat to archivists, they did the same thing. But the cataloging done by archivists and that done by librarians did not follow the same pattern. The librarians' discrete item approach to cataloging was abandoned by the archivists who solved their problem by keeping related papers together, usually in the order in which they were created. In such fashion, tens of thousands of pages could be meaningfully described in a single brief entry in a catalog or guide. Without such an approach it would be impossible today to handle the 1.4 million cubic feet of records held by the National Archives or to describe the more than 1,000 cubic feet of paper of a single governor of Michigan.

The nature of the prospective clientele was another factor leading to the divergence of librarians and archivists. Archives were in a real sense the creation of historians, and thus were organized to aid historians and the government agencies which created the records. Libraries had all of society for their clientele and needed different methods and practices.

MODERN CONVERGENCE

While it is both useful and necessary to understand the divergent histories and some of the differences between libraries and archives, the theme as I see it today, from my perspective of archivist turned library school dean, is one of convergence. The archival and library professions are increasingly growing together, and I believe that trend will accelerate. For both of these groups to gain maximum benefit from this convergence, it should be understood, nurtured, written and discussed.

Convergence is taking place, not because the differences in ways the professionals do their jobs have been eliminated, but because the major problems facing both are in many cases identical. Both professions are fairly weak politically and economically, although the problem of low salaries seems to be improving. Both have an undeserved image problem: they are thought of as refugees from the real world, passive managers whose main contact with their patrons is to tell them to be quiet (librarians) or to use only pencils when taking notes (archivists).

Perhaps first among the common problems linking archivists and librarians is the enormous preservation issue confronting both professions. It is no secret that the holdings of libraries and archives are slowly disintegrating—what could be called "the quiet disaster." Modern paper, because of its acidic content, disintegrates in a relatively few years; photographs, because of the instability of the medium, fade, discolor, or buckle; even computer tape requires considerable attention if it is to be saved. The list of horrors could be expanded, but the point is clear: libraries and archives have the same problem. As a consequence both professions are beginning to share research data, sponsor joint educational programs on preservation, serve together on preservation committees and task forces, and join together to see that the American public is made aware of the enormity of the preservation problem and the technological complexities involved. The first common project of the two international components of the professions—the International Council on Archives (ICA) and the International Federation of Library Associations (IFLA)—came in 1985 when they agreed to sponsor jointly a workshop on preservation.

Another area where archives and libraries are growing closer is in the clientele they serve. Ironically, as already noted, archivists tended to reflect their historical bias: they were largely the creation of historians and saw them as their principal if not sole clients. Librarians understood from the beginning that their clientele was all of society, but in recent years archivists have had to learn to serve the general public too. By far the largest single group of non-government users of the National Archives today is not historians but genealogists—thousands of ordinary citizens from all walks of life wanting to learn more about their past. High school students are now commonly taking advantage of the archival resources all over the nation, and elementary school children are being introduced to the world of manuscripts and government records through mobile exhibits presented by imaginative docents at the National Archives. The lesson learned early by librarians is now being incorporated by archivists as they undertake to serve a broader clientele.

Archives and libraries are drawing together because of the increasing similarity of their materials. At the National Archives, for example, in addition to the 3,750,000,000 pages of records there are 81,000,000 feet of motion pictures, 5,000,000 still photographs, 1,600,000 maps and architectural drawings, 72,000 sound recordings, 180,000 books and 2,000,000 other printed items. In like manner, the Library of Congress has all of these materials including one of the world's great manuscript collections. In fact, virtually all major research libraries and many smaller college and university library systems have active archival and manuscript collections. The people who work in these areas may see themselves differently, but the public they serve and many of the administrators who fund them see them as part of an integrated entity.

The last point of growing commonality requiring mention is controversial and still undecided. This is the all important question of formal education for archivists and librarians. The education of archivists has been an issue for library schools only in recent years. It is fair to say that for most library schools, archival education was, and still is, an issue of little concern. What interest has been shown frequently has not been motivated by theoretical or philosophical questions of library education, but by market place concerns—adding numbers to a declining student body. Other reasons for the lack of great interest in archival education among library schools has been their serious self-study, and the change as schools strive to cope with the impact of the computer and other new information related technology which is bringing into being a new information society. Many library schools have changed their names and curriculum; a few have ceased to exist altogether.

For the archivist, however, the problem of professional education has been a major interest for many years and continues to be of primary concern today. Reflecting the historical origins of the profession, the general assumption in the early years was that history departments would take the lead in archival education. Writing in the mid 1930's, diplomatic historian Samuel F. Bemis outlined a comprehensive educational program for archivists centered, not surprisingly, in history.[4] The second Archivist of the U.S., Solon J. Buck, writing in 1941, also saw history as the foundation for archival education.[5] But the chief theoretician of archives in the United States, Theodore R. Schellenberg, came to a different conclusion. He advocated placing archival education programs in schools of library science. "The library and archival professions are not inseparable," he wrote. "While the principles and techniques of the two professions are distinctive, they are also . . . complementary. And the objective of the two professions are obviously the same. . . . The two professions should thus collaborate with each other—in the administration of their holdings, in the development of their methodology, and in the provision of training facilities."[6]

In any case, programs were slow in developing. A report I published in 1972 showed that there were only eight programs in the United States with more than two courses and all relied on part-time adjunct faculty.[7] This number has increased substantially, but marginality, lack of strong financial support, and non-permanent faculty are the general rule, not the exception. That is understandable. Most history departments in major research universities of the U.S. are principally concerned with research and teaching in their various fields of history. Training in archival theory and practice is not and probably should not be their major concern. Library and information science schools, however, have as a major focus research and teaching of the methods of handling a wide variety of information.

The historical development of the School of Library Science at The University of Michigan illustrates the educational dilemma. The School began in the College of Literature, Science, and the Arts, where it remained as a department for forty-three years. In 1969 it became an independent school, largely because its parent was interested in the content of the scholarly disciplines and was little concerned with an area which focused much of its attention on methodology. The separation proved beneficial to both.

Looking ahead to the next five or ten years, what will be the configuration and relationship of the two professions? No one has the answers, but one may venture some hypotheses. While specific differences will remain in approaches to their jobs, archives and librarianship will both increasingly become subcomponents of a larger discipline of information handling. This development has both theoretical and practical roots. Theoretically, both librarians and archivists have to realize that both are concerned with the collection, storage, and access to information in a wide variety of formats to meet divergent publics and responsibilities. The form of the information, a distinction so important in differentiating the work of archivists and librarians in earlier years; is becoming less important, and in many cases the distinction is disappearing entirely. In effect, both professions are becoming components of the "information profession." A recent Library of Congress publication discussing experiments in the use of the optical disc in storing information clearly exemplifies this point by stressing that the reader of the future need no longer go to different reading rooms for different kinds of materials. "In the optical disc document delivery system, manuscripts, maps, and music, as well as regular print material, can be accessed via the same terminal.''[8] The reader might not need even to leave his or her own office to do the reading.

An interesting and instructive example of the drawing together of the library and archival professions is illustrated by their views of a third component of the information handling discipline: records management. Records management was born in the National Archives during the World War II years. Archivists and records managers shared, at least in the National Archives, a common theoretical base, namely the life cycle of records concept which saw archives as part of one long continuum from their creation to their ultimate disposition. For several years, the Society of American Archivists and the American Records Management Association (now the Association of Records Managers and Administrators), held concurrent meetings. In the last decade however, there has been a growing apart of the two. No longer do they meet jointly, and the formal interaction between SAA and the ARMA is minimal. At the same time, library and information educators have grown more interested in records management. Records managers have devised their own certification requirements and procedures, but their education has been somewhat "up for grabs," dispersed in community colleges, business schools, and library schools. In the latter category, Michael K. Buckland, former dean at University of California, Berkeley, has taken a leadership role in bringing records management into the library structure and curriculum, seeing it quite correctly, as another important and appropriate component of education for the emerging information society. Thus we may well be on a path of reconvergence of archives and records managers, not under the sponsorship of disinterested history departments, but in schools of library and information science which increasingly see records management as part of the theoretical and practical components of their program.

A COMMON EDUCATION?

In the final analysis, I believe that it is in the area of education where archivists and librarians will finally come together, but my conclusion is hardly universally accepted. There are strong and articulate voices, particularly in the archival community, who envision other arrangements. My immediate predecessor, the 5th Archivist of the U.S., James B. Rhoades, in the first Walter Rundell lecture to the Society for History in the Federal Government, advocated the establishment of an interdisciplinary program, centered in an archival education institute affiliated with one of the universities in the Washington D.C. area and with strong support and ties from the National Archives.[9] Mary Jo Pugh, my former colleague at the Bentley Historical Library, in a thoughtful paper delivered at the 1985 meeting of the SAA in Austin, advocated an archival education program which, while allied with both history and library science, was essentially separate.[10] These are valid positions which merit careful consideration. At one point in my own thinking I would have advocated a similar program, but now I suspect this is an idea whose time has passed, made somewhat obsolete by fast moving technological change which has diminished the theoretical basis and need. The challenge of the future will not be to particularize and specialize the various segments of the information continuum and call attention to their differences, but instead to see how they can be theoretically and practically brought together and how much they interrelate.

For greater usefulness, prestige, importance, and yes, economic rewards, all goals of both professions, it will be important, even necessary, to develop clear, sophisticated core concepts that become the foundation for all information handling professionals. The logical site for this development to occur is in schools of library-information science which already possess archival components and for the most part are located in major research-oriented universities. To be sure, there is as yet no such program, and no agreement on the content and format. That is not unexpected. In looking ahead to a new curriculum, there will need to be considerable experimentation, debate, and probably a few failures before the new integrated course of instruction emerges. Undoubtedly these programs will be interdisciplinary. In the development and articulation of the new curriculum, other disciplines and expertise outside traditional librarianship and archival administration will be needed. In fact, this interdisciplinary quality is already accepted and is expanding in existing library information programs. For example, deans of library-information schools at Syracuse, Maryland, UCLA, Texas and Michigan hold Ph.D.'s in fields other than Library Science. In building the new foundation curriculum applicable to both, librarians and archivists of the future will need economists, statisticians, management experts, and others to help do the job. This should cause no real problem (except for locating the right people and the funds to attract them!) to the library-information school. Librarianship is certainly, or should be, the most interdisciplinary of all professions, for it is needed by all and encompasses all.

It would be presumptuous to try to outline here a new curriculum of value and applicability to both librarians and archivists, but a few examples may at least get the debate under way. Preservation is an obvious example. As already noted, it is a problem for all persons trying to pass on the archival and library heritage of today and the future: librarians and archivists need to know the common scientific background of the problem; how to define it; what options are available to solve it; how to allocate resources in a practical way to bring solutions. Archival principles could be of great value to enrich this portion of the curriculum. Everyone agrees there are not enough resources available to save everything; selectivity is essential. Archivists already have done extensive studies of the intrinsic value of their materials, seeking to identify those documents that should receive intensive and expensive treatment to ensure their continued survival in their original form. Why not teach archival methodology of appraisal and records scheduling to help solve this critical problem of selectivity for preservation of books and printed material as well?

In addition to preservation, there are other examples of useful sharing of common curriculum components. Certainly an understanding of the various computerized databases would have common value. Both OCLC and RLIN are already heavily involved with nonprint material in their databases. The future of the two systems will not mean less involvement with such material, but undoubtedly much more. Economic questions, particularly the problems of economics of information, could be an important component of the core curriculum. Freedom of information issues, state and federal government policies for information, access questions, legal problems are of common concern, and both professions must have the knowledge to deal with them. General managerial education in all its components—personnel, short and long-range planning mechanisms, budget, politics and public relations, fundraising and grantsmanship—all are of common applicability and concern to librarians and archivists and could be part of a common curriculum assisted by other disciplines.

Even the field of cataloging, which was historically one of the principal areas separating librarians and archivists, offers potential for a more unified approach. If cataloging were viewed theoretically, as a comprehensive system to control all kinds of information by various approaches, including both the archival systems as well as traditional library cataloging, students in both areas should find the broader view of considerable value.

CONCLUSION

There will always be specific problems unique to librarians and unique to archivists which can not be shared and which will require special knowledge and skills. Increasingly, however, those entering the professional world of librarianship, archives, and record management will be generalists in the world of information. They will not be technocrats or systems engineers, but will still be humanists committed to humanistic values. They will be bright with a good general undergraduate education, able to communicate effectively, talented in organizing and with a sense of service that has always been a hallmark of both archivists and librarians. They will understand information theory and all aspects of handling information, be able to understand and use the latest technology, and deliver it in the most useful fashion to whatever public they serve. Those who channel their abilities into mastering a single technology or subdiscipline will be experts for a time but face early obsolescence. New technologies are making many long cherished concepts held by all information handlers—librarians, archivists, record managers—seem mere provincialisms rather than sacred theory or immutable principles. The future holds more commonality between archivists and librarians in which both will share a broadly based core of general principles and theory which will stand them in good stead in the increasingly complex but interrelated information world of the future.

FOOTNOTES

1. T. R. Schellenberg, *The Management of Archives* (New York: Columbia University Press, 1965), pp. 5–6.

2. C. H. Cramer, *The School of Library Science at Case Western Reserve University, Seventy-Five Years, 1904–1979* ([Cleveland]: School of Library Science, 1979), p. 10.

3. *Ibid.*, p. 36.

4. Samuel Flagg Bemis, "The Training of American Archivists," *American Archivist* 2 (1939): 154–161.

5. Solon J. Buck, "The Training of American Archivists," *American Archivist* 4 (1941): 84–90.

6. T. R. Schellenberg, "Archival Training in Library Schools," *American Archivist* 31 (1968): 165.

7. Robert M. Warner, "Archival Training in the United States and Canada," *American Archivist* 33 (1972): 347–358.

8. Ellen Z. Hahn, "A Report on the Print Project Archives," *The Library of Congress Optical Disk Pilot Program* (leaflet, October 31, 1983), p. [1].

9. James B. Rhoades, "In Quest of the Keystone: Some Thoughts on the Future of Archival Education," Unpublished Paper, 1984, in possession of Robert Warner.

10. Mary Jo Pugh, "Archival Education: Promise and Performance," Unpublished Paper, 1985, lent to me by the author.

Abbreviations and Acronyms

AA	*The American Archivist*
AACR	Anglo-American Cataloging Rules
AHA	American Historical Association
ALA	American Library Association
AMC	See MARC AMC
ARL	Association of Research Libraries
ARLIS/NA	Art Libraries of North America
ARMA	Assocation of Records Managers and Administrators (formerly: American Records Management Association)
ASIS	American Society for Information Science
CLR	Council on Library Resources
CONSER	Conversion of Serials
CRL	*College and Research Libraries*
EDUCOM	Education Communications
GPO	Government Printing Office
GPR	*Government Publications Review*
ICA	International Council on Archives
IFLA	International Federation of Library Association
LC	Library of Congress
MARC	Machine-Readable Cataloging
MARC AMC	MARC Archives and Manuscripts Control (format)
NAGARA	National Association of Government Archives and Records Administrators
NARA	National Archives and Records Administration
NASARA	National Association of State Archives and Records Administrators
NCLIS	National Commission on Libraries and Information Sciences
NEH	National Endowment for the Humanities
NHPRC	National Historical Publications and Records Commission
NISTIF	See SAA NISTF
NSF	National Science Foundation
NUC	*National Union Catalog*
NUCMC	*National Union Catalog of Manuscript Collections*
OCLC	Online Computer Library Catalog, formerly Ohio College Library Consortium

RECON	Retrospective Conversion
RLG	Research Libraries Group
RLIN	Research Libraries Information Network
SAA	Society of American Archivists
SAA GAP	SAA Committee on Goals and Priorities
SAA NISTF	SAA National Information Systems Task Force
SIBIS	Smithsonian Institution Bibliographic Information System

Index

Abstracting. See Description
Academic archives. See University archives
Access 26, 38–9, 57, 63–5, 67, 81, 117, 148, 162 Physical access 132–4
    See also Preservation
Subject access 28, 40, 65, 81, 108
See also Cataloging, Indexing, MARC
Accessions. See Collection development
Acquisitions. See Collection development
Administration, structure 9, 18, 29, 35, 41–3, 63, 67, 84–5, 138
American Association for State and Local History (AASLH) 2, 46, 151
American Historical Association (AHA) 168
American Library Association (ALA) 168 MARBI 105 See also Association of College and Research
    Libraries (ACRL)
American Records Management Association. See Association of Records Managers and Adminis-
    trators
Anglo-American Cataloging Rules (ACRL) 42, 62 81, 84, 104
Appraisal 52, 65, 116, 161 See also Collective development Archives and Manuscripts Control
    Format. See Cataloging, MARC See Also Description, Standards
Archives programs 19, 148 Evaluation. See standards See also type of archives: Corporate, State,
    etc.
Arrangement 119 See also Description
Association of College and Research Libraries (ACRL) 76, 109 Rare Books and Manuscripts Section
    (RBMS) 76
Association of Records Managers and Administrators 173
Association of Research Libraries (ARL) 146
Austin, Erik W. 94, 128
Authority control 54, 73, 75, 78–9, 83–5, 96, 107, 110 See also Cataloging, Standards
Automation 54, 61–2, 69, 89, 97, 120
Avram, Henriette 99
Barr, Pelham 141
Battelle Technical Report (1980) 109
Bearman, David 11, 33, 99–110
Becker, Joseph 99, 101
Belknap, Jeremy 168
Bemis, Samuel F. 171, 176
Bentley Historical Library 1, 5, 159 Modern Historical Documentation Program 1
Berner, Richard 38–40, 44, 46, 59–60, 97, 124
Bicentennial 143
Blouin, Francis X, Jr. 12, 94, 128, 155–166
Boles, Frank 94, 127
Bookbinding 136–7 See also Preservation
Boss, Richard W. 93, 95
Brichford, Maynard J. 125
Bridges, Edwin C. 46
British Museum Documentation Association 102
Brown, Thomas E. 94
Buck, Solon J. 171, 176
Buckland, Michael K. 173
Budget. See Resource allocation
Burke, Frank G. 32, 38, 46, 60, 93, 123, 126

Burkel, Nicolas 36, 45–6, 125
Business archives. See Corporate archives
Campbell, Ann Morgan Dedication, 8, 94
Canada, Public Archives 148
Canadian Museum Inventory Project 102
Cataloging 53–4, 58, 64, 66, 76, 102, 133, 160, 175 Retrospective conversion 62, 90 See also Classification, Description, MARC
Certification. See Education See also Employment, Personnel, Professionalization, Standards
Child, Margaret S. 94, 121–2, 127
Circulation 57–8 See also User services
Clark, Robert L. 7, 13, 32, 45, 110–11, 123
Classification 28, 38–9, 57–8, 77, 79, 160 See also Access, Cataloging, Arrangement, Description, MARC
Cline, Hugh 131
Collection development 20, 32, 51, 65, 129–30 Accessions 20, 38, 51–2 Acquisitions 20, 38, 51–2 Policies 115–6, 125, 129 See also Preservation
Computers. See Automation See also Cataloging, MARC, Networking
Communications Public communications 147, 151 See also Public image Technical communications 27, 100
Confidentiality. See legal concerns
CONSER 101
Consulting 146
Cook, J. Frank 36, 45, 123
Cook, Michael 93
Cooperation 31, 59, 61, 70, 81, 111, 144, 151, 164, 167 Collections 20–1, 114–5 See also Collection development, Networking
Corbett, Bryan 127
Council on Library Resoruces (CLR) 109
Cox, Richard 1–2, 11, 111–28
Credentials 23–4, 42 See also Education, Professionalization
Cuadra, Carlos 99
Darling, Pamela 141
Databases. See Machine readable records
Dean, John 2, 12, 129–41
Description 28–9, 35, 38–9, 51, 56–7, 60, 74–6, 78–9, 161 Elements 51–60 See also Cataloging, Indexing, Standards
Dewey, Melville 168
Documentation strategy 116–7 See also Collection development
Dodd, Sue 95
Donors relations. See Solicitation See also Collection development
Duchein, Michael 97
Durr, W. Theodore 127
Education 12–3, 22, 63, 85–91, 97, 122, 155–66 Archival education 12, 19, 23–4, 28, 32, 112, 157, 169–72 Library education 12, 67, 165, 167–8, 172 Historical studies 12, 168 See also Professionalization, Standards
EDUCOM 99, 108
Electronic publishing 30, 83, 95, 166
Employment 23–6, 42, 67, 111–2, 165 See also Education, Professionalization
Engst, Elaine D. 60
Environment 133–5 See also Preservation
Epstein, Susan B. 95, 97
Evans, Max 93, 96, 110, 120, 127
Federal programs 144–5, 147 See also National Endowment for the Humanities, National Historical Publications and Records Commission
Fleckner, John A. 125
Ford, Barbara J. 124
Freeman, Elsie T. 126
Frost, Eldin 127

Fry, Bernard 118, 124
Funding 144, 147, 149 See also Federal programs
Fussler, Herman 133, 141
Galleries. See Museums and galleries
Galvin, Thomas 109
Geda, Carolyn 94, 128
Gill, Michael 94
Goals. See SAA Task Force on Goals and Priorities
Government documents 12, 90, 97, 111–28
Government Printing Office (GPO) 114
Government publications. See Government documents
Gracy, David 33, 46, 126
Grants. See Funding, NEH, NHPRC
Hackman, Larry J. 123, 125
Hahn, Ellen Z. 176
Ham, F. Gerald 22, 24, 70, 95, 117, 123, 126
Hayes, Robert 99, 101
Hedstrom, Margarit 94, 128
Henderson, James 129, 141
Hensen, Steven L. 60, 96, 110
Hernon, Peter 124, 128
Hesselager, Lisa 128
Hickerson, Thomas E. 93, 109, 127
Hinding, Andrea 41, 46
Historical associations. See American Historical Assn., American Assn. for State and Local History
Historical societies 2–5, 10, 19, 37, 45, 76, 159, 168 See also State archives
Historical studies 12, 168 See also Education
History, profession, 12, 24, 111, 123 See also Education, professionalization
Imaging 54, 78, 153
Indexing 39, 65, 71, 74, 77–9, 96 See also Access Cataloging, Description
Information management 31, 69–70
Information science 11, 62 See also Library science
Information systems 54–5, 65, 69, 82, 85, 89
Institutional evaluation. See standards See also SAA Task Force on Institutional Evaluation
International Council on Archives (ICA) 170
International Federation of Library Associations (IFLA) 170
Jones, H. G. 125
Kent, Allen 109
Kesner, Richard 86, 93, 95, 123, 127–8
Kilgour, Frederick 99
Klaassen, David J. 3., 9, 35–47
Kraft, Margarit 132, 141
Labor. See Employment See also Personnel, Professionalization
Lane, Margarit T. 128
Legal concerns 53, 56, 76, 162
Levy, Signey. Report. 9, 26, 32, 36, 45 See also Public image
Libraries 2, 5, 27, 60, 99, 101–2, 159, 171
Library of Congress, 27, 39, 60, 99, 101–2, 171 Manuscripts Division 39 National Union Catalog of Manuscript Collections (NUCMC) 28, 42, 63, 81, 103 Subject Headings 28, 81, 84, 108 See also Access, Cataloging, Description, Standards, MARC
Library Science 12, 19, 24, 67, 157 See also Education, Information Science, Professionalization
LINK project 61, 105
Lobbying 147 See also Administration, Public image
Lutzker, Michael A. 47, 127
Lynch, Clifford A. 153
Lynch, Karen T. 97
Lytle, Richard 7, 39, 46, 96, 110, 123, 158 See also Access, Indexing, Provenance
Machine-readable Cataloging (MARC) 42, 54, 60–1, 71, 77–9, 80–1, 99, 102, 120 Archives &

Manuscripts Control Format (AMC) 28, 42, 54, 61, 73, 80–1, 104–6, 120, 122 See also Cataloging, Library of Congress, Standards
Machine-readable records 66, 83, 166
McCarthy, Paul H. 3, 9, 17–33
McClure, Charles R. 125–6
McCoy, Donald 126
McCrank, Lawrence J. 3–4, 11, 14, 16, 32, 60, 61–97, 95, 127
McGrath, William 131, 141
Magrill, Rose Mary 131, 141
Maher, William 47, 97
Malenconico, S. Michael 97
Management 63–4, 72 See also Administration, Information management, Personnel
Manuscripts. See Special Collections See also ACRL Rare Books and Manuscripts Section
Manuscripts Society 5, 76 See also Historical societies
Martin, Susan K. 95
Mason, Philip 123
Microfilming 44, 136
Midwest Archives Conference (MAC) 3, 46
Minnesota Educational Computing Consortium 99
Models 50, 73, 82, 95, 114, 163
Morrow, Carolyn Clark 141
Mosher, Paul H. 125
Museum Computer Network 99 See also Networks
Museums & galleries 99, 102, 107–9
Naisbitt, John 69
Nakata, Yuri 125–6
National Archives and Records Administration (NARA) 5, 30, 127, 145, 147, 168, 171
National Association of Government Archives & Records (NAGARA) 146, 153
National Commission on Libraries & Information Sciences (NCLIS) 100–1, 109
National Coordinating Committee for the Promotion of History 150
National Endowment for the Humanities (NEH) 102, 104, 109 See also Federal programs
National Historical Publications and Records Commission (NHPRC) 3, 5, 30, 61, 103, 122, 143, 145, 151–2 Directory of Archives and Manuscripts Repositories 5, 146, 153 See also National Archives and Records Administration, Federal programs
National programs. See Federal programs.
National Science Foundation Computer Network 99
National Trust for Historic Preservation 148, 151
Networking 8, 10–11, 16, 28, 50, 59, 61, 63, 70–1, 87, 99–109, 114, 144 See also Cooperation
Office automation. See Automation, Technology
Online Computer Library Catalog (OCLC) 61, 81, 141, 175 Oxford Project 61
Optical scanning & storage 78, 153 See also Imaging
Organization. See Administration
Original order. See Description See also Provenance
Personnel 8, 22–25, 64, 72, 85 See also Employment, Professionalization
Peterson, Trudy Huskamp 94, 128, 166
Posner, Ernst 123, 125
Preservation 2–3, 12, 22, 43–4, 64, 68, 75, 77, 96, 129–141, 150, 170, 174 See also Bookbinding
Privacy. See Legal concerns
Professional development. See Education See also Personnel, Professionalization
Professionalization 13, 19, 22–4, 28, 42, 49, 65, 67, 92, 164, 167–9 See also Employment, Personnel
Provenance 35, 38–40, 74, 119, 158 See also Access, Cataloging, Classification, Description
Pruitt, Linda V. 127
Public image 9–10, 26, 32–3, 36, 49, 70, 147 See also Levy Report
Publishing. See Electronic publishing See also Research and publishing
Pugh, May Jo 126, 166, 173
Rapport, Leonard 126

Rare books and manuscripts. See Special Collections See also American College and Research Libraries RBMS
Records management 41, 51, 60, 116 See also Association of Records Managers and Administrators
Reference 51, 55–8, 74, 77, 85, 91 Reference Management systems 51 See also Users services
Reed-Scott, Jutta 93, 125
Reporting. See Standards See also SAA Committee on Standard Reporting
Research & publications 27, 71, 86, 120, 127
Research Libraries Group (RLG) Research Libraries Information Network (RLIN) 43, 61, 81, 84, 105–6, 122, 134, 136, 141, 175
Resource allocation 8, 18, 26, 36, 42, 174
Retrieval, information 70–5, 78, 85 See also Information management
Retrospective conversion. See Cataloging
Rhoades, James B. 96, 173, 176
Rizzo, John 7–8, 16
Roberts, Andrew 109
Rundell, Walter 4
Rush, James E. 109
Russell, Mattie U. 123
Sahll, Nancy 47, 93, 110, 123, 127
Sampling 78, 149
Schellenberg, Theodore R. 115–6, 119, 126, 171
Schlereeth, Thomas J. 46
Schwarzkupf, LeRoy C. 127
Selection & evaluation. See Appraisal See also Collection development, Weeding
Shera, Jesse 129, 141
Simon, Julian 133, 141
Sinnot, Loraine 131
Slotkin, Helen W. 97
Smithsonian Institution 4, 54, 60 SIBIS 60
Society of American Archivists (SAA) 1, 7, 9, 19, 27, 46 Committee on Standard Reporting 29, 46 See also Archives programs, Standards Education & Professional Development Committee 1, 7, 19 See also Professionalization National Information Systems Task Force (NISTF) 1, 28, 33, 42, 54, 94, 103, 110, 120 Task Force on Archives and Society 45 Task Force on Goals and Priorities 30, 33, 146, 150, 162 Task Force on Institutional Evaluation 29, 46
Solicitation 20–2, 52, 50 See also Collection development
Special Collections 10, 17, 37, 41, 76
SPINDEX 103 See also Indexing
Standards 101–2, 148 Description 29, 33, 50, 54, 60, 73, 96 See also Cataloging, Description, SAA Institutional Evaluation
State archives 2, 25, 45, 111, 123, 125, 145, 150 See also Historical societies
Stevens, Norman, 109
Stieg, Margarit F. 124
Storage. See Preservation
Subject access. See Access See also Description, Indexing, Library of Congress Subject Headings
Surveys. See Records management
Szary, Richard V. 4, 11, 49–60
Taylor, Hugh 124
Technology 8, 10, 13, 28, 31, 62, 69–72, 82, 96–7, 123, 155, 157
Terminology. See Authority control, Cataloging, Description, Standards
Tomer, Christinger 136, 141
Turner, Dechard 140–1
UNISIST 102
UNIX 71
Universities 2–5, 17, 41, 135, 138, 140, 159, 172
University archives 36, 41, 82, 145, 159
US MARC See MARC
Use studies 53, 65–7, 64, 86, 91, 97
User services 8, 55, 63, 74, 86, 89, 94

Vendors 86–7
Vocabulary control. See Authority control See also Cataloging, Description, Standards
Vogt, George L. 4–5, 12, 143–53
Warner, Robert W. 5, 13, 167–76
Weber, Lisa B. 93, 110, 127, 152
Weech, Terry L. 124
Weeding 132 See also Appraisal